I0085878

First published by Barry Collier, 2018

© Barry Collier 2018

National Library of Australia Cataloguing-in-Publication entry

Creator: Collier, Barry, author.

Title: Collier for Miranda: The 1999 Labor Campaign / Barry Collier.

ISBN: 978-0-6484393-0-1 (paperback)

ISBN: 978-0-6484393-1-8 (ebook)

Subjects: Collier, Barry.

New South Wales. Parliament — Officials and employees — Biography.

Politicians — New South Wales — Biography.

Australia.

Book cover design and layout by eMatti

Cover photograph: The Sydney Morning Herald, 29 March 1999

Printed and distributed by IngramSpark in Australia

Keywords:

> Politics
> Preselection
> Campaigning
> Elections
> Government
> Leadership
> Australian Labor Party

COLLIER FOR MIRANDA

The 1999 Labor Campaign

by

BARRY COLLIER

To my wife, Jeanette

and our children, Sarah and Michael,

for their love and support,

and to our grandchildren,

Taylah, Lucia, Joseph and Alexandra.

and

To all the local Labor Branch Members,

Volunteers and Supporters

who walked 'the Miranda Road' with me in 1999.

"All politics is local"

Thomas Phillip "Tip" O'Neill Jr (1912-1994)

Speaker, US House of Representatives (1977-1986)
Democratic Party

ACKNOWLEDGEMENTS

This book is my account of the journey I took as an aspirant for a seat in the New South Wales Parliament in 1999. The path I travelled would not have been possible without the encouragement, the hard work and the commitment of so many.

I sincerely thank all the local Labor Branch members, supporters and volunteers who believed in me and worked with me during our journey together down 'the Miranda Road'.

But there are those who deserve special mention – starting with my family: my wife Jeanette, our daughter Sarah, and son Michael. Without their backing, love and support, I wouldn't have made it to the starting line, let alone to journey's end.

I remain grateful to my outstanding Campaign Director, Bob Rogers, for the skill and experience he brought to our quest to return Miranda to Labor after 15 years in the political wilderness. I especially thank (then) Sutherland Shire Councillor, Paul Smith, for his first-class strategic advice and input on key local issues.

I thank Premier Bob Carr for his early encouragement, and Ministers Egan, Shaw, Knowles, Whelan and Scully for their support and visits to Miranda during the campaign. I also acknowledge the assistance and teamwork of my neighbouring Labor candidates, Ian McManus MP (Heathcote) and Alison Megarrity (Menai). My thanks also to *the Tradies* for the Club's support. When it comes to recording our journey, I am grateful to Jeanette for her careful reading of numerous drafts (not to mention her patience and understanding during my writing).

CONTENTS

IMAGES & PHOTOGRAPHS

PREFACE

Whether you are an aspirant seeking a seat in Parliament for the very first time or a reader with a general interest in Australian politics, you may well ask: Why write this book? What has *your* journey as a Labor candidate in 1999 got to do with elections today?

The answers derive from a question I was asked in 2015 by a sitting MP in a 'safe seat' feeling under threat as the State election approached: "How do you do doorknocking?"

Astonished as I was, I outlined my approach to this very basic campaigning technique, using examples from my encounters with voters at thousands of front doors in my quest to win a seat in the NSW Parliament in 1999. During our conversation, it became very clear that this nervous MP had set out on a very different pathway to Macquarie Street than me. I had to learn the hard way.

But that conversation carried with it the kernel of an idea for this book. Clearly, there is much more to running for a seat in Parliament than doorknocking. The more I thought about the challenges facing candidates, the more important it became for me to record my personal account of our 1999 Labor campaign for Miranda: the story of an unknown, first-time political aspirant who set out to win this southern Sydney seat from a very high-profile Liberal MP who'd held it for 15 years. To me, this was a book that just had to be written.

The book is the detailed account of my path to the NSW general election in March 1999. I've recorded my experiences, my conversations with voters, my observations and the key lessons I learnt along the way. I've provided advice about campaigning which I believe will assist not only first-time political aspirants but also some sitting MPs. After all, and as recent times clearly demonstrate, there is no such thing as a truly 'safe seat'.

I don't for one moment suggest that this book is the 'be all and end all' of modern campaigning. It's a book of its time, before the Internet really took hold and before campaigning in cyberspace began. Even so, many of today's aspirants on both sides of the political fence will have to overcome much the same obstacles, face much the same challenges and make much the same sacrifices as I did back in 1999.

But this book is more than just my story. It's also the story of a journey which would not have been possible without the extraordinary hard work, commitment and belief of so many local Labor Branch members, volunteers and supporters. It's their story as much and as it is mine, and this book stands as my testament to them. I've taken the liberty of mentioning some of their names throughout the book, and listed many of their names in the Appendix. It is to them, and to my family, that I remain eternally grateful for the journey of a lifetime.

Barry Collier OAM
22 October 2018

PART A: THE STARTING LINE

1. LABOR ASPIRANTS ... AND ME

1.1. Getting into politics

The memoirs and biographies of major political figures often begin with several chapters about the things that shaped them— their family background, early lives, education, early career— and the role that each of these played in their decision to stand for Parliament.

In those early chapters, the recently retired (or recently defeated) MP tends to look back with rose-coloured glasses. He might remember, as a boy, overhearing Dad and his mates discussing what he later learnt was "politics" around the kitchen table. The former MP may well recall standing at the front gate with Mum, waving Dad off to some important "political meeting" or putting pamphlets in letterboxes down the street for one of his Dad's mates around election time.

Our former high-profile political figure might refer to some vague memory of his grandparents praising some long-dead Premier or Prime Minister at the Christmas family get-together. He may tell of his surprise when, as a teenager, he was introduced to a well-known political figure who turned up out of the blue at his family home for a cup of tea. Our retired political giant may give a detailed account of taking up some just cause or his key role in some protest movement whilst at university.

Somewhere, and sometime, in all that mix the young man decided (or was persuaded) that one day he should "go into politics" and become an MP.[1] And so, he joined the "appropriate" political Party. At the "appropriate" time, he sought and easily gained the support of Party Officials — going on to win a 'safe seat' in Parliament and to later make his mark in political history.[2]

Reading these memoirs and biographies — or maybe even watching the TV series in some cases — you might get the distinct impression that, for this former high-profile MP at least, his ascension into Parliament was his destiny. For him, being an MP was just 'meant to be,' as if pre-ordained by some higher power.

The reality is, of course, very different. As most State Labor MPs will tell you, gaining a seat in the New South Wales Parliament — be it the Legislative Assembly or the Legislative Council — is not quite that easy or quite that simple.[3]

You should note that much of what I say about Labor aspirants in the next two sections of this Chapter [Sections 1.2 and 1.3] applies equally to those seeking to represent the Liberal and National Parties in the NSW State Parliament.

---

[1]   And these days, thankfully, we can add *the young woman*. The gender imbalance is something both major Parties are yet to fully address in all Australian Parliaments.

[2]   A "safe seat" in Parliament is one traditionally held by an MP representing the *same* political Party by a healthy margin of votes at successive elections. As NSW and Queensland State elections have shown in recent times, no seat can truly ever be regarded as 'safe' or impossible to lose!

[3]   The NSW Parliament consists of two Houses: the *Legislative Assembly* (or Lower House) and the *Legislative Council* (or Upper House). The Party which commands the majority of the 93 seats in the *Legislative Assembly* forms the State Government.

1.2. Labor aspirants and the bodies

The footpaths along Macquarie Street are littered with the bodies of former political aspirants who never made it into Parliament as a Labor MP.[4]

There are those who, despite their talent, education, experience or potential were overlooked, undermined, stepped on (or stepped over) by other Labor aspirants or by the Party machine itself. There are those who fell victim to the media or Party gossip as well as those whose past indiscretions came back to haunt them as a result of 'whispering campaigns' orchestrated by other aspirants on both sides of the political fence.

There are also those enthusiastic Labor aspirants who were prevailed upon by Head Office (aka Sussex Street) to wait and 'take their turn', which never came.[5] Then there are those who were persuaded by Head Office, the Party Leadership, their faction or their Union to stand aside for another (often less-deserving) candidate, even when their turn *did* eventually come.[6]

There are those loyal, deeply committed Labor candidates who simply 'flew the flag' — having had the courage to put up their hands and run for safe Liberal and National Party seats, knowing full well they had absolutely no chance of winning.

---

[4]   *Macquarie Street* is the short-hand or colloquial reference to NSW Parliament because of its physical location in that Sydney Street. The term is often used by the media to refer to the State Government itself.

[5]   These names are often used interchangeably. The NSW Labor Party's *Head Office* — its administrative headquarters — is located in *Sussex Street Sydney*. All Labor candidates must be *endorsed* (or approved) by Head Office before they can represent the Party at a State election.

[6]   All State Labor MPs themselves formally belong to either the *Right* faction or the *Left* faction. The media often refer to these as the 'Right Wing' and 'Left Wing' (respectively). Many local Labor Branch members also identify with a faction.

But there are also those Labor aspirants who *could have* won a seat from the Coalition, but didn't work hard enough in months leading up to the election.[7] Some of these simply ran hopeless campaigns based on poor advice— sometimes from Head Office, sometimes from previously unsuccessful candidates, but all too often from well-meaning local Labor Branch members.

There are those Labor aspirants who, sadly, and despite their best intentions, simply didn't have what it takes to be a Member of Parliament—and the *voters* knew it. But there are also some very promising candidates who didn't get the help and full support they needed (and deserved) during the election campaign from their own local Labor Branch members for a host of reasons—not least of which was the candidate's membership of a different faction to their own.

Again, there are some Labor aspirants who, at a different time in the electoral cycle would have taken a seat in Parliament and been excellent local MPs.[8] These aspirants missed out, not because of any personal shortcomings, but because they stood for Parliament at a general election when 'a big swing was on' against the Labor Government itself.

These swings occur when, for a variety of reasons, the voters of NSW as a whole have decided to toss the ruling Labor Party out of Office, and 'give the other side a go.' As they 'swing' their support behind the Coalition, the dramatic State-wide fall in the Labor vote translates into a huge loss of seats held by the Party.

---

[7] In NSW, "the Coalition" comprises the *Liberal Party* plus *the National Party*. MPs often refer to these as "the Libs" and "the Nats," respectively. The *Libs* generally represent city and suburban areas; the *Nats* typically represent country and regional NSW.

[8] In NSW, there is the inevitable sequence of Labor Governments being followed by Coalition Governments and vice versa. Effectively, it's the Parties 'taking turns' at being in Government and then being in Opposition.

Having lost its majority in the Legislative Assembly, Labor is swept from Office in a 'landslide' – along with any chance the promising aspirant might otherwise have had for a seat in Parliament.

Big swings affect the fortunes of both the Labor and the Coalition Parties and typically occur when the ruling Party has been in power for two or three terms (8-12 years).[9] That, of course, is cold comfort to the hard-working Labor aspirants who are beaten before they start by an electorate that considers their Party to be 'on the nose.'

1.3. Labor pathways into NSW Parliament

But what about the successful political aspirants? How did they become State Labor MPs?

It is trite to say they got elected to Parliament! The better question is: how did they each get their name on the official voting paper as the Labor candidate for the seat first time around?

Of course, the successful aspirants will each have their own individual tale as to how they got over – or, in some cases, around – Party's initial administrative hurdle of preselection to gain endorsement (the imprimatur of Head Office) as the official Labor candidate for a seat in Parliament.

Even so, and with the benefit of hindsight on my part, I believe we can identify some of the major, more 'traditional' Labor pathways into Parliament. I've labelled these as the family

---

[9] Members of the NSW Legislative Assembly are elected for a *fixed* four-year term. The NSW Constitution requires a General Election to be held on the last Saturday in March at the end of each four-year term.

dynasty, the local councillor, the star candidate, the factional warrior, the union boss, the big Party fundraiser and the Head Office heavy.

Before we begin our brief journey along each of these paths, I need to make some general points. Firstly, with the exception of the 'union boss,' each of these Labor pathways has its counterpart in the Liberal and National Parties.

Secondly, these pathways are not mutually exclusive. The local councillor with aspirations of becoming an MP, for example, may well have strong factional allegiances—as might the union boss seeking a place on the Parliamentary benches.

Thirdly, regardless of the time taken by individual Labor aspirants on their journey into Parliament, their pathways inevitably cross and conflict with those of other Labor aspirants— generating bitterness, hatreds and rivalries that forever remain unforgotten and unforgiven.

Finally, it is beyond the scope of this book to identify any former or serving MP as having taken one or more of these pathways into Parliament. You can attempt that for yourself, if you wish.

What follows is merely a general guide to the more common routes taken by Labor aspirants who actually got there—beginning with those who took their first steps on the road to Parliament with the advantage of inherited history.

The family dynasty

For some, becoming a Labor MP simply meant following in their father's or their grandfather's footsteps, and continuing the family dynasty.

These aspirants grew up in a 'political family', having one or more relatives who were former Labor MPs, Ministers or Party Leaders. Schooled in politics, these aspirants had every reason to expect that, when the time was right, their well-connected relatives would be their (very effective) advocates, doing everything they could to secure a seat in Parliament for them.

And their expectations would prove correct. The dynasty founders and family members are more than willing to put a word in the right ear, call in favours, draw on long-standing loyalties, make promises, and, if necessary, weigh into preselection battles: anything to promote their aspirational descendants.

The Labor family dynasties are not interested in securing just *any* seat for their descendants; it has to be a *safe* Labor seat. Marginal Labor seats are simply out of the question.[10] But what if the time is right and there are no safe Labor seats available for their 'deserving descendants'? The family dynasty still goes into action, working behind the scenes within the Party (and even across the factions) to 'create a vacancy' by encouraging a long-serving Labor backbencher to retire earlier than he or she would otherwise have chosen personally.[11]

The local councillor

For those without family connections or other key Party roles, securing a seat in the NSW Legislative Assembly can mean a slow, hard, and at times treacherous slog along the path of local government.

---

[10] Marginal Labor seats are those held by the Party with a margin of less than 5%.
[11] *Backbenchers* are MPs who are not Ministers. Whilst Ministers sit on the 'front benches' of the House, other Members sit in the rows behind them — on the back benches.

Aspirants taking this path often began their journey by joining the junior arm of the Party, *Young Labor*. They'd later attend innumerable monthly meetings, slowly and cautiously making their way up into leadership positions in their Branches and working their backsides off for every local Labor candidate at every election and at all levels for years on end.

These are the hard-working, long-serving, and committed Labor Branch members, some of whom decide that, one day, they'd like to run for the local council. While some of them only see this as a means of serving their communities at the local government level, others see a spot on the local council as a stepping stone into State Parliament itself. After all, they reason, what better way to get the experience and the public profile they need to get elected to Parliament and be an effective local MP, than spending a term or two on the local council?[12]

And so, when the Party calls for nominations, our long-serving and hard-working Branch member puts up his or her hand, knowing full well that a preselection may be in the offing. That, in itself, is not for the faint-hearted. A preselection battle to secure the number 1 spot on the Labor ticket at a local council election may prove to be just as tough, brutal and divisive as a preselection for a seat in the Parliament itself.

Once elected to council, those with eyes on Macquarie Street work to improve their public profile and popularity within their local community by being accessible to ratepayers and establishing a reputation for 'getting things done.'

---

[12] Councillors in NSW are elected to serve the residents of a defined Local Government Area (LGA) for a four-year term. They each represent a particular *Ward* or geographical portion of the LGA.

But, for the local Labor councillor, the pathway into Parliament is likely to be a long one, particularly where the seat involved is a safe Labor seat and the sitting MP has no intention of retiring any time soon. Even then, the aspirant must hope like hell that the local MP they've faithfully supported for years will effectively anoint him or her as their successor when 'the time comes' to call it quits.

There's no guarantee, of course, that the retiring MP will provide such endorsement. And, in any event, other unexpected circumstances and unanticipated political forces may come into play, ending the local councillor's Parliamentary ambitions. As many have learned to their great disappointment, the local government pathway to Macquarie Street is a dead end.

The star candidate

Of the other pathways into State Parliament, one in particular strikes fear and loathing into the heart of the local Branch member who has worked so hard and waited so patiently for that one shot at becoming a Labor MP.

This is the star candidate: the one with the high public profile who is "recruited" by Head Office (when Labor is in Government) and is effectively parachuted in as the Party's candidate for a 'safe seat' shortly before the election. The attraction? The personal promise, directly or indirectly, by the Party Leader that 'the star' will be sworn in as a Minister in the next Labor government — after he or she easily wins the chosen seat (as expected).

When recruitment begins, the star typically does not live in the electorate, has absolutely no connection with the people of the area, and often is not even a member of the Labor Party itself.

But, the deal done, the star moves to a rented flat in the electorate. He or she then joins the Party in record time: without serving out the usual waiting period and without attending the required number of Branch meetings. The star is then quickly endorsed as the candidate by Sussex Street, having been preselected unopposed by Branch members or effectively preselected by Sussex Street itself, by virtue of the Party Rules which allow Head Office to ignore and override the wishes of the Branch members.[13]

Meanwhile, the Labor MP who occupies the 'safe seat' is quietly 'tapped on the shoulder' by Head Office. He or she may be persuaded to make way for the star and 'retire' from Office with the vague hint—or even the firm promise—of 'a job' after the State election.

The 'fix is in.' The sitting Labor MP then publicly announces his retirement, seemingly out of the blue, giving a host of very sensible reasons. And, while supporting the star's candidacy until voting closes on election day, the sitting Labor MP steps back from public life and 'goes quietly.'

The star is easily elected, and, his appointment having been rubberstamped by the Parliamentary Labor Caucus, is sworn in as a Minister of the Crown, with all the security of a 'safe seat', much to the despair of the hardworking local Branch members and councillors—not to mention the chagrin of those returned backbenchers who had long been hoping for a spot in the Ministry.

While his or her addition to the front bench adds credibility to the Labor Government itself, the transition from high profile public figure to the Ministry can be a very difficult one for the star

---

[13] Such decisions are made by NSW Labor's powerful *Administrative Committee*.

personally. Despite all their promise, the brightest stars in the Labor firmament often burn out completely, and very quickly.

The factional warrior

There are those whose path to Parliament took them via the factional stepping stones.

For these Labor aspirants, the (Right or Left) faction was far more than just a vague philosophical leaning; it was also their meal ticket. It was the faction which provided them with paid work in the office of a Labor MP, Minister or affiliated Union with the same factional alignment.

These aspirants are the factional warriors. Regardless of their faction, all of our major warriors have similar histories. Joining the Party in their teens, they worked their way up into leadership positions in Young Labor and went on to establish close associations with those at the top of the Head Office hierarchy-namely, the General Secretary or an Assistant General Secretary.

Having proven their loyalty to the faction and the Labor leadership at all levels and at every turn, our factional warriors would later be shoe-horned by Sussex Street into a 'safe seat', or at the very least, be preselected unopposed for a seat the Party is odds-on favourite to win, with the help of significant financial assistance from Head Office coffers.

For the long-time local Branch members effectively sidelined by the preselection of the factional warrior, the whole process was, and remains, unpalatable. After all, the factional warrior earmarked for their local seat has (usually) had very limited life experience and virtually no work experience beyond the Party machine or its affiliated Unions. Like the star candidate, the factional warrior has typically had very little, if any, previous connection with the Branch, let alone the community they now say they are committed to represent in State Parliament. Not surprisingly, it was not uncommon for Sussex Street to invoke the Party Rules which permit the endorsement of the factional warrior as a Labor candidate without a 'rank and file' preselection ballot.[14]

For the factional warriors, becoming a Labor MP was not just their reward for past services. Their elevation into Parliament carried with it the expectation that they'd continue to support their faction in the Labor Caucus and strengthen the power bases of their various patrons — without question.

The union boss

The Australian Labor Party grew out of the Trade Union movement in the 1890s and the two have been closely associated ever since.[15]

The unions have long had an input into the Party's policy-making and contributed to its election war chests. Many union members are also members of the ALP. Accordingly, it should also come as no surprise that more than a few Labor MPs took their first steps on their own pathway into Parliament having held a senior position in an affiliated Trade Union. There are, of course, plenty of examples of union leaders playing a major role in Australian politics. The most obvious of these is Bob Hawke, who, after 14 years as the President of the Australian Council of Trade

---

[14] A *rank and file preselection* occurs when the candidate is chosen by a vote of all eligible local Branch members alone.

[15] Even today, the Sussex Street building which houses State Labor's Head Office is owned by Unions New South Wales itself!

Unions (ACTU), went on to become the nation's longest serving Labor Prime Minister.[16]

Unions operate at a national and state level. For the most part, the bosses of NSW-based Unions anointed by Sussex Street typically go on to occupy the plush red leather benches of the Legislative Council (the State's Upper House) for eight years.[17]

One of the features of this pathway is that, unlike those seeking a seat in the Lower House, you don't have to slug it out in a tough preselection battle or campaign out there in the heat going from door-to-door or spend hours on a polling booth. You don't even have to worry about serving the people in one of the 93 geographically defined NSW electorates.

Under the proportional system of representation in which the whole State is treated as a single electorate, the key to your ascension into the Upper House at a general election is your spot on the Party's official ballot paper. The closer your name is to the top of the listed Labor candidates, the more likely it is you will be sworn in as one of the 42 Members of the NSW Legislative Council (MLCs).

Just how your particular spot is determined on the ballot paper is another matter altogether. But it's not unknown for the Party, when in Government, to go out of its way to attract high-profile NSW Union leaders into Parliament to fill a casual Labor

---

16   Bob Hawke was Prime Minister from 1983 to 1991. Ben Chifley, Labor Prime Minister from 1945 to 1949, was also a prominent Trade Union leader before entering politics.

17   For the most part, the Presidents and Secretaries of National Unions who make it into Federal Parliament have a seat reserved for them in the Australian Senate for six years.

vacancy in the Legislative Council with the tempting offer of a Ministry.[18]

Labor Premiers often see it as important to keep the union movement 'on side' when there are likely to be decisions made by the Government affecting the union membership. There is also the conventional wisdom that it is better to have a vocal union leader with a strong media presence "inside the tent" as a member of the Labor Ministry—rather than "outside the tent" criticising the Government.

The big Party fundraiser

Election campaigns don't come cheaply, and raising money to help finance them is something expected of every political aspirant.

From time to time, there are some whose enormous contributions to the Party coffers—through soliciting donations and promoting formal fundraising events—are such as to distinguish them from other aspirants and give them the edge when it comes to getting a spot on the Labor ticket for NSW Upper House.

Aspirants who take this particular pathway are typically wealthy Party members with extensive business contacts who enjoy the patronage and influence of Labor powerbrokers. But their value to Sussex Street and the Party leadership goes beyond their extraordinary fundraising abilities. These aspirants are often well-respected, high-profile leaders of particular cultural communities and are generally seen by the Party as a means of

---

[18] A 'casual vacancy' occurs in the Legislative Council when a sitting Member dies or resigns during his or her term of Office. His or her replacement is not elected by the people. The casual vacancy is simply filled by a nominee belonging to the *same* Party as the Member who dies or resigns.

attracting the so-called 'ethnic vote.' They are also regarded by the factional heavyweights as the perfect vehicle for attracting new members to the Party, if not particular Labor Branches themselves.

Over time, and with the support and assistance of Parliamentary Leaders and Head Office, the aspirational big fundraisers raise their profile within the Party. Their continued contribution and apparent loyalty are such that they may well be rewarded with a spot high up on the Labor ticket for NSW Upper House at a general election.

With the strong support of the Head Office heavies, the aspirant who set out on the fundraising road secures a comfortable seat in the NSW Legislative Council, and may even go on to be a Minister of the Crown in a Labor Government.

The Head Office heavy

It really should come as no surprise to find former Sussex Street heavyweights occupying the Parliamentary benches — usually in the NSW Upper House.[19]

Indeed, that is the destiny (if not the reward) awaiting those who work their way up through the factional maze and intrigue of Head Office to become the General Secretary of the NSW Branch of the Australian Labor Party.

Once in Parliament, these organisational high flyers can expect a further step up to the Ministry as soon as a vacancy appears, or in some cases following a general election, from the word 'go.'

---

[19] Some make it into the Federal Parliament as members of the Australian Senate.

These aspirants typically set out on their pathway into Parliament by joining Young Labor, working as union organiser and later picking up a job in Sussex Street.

And, like every other major organisation, Labor Head Office has a structure which provides both the pathway to the top and the rules for the succession once the head honcho moves on to Parliament. After years working in the bowels of Sussex Street, our aspirant is appointed as a 'State Organiser', and goes on to secure one of the two Assistant General Secretary spots: one for each of the factions, Right and Left. While the final rung on the Head Office ladder – that of the NSW General Secretary – is reserved exclusively for those Assistants on the Right, those on the Left who take on the role of Assistant General Secretary later also go on to enjoy the rarefied atmosphere of a seat in the Legislative Council.[20]

One should never underestimate the incredible power and influence of the General Secretary of the NSW Labor Party. They are at once major factional players and key power brokers – playing a role in everything from the selection of Labor candidates to the appointment of Labor Ministers, and capable of making and breaking Labor Premiers and Labor Prime Ministers.

The General Secretary also plays a key role in the development of Labor Party policy and, whilst having very strong connections with the Union leaders, is often the point of access for big business to the Labor Government itself. Those holding the top Sussex Street job naturally control overall Party funding and assume the role of the State-wide Labor Campaign Director at each general election.

---

[20] The majority of Labor Party members and Labor MPs belong to the Right faction.

To many within the Party, the General Secretary is something of a protected species. Regardless of their successes or their failures, this aspirant is odds-on favourite for a seat in the NSW Upper House, at the very least.

1.4. One anomaly...Me!

Let's now turn the clock back to 1998. What about me? Which of the seven more 'traditional' Labor pathways we've just discussed would I take in my own attempt to become an MP?

The answer to this oversized, multiple-choice question is simply: none of the above!

You see, so far as getting into politics goes, I was something of an anomaly. Explaining that requires me to talk about a little about my own history. Unlike Alice in Wonderland, I'm not going to "begin at the beginning." I really only want to touch upon so much of my early life and background that led me to answer the multiple choice question the way I did.

A thumbnail sketch

My earliest childhood memories begin around five years of age, living with my parents, Joe and Joyce Collier, and baby brother Allan in a semi-circular tin hut on the edge of the Darwin Air Force Base.

Like many young Australian men of his time, my father put up his age to join the RAAF during World War II and after War's end served with the British and Commonwealth Occupation Forces in Japan.

In the mid-1950s, and shortly after I started school in Darwin, we returned to Sydney. There we shared an old terrace house with two other families (including my younger cousins) in what was (then) the far-from-socially-desirable and decaying inner city suburb of Redfern.

Sadly, it wasn't long before Dad developed a condition rendering him medically unfit for further service in the RAAF he loved. He had no choice but to go out and find other work, becoming a travelling salesman selling car and truck tyres.

But he did manage to get a War Service Home Loan and in the late 1950s we moved from that overcrowded Redfern terrace with its small, lifeless cement backyard to a new two-bedroom fibro on a quarter-acre block in the working-class Sydney suburb of Revesby. While Dad sold tyres, Mum worked in a nearby factory.

In the early 1960s, Dad took on the role of a country traveller and we spent about four years living in Cessnock and Orange before finally returning to our Revesby fibro. That, of course, meant a disrupted education for my brother and me. By the time I left school in Year 10 — contrary to the wishes of my parents and the advice of my teachers — I'd changed schools seven times.

After two years of monotonous and mind-numbing work with nothing to look forward to beyond going surfing with my mates every weekend, the penny dropped: I just had to get an education! In 1968, at age 18, and with the support of my parents, I left my job, put my surfboard under the house and undertook the day-matriculation course at Sydney Technical College.

I completed the two-year Higher School Certificate (HSC) course in one year and won a Teaching Scholarship to the

University of New South Wales, where I'd be awarded a Commerce Degree (with Merit) majoring in Economics and go on to complete a Graduate Diploma in Education.

Like most people my age back then, I lived at home with my family until my wedding day. In January 1972, at age 22, I married a Sutherland Shire girl, Jeanette Carter. And, like many young newly-weds of the day, we lived with her parents, Neville and Elizabeth, in the southern-Sydney suburb of Miranda until we got on our feet. At the time, I'd just finished my Commerce Degree and was just about to start on my graduate training to become a State high school teacher.

During my 17-year teaching career, I also served as the Education Department's State Consultant in Economics, chaired the NSW HSC Economics Examination Committee (which sets the annual papers) and wrote five textbooks on the subject for Year 11 and 12 students.[21]

Whilst teaching, I studied law at night, becoming a solicitor practising criminal law with the Office of the Director of Public Prosecutions (DPP) and later with the Legal Aid Commission of NSW. I went on to be admitted as a barrister specialising in criminal law in the higher Courts. So much for my careers in education and the law.

None of these career achievements would have been possible without the love, patience and ongoing support of my wife, Jeanette, for which I shall always be grateful. We had two beautiful children, Sarah and Michael, both born at Sutherland Hospital and now have four beautiful grandchildren.

---

[21] Barry Collier, *Introducing Economics*, Jacaranda-Wiley, 1988 (first edition).

My Dad died in 1986 aged 60, after a long battle with cancer. Mum suddenly passed away in 1991 at 64 from leukaemia. Allan had been killed earlier in a motorcycle accident in 1978 aged 23. I'd also had a sister, Susan, who had died soon after birth.

Jeanette's supportive parents, Neville and Elizabeth Carter, had passed away in 1985 and 1996 respectively. Jeanette was an only child, and so, by the time I thought about putting up my hand for a seat in Parliament in 1998, our family circle was, sadly, a very small one indeed.

Family politics

I wasn't the product of a political family. Looking back, I don't ever remember any conversations around the kitchen table about politics or political Parties or about how we should right the wrongs of the world.

Like most families in Revesby in the 1950s, 1960s and early 1970s—and like most families today—we just got on with our lives. The only comment I recall coming even close to a political discussion at home was Dad telling me, one ANZAC Day after the dawn service at Panania RSL, that:

> "I really liked Ben Chifley. But John Curtin was our greatest Prime Minister. You know why? Because he told Churchill to go to buggery and brought our boys back from overseas to fight for Australia."

I don't know whether my parents even knew who their local MP was, and if they did, they never talked about him in front of me. Sure, I saw all the posters up at the local public school from time to time on the way to play soccer on a Saturday morning and I heard Mum remind Dad they had to "go up and vote," but that was where the conversation ended. I never accompanied them when they went to vote. I never knew how they voted and it never even occurred to me to ask.

I don't ever recall learning about Parliament, or democracy at any of my seven Catholic schools, let alone going on a school excursion to Macquarie Street or to Canberra. We never had a Member of Parliament visit any of my schools, and I certainly can't recall any candidate ever knocking on our front door.

The thought of going into politics never even crossed my mind until the ripe old age of 48. I well recall visiting my 98-year-old maternal grandmother, Violet Donnelly, at her Chippendale home, and telling her I'd joined the Labor Party and hoped one day to stand for Parliament. Her reply?

> "That's nice, dear. The Labor men were very good to your Pop and me during the Depression. They used to come around and give us fruit and vegetables for the kids when we lived in Granville. Would you like a cup of tea?"

That was all she said. Nanna had never before mentioned any political Party or said anything even remotely political, let alone mention the Great Depression! But I already knew that Nan and Pop Donnelly had really struggled to bring up six daughters in the 1920s and 1930s. After Pop became an insulin-dependent diabetic, Nan kept the family going by scrubbing floors at the local hospital. Now, I could add the fact that the Labor Party had helped my family through the toughest of times.

In her own way, my very polite and unassuming grandmother had not only given me her seal of approval, but extra pride in the fact that I was a member of the Labor Party — and a reason to believe I had chosen well! But so much for family discussions about politics and my non-existent political heritage.

Joining the Party

Gough Whitlam's election win in December 1972 after 23 years of Labor in Opposition carried with it, great hope for the future of our nation. But his win also secured the future for Jeanette and me personally.

Whilst at University, I'd won the lottery no student wanted to win: my birthdate came out of the conscription barrel. I'd been officially notified, towards the end of my studies, that I'd be joining the Australian Army in the January 1973 intake, whether I liked it or not.

Within days of his election, and as he had promised, Prime Minister Whitlam abolished conscription, effectively allowing me to get on with family life at home with Jeanette and begin my career as a high school teacher. And who knows, with the Vietnam War continuing, Mr Whitlam's victory may have even saved my life![22]

Gough Whitlam was both charismatic and inspirational. Ask anyone why they joined the Labor Party in the early 1970s, and they'll answer you in just two words: "Gough Whitlam!" I was among the many who became a member in the wake of the great man's historic victory.

In April 1973, Jeanette and I went along to our first meeting of the Miranda Branch of the ALP, at the Sutherland District Trade

---

[22]   To this day, I nevertheless remain appalled at the way so many of our Vietnam Veterans were treated after they returned home, having served Australia with courage and pride.

Union Club (better known as *the Tradies*) in Gymea. Our membership was short-lived. Having begun studying law part time at night, and teaching throughout the day, I just didn't have the time to continue attending Party meetings.

Come 1995, I was working as a Legal Aid Solicitor at Sutherland Local Court and was a big fan of Labor Prime Minister, Paul Keating.[23] Bob Carr had just been narrowly elected as NSW Premier, and during a discussion with a neighbour living across the road, Alan Bell, I discovered that, when it came to politics, we were of like minds. He was a member of a nearby Labor Branch and invited me attend a meeting with him.

At the time Jeanette and I joined the Como-Jannali Branch of the ALP in 1995, I did so without any thought of standing for Parliament. This was a very active Branch, and, like any committed Party member, I soon got involved in supporting our local candidates — letterboxing pamphlets, attending fundraisers, helping out at street stalls and handing out 'How to Votes' at Federal, State and Council elections.

My profile: Zilch!

The day would come when I decided to put up my hand and take my very first steps on a pathway that I believed would take me into Parliament.

Prior to setting out on any such path, of course, every aspirant needs to think about the kind of political profile they have: their attributes which might lead their Party to choose them over other competing aspirants as the candidate for a particular

---

[23] From an *Economics* standpoint, I still regard Paul Keating as Australia's greatest ever Federal Treasurer.

seat as well as those individual qualities which might encourage people to actually vote for them.

When the day did in fact arrive for me to think about standing for public office, I was a complete unknown. I had no political experience to speak of, no Party or factional profile, and no real profile within my local community.

Unlike many of those aspirants on the Parliamentary path for the first time, I hadn't served as a local councillor. Neither had I put in the many years of hard slog for the Party as a Branch member. Indeed, my Labor membership number begins with the number 95 to indicate the year I'd joined the Party (1995).

Prior to putting up my hand, I'd never spoken to the then General Secretary, John Della Bosca or to any of his offsiders. I'd never met the Premier, any of his Ministers or even any Labor MP— other than the Federal MP Robert Tickner who attended the Branch meetings from time to time.[24] And, while it will horrify some, I'd never attended the NSW Party's Annual Conference at the Sydney Town Hall, or even visited Head Office.

Astonishing as it may sound, I would set out on my aspirational path without factional allegiances or patronage of any kind. I wasn't a member of a faction and had never been so. Factionalism was not something I'd encountered, or openly discussed, at Branch meetings. Indeed, by the time I first put up my hand, I really had no basic knowledge or awareness of the Right and Left factions or the philosophical differences between them (whatever they're supposed to be).

---

[24] Hon. Robert Tickner MP was the Member for Hughes from 1984 to 1996. He was Minister for Aboriginal Affairs in the Hawke and Keating Governments.

I wasn't a 'star candidate' by any stretch of the imagination. Indeed, my public profile matched both my political heritage and my political experience: nil!

Apart from playing sport for local soccer, hockey and cricket clubs, I'd never been actively involved in any local community group or organisation in the Sutherland Shire. And, while I'd worked as both a high school teacher and as a Legal Aid Duty Solicitor in the Shire before becoming a barrister, the stark reality was that no one out there in voter-land had ever heard of me.

With me supporting a family and surviving as a barrister on Legal Aid criminal work, there was no way I would ever fall into the category of a big party donor.

At the time I put up my hand, I didn't even meet the usually strict requirement of being a member of a Trade Union, let alone a Union boss! My escape clause here was the fact that barristers, by definition, don't have a union — and I'm sure the Bar Association of NSW would frown upon any suggestion that it was one!

As odd as it may sound, starting off in politics as a complete unknown is not necessarily a bad thing. Being an unknown means that you don't carry any political baggage to begin with.

What follows now is my story: the pathway I took in seeking a seat in Parliament. I don't for one moment suggest I'm special or somehow unique. But as one former Labor Minister would agree many years later, I was something of an anomaly!

2. FIRST ATTEMPT

2.1. Putting up my hand

From the time I first became interested in politics, my focus had been on the Federal scene. After joining the Como-Jannali Branch in 1995 and working on the local Federal campaign in 1996, I was elected as a Branch delegate to the Federal Electorate Council (FEC) for *Cook*, the electorate in which I lived.

FECs are an important part of the local Labor hierarchy. It is to the FECs that Branch motions are sent and debated. If passed by the FEC, these motions have the potential to become Federal Labor Party policy — something not lost on the delegates after the loss of government to the Liberals under John Howard in 1996. With the need to restore Labor to the Treasury Benches and the likelihood of a Federal election being called in late 1998, debates at Cook FEC meetings were particularly vigorous, and at times, heated.[25]

I enjoyed participating in the FEC debates, and I thought that one day, I would like to be a Federal MP. I decided that, if the opportunity ever arose, I'd give up my work as a barrister and have a go at running as the Labor candidate for Cook, long held by the Liberal Party.

---

[25] The term 'Treasury Benches' technically refers to the front benches in the (Federal or State) Lower House to the right of the Speaker occupied by the Prime Minister or the Premier, the Treasurer and other Ministers. The term is often used generally to refer to the Government of the day.

You?

I well recall attending one of the monthly Como-Jannali Branch meetings in the drafty little Oyster Bay Community Hall on a very cold and wet winter's night in 1998.

True to form, the meeting followed its rather strict, inflexible agenda despite the dreary weather outside. 'Correspondence inwards' included a note from Head Office that nominations would soon open for candidates wishing to stand for seats at the forthcoming Federal election.

> "So, we're looking for a candidate for Cook," the Branch Secretary said, with a little smirk and a knowing look. "Anybody interested?"

> "Yes, I am!" I said, sitting at the back of that small, dimly-lit hall on one of the battered, wooden school-room chairs provided by the local Council for the public.

Several members turned and looked at me with a mixture of surprise and disbelief, along with body language which effectively said:

> "Oh yeah, right! You're kidding, aren't you? As if *you* could win Cook! You're wasting your time!"

There were several messages in this for me. For a start, it seemed that the Como-Jannali Branch of the Australian Labor Party had resigned itself to never winning the seat of Cook back from the Liberals.

By 1998, Cook was regarded as a 'blue-ribbon' Liberal seat. Since its creation in 1969, Cook had only been held by Labor for a short three-year period. In 1972, and in the wake of the famous *It's Time* campaign, Sutherland Shire President and Labor candidate Ray Thorburn took the seat from the Liberal's Don Dobie.[26] Thorburn lost Cook to Dobie at the double dissolution election which followed the 1975 dismissal of the Whitlam Government. Despite three attempts by Thorburn to win the seat back for Labor, Dobie went on to hold Cook until his retirement in 1996.[27]

The Branch members were understandably justified in doubting that someone with my credentials could actually return the seat to Labor. After all, so their reasoning probably went, I'd only been a member of the Party for three years. I wasn't just a newcomer to the Party; I was a newcomer without any public profile and without any apparent support across the local Labor Branches. In short, I was a complete unknown and, in the unlikely event of being preselected, I'd probably lose anyway!

The process

But I have never been one to give up so easily. I'd never read the official ALP Handbook – let alone own a copy – and had no idea how to get to the preselection starting line. And so, meeting over, I asked Branch President, Trevor Romer, about the process.

Among other things, I'd have to persuade at least five paid-up, *bona fide* Labor members residing in the Cook electorate, and who had attended a specified number of Branch meetings over the previous two years, to nominate me by signing the official form. Each nominator's eligibility having been certified by the Branch

---

[26] The term *Shire President* was later replaced with *Shire Mayor*.
[27] At the time of writing, the seat of Cook had been in Liberal hands for the 43 consecutive years since 1975.

Secretary, I needed to lodge the form along with an upfront fee of $100 with Head Office.

Trevor told me that if I was the only one to nominate, and I was endorsed by the Party's Administrative Committee, I'd be the candidate for Cook. But if more than one candidate nominated, I would have to win a preselection ballot in which all eligible Branch members get a vote.

2.2. Nominating

The first problem for me was: who could I get to nominate me? There was my neighbour, Alan Bell, who'd taken me to my very first Como-Jannali Branch meeting.

Two other Branch members I spoke to after the meeting were also happy to sign my nomination form. One did so with the proviso that, while nominating me, she "might end up *not* actually voting for me" in a preselection ballot, because she "did not yet know who else would put up their hand!" That was three.

Some early advice

There were also two Members of other branches with whom I'd gotten on quite well at the Cook FEC meetings: Paul Ellercamp (Gymea-Grays Point Branch) and Tony Iffland (Miranda Branch). Their views on major issues generally aligned with mine and I sought both their advice and their support.

A former media adviser to Prime Minister Bob Hawke, Ellercamp had stood unsuccessfully in a preselection ballot for Cook in the lead up to the 1996 Federal election. Bitter about losing that preselection battle by only one vote, Paul was said to hold a grudge against several local Branch Members who, having committed to vote for him, switched their votes at the last moment to his opponent, Mark McGrath.

No doubt McGrath's very poor performance in the subsequent Federal poll— losing to first time Liberal candidate Stephen Mutch with a swing against Labor of 8.8% —rankled Paul even further. McGrath's disappearance from the local Labor scene immediately after his election loss, never to be seen again, added fuel to Paul's argument that McGrath was just another self-interested blow-in who didn't really have the Party's interests at heart, and so shouldn't have been our candidate for Cook in the first place.

Tony Iffland came from a very strong Labor family, including uncle and Party fundraising legend, John (Johno) Johnson MLC.[28] Tony had been our candidate for the seat of *Miranda* at the disastrous 1988 NSW State Election, which saw the defeat of Labor Premier, Barrie Unsworth. Tony delivered 38.5% of the final vote — a very creditable performance against sitting Liberal MP Ron Phillips in what was, until 2011, described as "the worst Labor performance, and best Coalition result, since the Lang era of the 1930s."[29]

Having 'been there and done that' both Paul and Tony knew the ropes. Both were happy to nominate me for preselection and to assist me throughout the process. They also gave me the names of Branch members they believed were likely to nominate me and vote for me should I ask them (and I certainly did that).

---

[28] Hon John Johnson was a Member of the NSW Legislative Council (Upper House) and its President from 1978 to 1991.
[29] *Antony Green*, NSW Parliamentary Library Research Service (October 1998). The 1988 Labor result would be eclipsed by the Party's disastrous 2011 State Election result.

A factional baby

I'd later learn from other Branch members that both Paul and Tony were members of the Party's Right faction and both were said to have been "done over by the Left." It was "several local Lefties" who'd switched their votes at the last minute to deny Ellercamp a shot at Cook. And it was "the same Lefties" who'd refused to help Iffland after he won preselection for Miranda, leaving him to run his entire election campaign out of his garage at home—simply because he wasn't a member of their faction.

In 1998, and when it came to factions, I was really just a baby. At the time I nominated for preselection, I was not just factionally unaligned, I was completely unaware of the existence of factions within the Labor Party itself.

Interestingly, neither Paul nor Tony ever hinted at their factional allegiances to me throughout my quest for preselection. You may well regard it as naivety on my part, but I do not believe, for one moment, that their overriding motivation in supporting me was driven by a need to exact revenge on the Left. I just really appreciated all the help and advice Paul Ellercamp and Tony Iffland gave me as I sought preselection for Cook.

Two preselection hurdles

Having gotten around, and signed up the required number of nominators, I personally lodged my nomination form and paid the requisite fee at Head Office. It was my very first visit to Sussex Street.

At the time, I hadn't heard of anyone else standing for preselection and I thought, somewhat naively again, that I might well be the only candidate. Yet, within an hour of nominations closing, I got a call from Ellercamp saying Peri Young from the Miranda Branch had put up her hand at the last minute. A ballot would be called to decide the Labor candidate for Cook in 1998.

Ellercamp was quick to point out, however, that a preselection contest against a female candidate presented another hurdle for me. In keeping with the Party's *Affirmative Action Policy*, Peri would receive a 25% loading on each vote she received in the preselection ballot. In other words, every single vote for Peri would count as 1.25 votes for her as against every single vote for me. To get across the line, I had to get 25% more votes than Peri.

Personally, I had no problem with the fact that gaining selection would require a very convincing win over Peri by me. I had always favoured the idea of having more women in Parliament and accepted the preselection loading without question or complaint.

While I don't recall having met her before she nominated, Peri Young had been around for a while and, as Ellercamp pointed out, was much better known around the traps than me. That, on top of her Affirmative Action loading, would raise the preselection bar even higher for me — especially given my relatively short time as a Party Member, my relatively low profile across the Branches and my zero profile in Sussex Street. But I was no stranger to hard work and I remained undeterred.

2.3. Getting to know you

Under Labor Party Rules, the announcement of a preselection battle is accompanied by a procedural timetable leading up to and including the ballot itself. The first step is to determine just *who* can vote on the appointed day, a process known as *credentialing*. Branch Attendance Books are opened and independently examined, members' financial status checked and a list of all eligible Cook preselectors produced.

The list of names and contact details included those of ALP Life Members within the electorate. While these were rarely, if ever, seen at local Branch meetings, Life Members were entitled to vote in preselection ballots by virtue of their status alone.[30]

For me, the names presented a real challenge. Beyond my own Branch members and those I'd met at FEC meetings, I knew very few of those on the eligibility list. While Paul Ellercamp and Tony Iffland provided me with background on several of them, it really all came down to me.

Making a phone call to each preselector clearly wasn't enough. I had to get out and meet each of them personally. Clearly, if I wanted preselectors to vote for me, I had to get to know them! That meant taking a week out of Court, passing several briefs to other junior barristers in my Chambers and visiting preselectors' homes.

At times, these visits were prearranged with a phone call. But at other times, and especially with those listed as retired or as Life Members, I turned up unannounced, believing they'd most likely be at home. Lobbying the preselectors at their homes would also serve as my personal introduction to the rigours of doorknocking, should I be fortunate to gain preselection as the Labor candidate for Cook at the forthcoming Federal election.

---

[30] Life Membership is bestowed on those who have held continuous membership of the Australian Labor party for at least 40 years.

Tough going...at times

I followed the list of preselectors methodically. I'd turn up at their homes, introduce myself and talk with them with a broad, flexible agenda in mind — all of which I hoped would eventually encourage each of them to say "yes" when I eventually asked them to vote for me.

We'd talk about them and their families, what they saw as important local issues and national problems and, of course, discuss the failures of the Howard Liberal Government. I'd tell them about my background and my family, my reasons for wanting to represent them and the issues I'd focus on if I won preselection and eventually became the MP for Cook. I was, of course, careful to avoid criticising (or even mentioning) my preselection opponent.

Several of the preselectors I visited said they would vote for me. Some were reluctant to talk to me and some obviously made excuses not to do so. Others were up front in telling me they would not vote for me, saying they preferred Peri, usually without giving me any reason. Following the old political adage that "you can really only believe those who tell you they *won't* vote for you," I ruled a line through their names on my list.

But the vast majority of preselectors whom I called were completely non-committal when I asked for their vote, saying only that they'd "think about it." While that was, in reality, only to be expected given my relatively short time in the Party, I found this answer particularly disappointing in cases where I'd spent hours at a preselector's home seeking their vote.

I shall never forget my very lengthy and excruciating visit to the Lilli Pilli home of Richard — a long retired police officer. Sitting with him at the kitchen table amid a blue haze of stale cigarette smoke, Richard seemed to take some kind of pleasure in asking me an interminable stream of irrelevant and ultimately meaningless questions.

On and on he went, seeking my views on everything from the GST to the problems facing the Australian Cricket Team. As a criminal lawyer, I sat there feeling sympathy for every suspect who'd ever been interviewed by Richard during his time as a copper. I couldn't help thinking that some of these poor buggers must have given up and confessed to crimes they didn't commit just to bring their interview with Richard to an end!

After more than two hours, it was clear that Richard was just wasting my time. Whether that was deliberate or because he was a lonely man who suddenly had a captive audience in me, I shall never know. But as Paul Ellercamp would later point out, some preselectors will deliberately keep you talking for as long as possible: not because they are interested in what you have to say, but because they intend to vote for your opponent! While they're talking to you and taking up your time, these preselectors are effectively reducing the amount of time you have to talk to the "undecideds" who might actually go on to vote for you!

I'll never know if Richard actually voted for me. But as I later discovered, no candidate could ever really rely on him to vote for them. One Labor aspirant desperately seeking preselection for Sutherland Shire Council had personally driven Richard from his home to the preselection venue expecting, of course, that he would secure Richard's vote. A grateful Richard is known to have left the aspirant's car, gone into the preselection booth and promptly voted for the opposing candidate!

A very special preselector

Amongst all the preselectors I visited, one deserves special mention: Albert (Bert) Rhodes, a 74-year-old retiree living on the Princes Highway at Sylvania Heights.

Turning up at his front door in my suit and tie, I was met by Bert's wife, Iris. When I asked to speak with Mr Rhodes, she said "he's down the side working on the house. You can go around and see him if you like."

I thanked Mrs Rhodes and walked across the front lawn in the direction she'd indicated. Rounding the corner of the house, I saw this old bloke in shorts and a singlet standing in bare feet on the top rung of the ladder painting the guttering with his back to me.

"Mr Rhodes?" I said, standing near the foot of the ladder.

He turned and looking down, paintbrush in hand and said, "Who are you?"

"Barry Collier" I replied.

"What are you selling?" he asked gruffly.

"I'm a Labor candidate for the Cook preselection, so I suppose I'm selling myself!" I replied with a smile.

The old fella chuckled and said, "I thought you must be a salesman. We get a lot of them up here on the Highway! Give us a minute and I'll finish up."

"OK" I replied, pleased he would make the time to talk.

"Iris! Put the kettle on!" he yelled out loudly.

Bert, Iris and I sat at the kitchen table and had a good chat over a cup of tea. In contrast to Richard and some other preselectors I visited, Bert got straight to the point and didn't waste my time. He told me about his background and his family. I told Bert and Iris about my mine. He asked me a host of relevant questions, and I answered them as best I could.

Bert Rhodes was old school: a strong family man, a strong Union man, and a genuine *True Believer*. He wanted to know if I, too, belonged to a Trade Union. I told him that before I was a criminal lawyer, I was a financial member of the NSW Teachers' Federation throughout all my 17 years as a State high school teacher, and I had represented Federation members on various Education Department Syllabus Committees for 8 of those years. I went on to explain that barristers don't have an affiliated Union, but they do have the Bar Association to represent their concerns to the government, and that I was a paid-up member of that. Bert's nod signalled that my answer was acceptable to him.

While I'll never know whether he voted for me in the preselection ballot, Bert Rhodes would turn out to be one of my best and most loyal grassroots supporters.[31]

The question not asked

Canvassing for preselection votes taught me much — not just about doorknocking, but about the local Labor Party psyche. I was asked a wide variety of questions and came across many differing views and ideas that I would later reflect upon. These not only helped me

---

[31] Indeed, the day would come many years later when Bert's family would give me the honour of delivering the eulogy at his funeral.

determine my own stance on particular issues, but served to guide me in my subsequent discussions with other preselectors and to assist me in my later presentations to local Branch members.

Interestingly enough, and looking back, however, the one question I *wasn't* asked by any preselector was: "Which *faction* do you belong to?" It was a question I could not have answered at that stage anyway. Indeed, the fact that this question was never asked of me only served to reinforce my general ignorance of the factions and the role they ultimately played in determining Labor candidates, Ministers, Premiers and even Prime Ministers.

2.4. Candidate Forums: testing times

The process of gaining preselection went beyond lobbying, telephoning and doorknocking preselectors. In the lead-up to the ballot, each Branch held its own Candidate Forum in conjunction with its regular monthly meeting.

The Forum format required both Peri and I to turn up at the appointed time, address the Branch members present and then answer a host of questions, without notice, from individual members. Questions were asked on everything from our family backgrounds and our campaign experience, to our reasons for standing and our support for 'Labor policies' — some of which did not exist and some of which probably never would.

There were, of course, questions as to how we would tackle local issues (some of which were hypothetical and many of which bore absolutely no relationship at all to Federal politics) and the type of campaign to which Branch members could look forward to, should either one of us be successful in gaining preselection.

The questions were often tough, and while many were only to be expected, there were other questions that seemed to have originated from somewhere beyond the known universe and could not have been anticipated even by the most astute and experienced politician!

Indeed, it was not uncommon to face a barrage of questions from at least one Branch member who was obsessed with one particular issue and was determined to cross-examine each candidate, machine-gun style, to determine whether they possessed the same intimate knowledge of the issue's history or at least the same sense of outrage that 'nothing was being done about it by either political Party'. At times, it was difficult to decide whether that particular Branch member was asking a question or making a speech. But you could tell by the number of other Branch members present who sat there patiently and rolled their eyes that they'd heard it all, many, many, times before. (The Labor Party, I'd discover, is clearly a 'broad church'!)

Again, I was never once asked about my factional allegiance at any of these Candidate Forums. In hindsight, and given my naivety as well as my lack of knowledge about Labor factions at the time, that was probably a good thing.

Yet, whatever the questions, the Branch members present gave no hint as to their satisfaction (or otherwise) with our answers, even when Peri and I were clearly on the same page. Members just seemed to sit there like so many judges hearing a barrister's submissions on the prisoner's sentence, giving absolutely nothing of their thinking away. Clearly, the Branch members wanted to 'keep their powder dry', preferring to make their decision closer to the preselection ballot, having considered all the pros and cons and having discussed our respective candidacies with the other local preselectors.

Not surprisingly perhaps, and while I thought I generally performed just as well as Peri—if not better in some instances—I found it very difficult to gauge the level of support for me among those attending these crucial preselection events.

Who is this Bob Rogers?

At the end of our questioning by Branch members, and before resuming their regular meeting, Peri Young and I were each given the opportunity to make a short closing statement. And it was here that I detected something troubling; something which I felt could well affect the outcome of the preselection itself.

If Peri and I agreed completely on anything at the Candidate Forums, it was our commitment to run a "grassroots campaign," and of course, we both reiterated that during our closing statements. But Peri always concluded her remarks with:

> "...and Bob Rogers has agreed to be my Campaign Director."

When she said this, I detected a collective sigh of approval, together with one or two winks and nods between the older Branch members in attendance.

"Who is this Bob Rogers?" I asked myself. I'd never heard of the bloke, much less met him. But, whoever he was, Peri's appointment of this Mr Rogers as her Campaign Director should she win the preselection appeared to be a big plus in her favour when it came to deciding the Labor candidate for Cook at the 1998 Federal election!

I'd later discover that Bob Rogers was something of a local Labor icon, living in the Sutherland Shire suburb of Grays Point, who was very well respected across the local Branches. Never having previously had a win under his belt as a local Campaign Director at any State or Federal election, he was not exactly an 'election guru'. Even so, Rogers was widely regarded as a very good organiser who could always be relied upon to mobilise the local Labor troops and run a very credible grassroots campaign.

Paul Ellercamp simply described Bob Rogers as "an election junkie" and dismissed his potential appointment as Peri Young's Campaign Director as having absolutely no impact on the outcome of the preselection ballot. I was not so sure.

2.5. Preselection day and beyond

Preselection day finally arrived with voting taking place at the unofficial home of Labor in the Shire — *the Tradies* — from 8.00AM to 6.00PM. While it would prove to be a very long day, I'd done everything I possibly could to get across the line first and thought I had a reasonably good chance of doing so.

I'd phoned all the 'undecided' preselectors, called those I thought would support me and organised transport to and from *the Tradies* for disabled preselectors and several Life Members who could no longer drive (including Richard). I'd even printed a 'How to Vote for Barry Collier' card to be handed out to preselectors before they went in to vote. That might sound over the top to you, but it was all about giving the preselectors the idea that, should I win, I'd adopt a professional approach to every aspect of the forthcoming Federal campaign.

I stood at the entrance to the booth all day greeting preselectors — with my wife, Jeanette, and daughter, Sarah, taking turns handing out with me. Most preselectors took my 'How to Vote' (HTV) in good spirits. But others just had to make it demonstrably clear to all and sundry as they went into vote that they were voting for Peri, not only by refusing point blank to take my card but by shaking their heads at us as they went in to vote.

Some preselectors rudely brushed past my family and me, apparently annoyed either that Peri actually had an opponent or that they had to come out to vote in a preselection at all! I'd seen far better behaviour than this by Labor booth workers towards the Liberals on an election day! Indeed, there were times when a casual observer would have found it hard to believe that Peri and I actually belonged to the *same* Party!

I was very disappointed by the fact that several preselectors who had committed to voting for me just didn't turn up at all. Neither did they return my mobile phone calls or messages I left throughout the day. What really rubbed salt into the wounds was the fact that none of these 'supporters' even had the courtesy, after the event, to offer any explanation for their 'no-shows'.

Voting in the preselection ended at 6.00PM sharp. The votes having been counted and scrutinised, the candidates and supporters gathered to hear the result declared by the returning officer. I was optimistic and, despite the no-shows, I still believed I would win. I was wrong. I'd lost by five votes!

In politics, as in sport, you have to be magnanimous in defeat. And so, I immediately and publicly shook Peri's hand. I congratulated her on her win and wished her good luck as our candidate for Cook. I thanked all the preselectors who voted, saying I accepted their decision without reservation. And most importantly, I promised I'd work as hard as I could to help ensure that Peri Young was elected as the Labor MP for Cook.

A brief post-mortem

All politicians, and all would-be politicians, who lose any ballot naturally ask themselves: what went wrong? Why did I lose? And so, I held a brief post-mortem with Paul Ellercamp and Tony Iffland after the supporters from both sides had dispersed. Why did Peri Young win?

Ellercamp was quick to attribute Peri's victory to "strong support from the Left," adding, "Arthur Gietzelt was probably on the phone calling in favours again." He didn't elaborate and I didn't respond. "Left? Arthur who?" I thought to myself, somewhat puzzled.

No one had mentioned 'the Left' or 'the Right' to me until that point and, while this would have horrified his acolytes, I knew absolutely nothing about Arthur Gietzelt at that stage. Indeed, I only recall Arthur's name being mentioned once during my preselection campaign when Ellercamp told me not to bother wasting my time seeking Gietzelt's support.

"Trust me, old Gietzelt won't vote for you. Arthur's a Peri supporter," Paul had said.

The factional penny finally dropped as Ellercamp explained that Arthur was "an old Leftie" who'd been around for years and who controlled the Shire Labor Branches.

Ellercamp went on to point out that every Labor candidate preselected for Cook had been a member of the Left — with the exception of Michael Addison (who was aligned with the Right). Likewise, Paul said, every Labor candidate preselected for the State seat of Miranda — with the exception of Tony Iffland — also just happened to be a member of the Left. The reason was quite simple, he continued: "Arthur controlled the numbers!" In short, Arthur Gietzelt was the local Labor power broker!

All this came as a complete revelation to me. I felt that I had not been beaten on merit, but by a group voting as a bloc under the direction of some factional heavyweight whom I'd never met. I must admit feeling a little hard done by as I left *the Tradies* with Paul, Tony and Jeanette.

Once home, Jeanette and I had a brief chat. On the positive side, I'd run a pretty close second, given the weighting. Not bad, we agreed, for a relative unknown who'd only been in the Party just over three years. But now, of course, I was far better known across the Branches. Ever the optimist, I thought I should give it another go if the opportunity came my way. Jeanette agreed.

A phone call

On the Monday night after my preselection defeat, the home phone rang. The caller introduced himself as Arthur Gietzelt. I was taken aback. This truly was the phone call out of the blue!

Gietzelt said he rang to tell me why he supported Peri Young in Saturday's preselection.

"I supported Peri because I wanted a female candidate," Arthur said.

"I was told it was because she was a member of the Left faction," I cheekily replied.

The conversation quickly changed direction, turning into what would be a history of the Labor in the Sutherland Shire starting with Arthur's first term as a Ward Councillor in 1956 and his nine years as Shire President, then moving on to his time as a NSW

Senator and Minister for Veterans' Affairs in the Hawke Federal Government. While I respected his obvious achievements and his contribution to the Labor Party, I could not help thinking that Arthur Gietzelt could talk under wet cement!

I had a brief to prepare for Court the next day and so, after an hour of this one-way conversation, I politely ended what would be my first and only conversation with Arthur Gietzelt.

In his autobiography published shortly after his death in 2014 and almost 15 years after the event, Arthur reflected upon Peri's preselection win. Having noted his role in changing Labor Party Rules to give 'women candidates an inbuilt 25% extra quota vote in ALP ballots for public office,' he went on to write: 'As a result, a youthful Peri Young was able to defeat a later well-known public figure in the preselection ballot to contest the Federal seat of Cook in 1998.'[32]

While Arthur put Peri's preselection victory down to her Affirmative Action loading, he didn't mention the name of the candidate she defeated! I'll leave you to figure out why.

2.6. Another local preselection battle

Mine wasn't the only Federal preselection battle going on in the Shire in 1998. The adjacent Federal seat of *Hughes* was also up for grabs. Hughes then covered the western half of the Shire and extended out to Liverpool.

Long held by Labor, Hughes had been won by the Liberal's Dana Vale in 1996. Robert Ticker had held the seat for 12 years and his defeat was attributed by many to the Hindmarsh Island Bridge

---

[32]   Arthur Gietzelt, *Sticks and Stones*, Warilla, 2014, page 351.

controversy towards the end of his six-year term as Minister for Aboriginal Affairs.[33]

While Tickner wanted to stand again at the 1998 Federal election, NSW Labor General Secretary, John Della Bosca would have none of it. Even before the Hughes preselection was called, Della Bosca made it quite clear to Tickner that Head Office would not endorse him. There was no point in Tickner putting up his hand again; his political career was effectively over.

Five other Labor aspirants presented themselves for preselection, including the high-profile boss of the ABC, David Hill, and Liverpool City Councillor, Alison Megarrity.[34] While I'd never met either and had no role to play in the preselection, I attended the Hughes Candidate Forum to hear what each of the contenders had to say.

As I'd expected, Hill was a very polished performer. But I thought Megarrity was, on balance, more impressive. At the end of the day, and when it came to the preselection ballot, however, her performance just didn't matter.

Hill had the numbers— thanks, reportedly, to a sudden rise in the membership of several supportive Labor Branches at the Shire end of the electorate, and to the fact that Head Office had made it widely known that he was its preferred candidate.

While David Hill went on to win the preselection battle, with Alison Megarrity running a creditable second, he did not go on to win the war. At the 1998 Federal Election, Hill not only lost every polling booth; Hughes was one of the few seats to record a swing

---

[33]   This was the so-called *Secret Women's Business Affair*.
[34]   At the time of the Hughes preselection, Alison Megarrity was one of only nine women to serve on Liverpool Council in its 140-year history!

in favour of the Howard Government itself! Being a star candidate is no guarantee of success at the ballot box.

Alison Megarrity would later go on to secure preselection as the Labor candidate for the newly-created seat of *Menai* at the March 1999 NSW State election. In hindsight, perhaps David Hill and Head Office did Alison a favour!

2.7. Don't spit the dummy!

Losing a preselection ballot after giving it everything you've got is not easy. But, however badly you feel, you can't be seen by the Party to take it personally. The members have spoken and moved on. You must do likewise.

The worst thing you can do, after losing, is to 'spit the dummy' — by criticising those preselectors you feel have let you down or by refusing to help the preselection winner in their subsequent campaign for the seat itself. If you want a future in politics, you must put the Party first: uniting behind the winner, giving the preselected candidate your full support and being seen to be doing so by all other local Branch members.

I was as good as my word so far as my pledge to help Peri Young after her preselection win was concerned. I letter-boxed her pamphlets, worked on her street stalls, handed out for her at railway stations and attended her campaign launch as well as her fundraisers. These included an event with special guest, Joan Kirner, former Premier of Victoria, arranged by *Emily's List*, a Labor-based organisation striving to increase the participation of women in Australian Parliaments.

On Federal election day, 3rd October 1998, I also handed out Peri Young's How to Votes (HTVs) at the Kareela booth and scrutineered for her after the polls closed.

A visitor to the booth

I well remember seeing my own State MP, the Liberal Member for Miranda, Ron Phillips, turning up at the Kareela polling booth with Peri's opponent, the Liberal Candidate for Cook, Bruce Baird.

A former NSW Transport Minister in the Fahey Government, Baird had replaced sitting MP Stephen Mutch as the Liberal candidate for Cook, after Mutch had served only one term.

It was common knowledge that Ron Phillips, a factional Liberal heavyweight, had been behind moves to roll Mutch and install Baird as the MP in the safe Liberal seat. Mr Mutch was reportedly very bitter at what he and his local supporters saw as treachery on Ron Phillips' part—something with the very real potential to come back and haunt the sitting Miranda MP.

2.8. Scrutineering: the numbers in Cook

At precisely 6.00PM, the doors of the Kareela polling booth closed and the counting began. Along with Peri's other scrutineers, I watched the count closely, challenging those Liberal votes which, at first sight, were incorrectly marked or upon which preferences were not filled in. Such votes were classed as 'informal' and would not be added to the Liberal tally.

Bruce Baird's scrutineers were, of course, just as active in trying to have votes favouring Peri Young ruled out as informal for the same reasons. Not surprisingly, and given the importance of securing every vote, challenges from both sides became quite heated at times.

As is the practice, however, disputes between each Party's scrutineers over the validity of individual votes were settled, as far as possible, on the night by the Presiding Officer appointed to run the booth.

In scrutineering for the first time, I was amazed to see the number of ballot papers left completely blank and the "messages" voters wrote on their ballot papers (some of which would make a wharfie blush). It was a sad commentary that so many Australians were just so completely disinterested in our democracy that they did not value their vote. Too many, it seemed, simply did not care who ran the country, regarding their attendance at a polling booth once every three or four years as an unnecessary chore and their political representatives as a 'waste of space' (to put it politely).

Scrutineering over, the formal votes tallied and the booth results agreed between the Parties and the Presiding Officer, our last task was to phone the Kareela booth results to Peri's Campaign Director, Bob Rogers, at her Caringbah campaign office. In the meantime, booth workers, Party members and supporters had gathered at *the Tradies* watching the election night coverage on TV.

The result in Cook at the 1998 Federal election was clear, very early in the evening. Having recorded only 31% of the primary vote, our candidate was easily defeated by Bruce Baird. Disappointed, Peri would be gracious in defeat, thanking Bob Rogers, local Branch members and booth workers for all their help and support in what was a tough campaign.

Peri Young stood again as the Labor candidate for Cook in 2001, this time having been preselected unopposed. With her primary vote down to 27%, she was again defeated by Bruce Baird. At the end of the day, however, it would be unfair to criticise Peri for failing to win what was becoming an increasingly safe Liberal seat in an increasingly conservative Sutherland Shire.

2.9.   What about Miranda?

As the evening drew to an end at *the Tradies* on Federal election night 1998, Jeanette and I were sitting in a small group with long-time Miranda Branch member, Martin Iffland (Tony's dad) and Bob Rogers.

Generally, the talk was about the campaign, the long day we'd all had, Kim Beazley's loss and what the return of the Howard government would mean for the Labor Party. Of course, we were all feeling a little down: we'd lost again and the prospects of Cook ever returning to the ALP looked bleak indeed.

During a lull in the conversation, Martin Iffland made a very unexpected observation:

> "You know, I think *you* could've won Cook today," he said to me.

> "Really?" I said.

> "Yes, really!" he replied, looking me squarely in the eye.

> "Well, the Branch members didn't think so," I said skeptically. "I didn't win the preselection!"

> Bob Rogers then chimed in with: "Well, *Miranda's* coming up soon. Why don't you think about that?"

"What about Peri having another go?" I said, believing she'd probably want to try for the State Parliament.

"She may not," Bob answered, adding "it's been a tough campaign. She's buggered, and it may be too soon for her to run again."

I'd never considered State politics but Bob Rogers said the NSW election would be held next March and the Party would call for nominations very soon. He encouraged me to think about it, adding: "it won't be easy. We haven't held Miranda for 15 years!"

While I agreed to give the idea some thought, it did seem a little odd that Peri's Campaign Director would be sussing me out as a potential candidate for the State seat of Miranda in March 1999.

But I took the suggestion as a kind of compliment, and I thought maybe — just maybe — this bloke might be *my* Campaign Director if I put up my hand a second time and actually won preselection!

3. MIRANDA, HERE I COME!

3.1. Miranda on my mind

Federal election over and Cook in the hands of the Libs for yet another term, it was back to my barrister's chambers and several waiting Legal Aid briefs.[35] But, having now been well and truly bitten by the political bug, the thought of putting up my hand for the State seat of Miranda was not all that far from my mind. Not surprisingly, the most basic question for me was: did I truly *believe* that I could win Miranda?

For me, standing for Parliament would never be about simply flying the Labor flag in a strong, blue-ribbon Liberal seat or about ingratiating myself with Sussex Street by putting up a credible (though clearly hopeless) campaign. Neither would it be about taking one for the Party by copping an inevitable hiding at the ballot box just so we can avoid media criticism that Labor didn't field a candidate. And for me, at least, standing for Parliament simply wasn't about campaigning in a safe Liberal seat with the (ultimately meaningless) aim of getting a swing against the incumbent, and so reducing the margin for the next Labor candidate at the next election.

No! For me, as one wanting to serve his community, standing for Miranda was all about one thing and one thing only: winning! If I was going to put up my hand for the seat at the State Election in March 1999, I *had* to believe in my heart of hearts that I

---

[35] My chambers, *Samuel Griffith*, was named after the first Chief Justice of the High Court of Australia.

could win! If I didn't personally believe that, then there was no point going through another tough preselection ballot!

If I truly believed that I could win in 1999, I'd put my heart and soul into the election campaign should I be preselected. Winning would mean giving it 150% on my part — something I'd always done for the things I really believed in.

3.2. Homework time

In politics, belief and reality often walk very different paths. It's not uncommon, for example, for those standing for Parliament for the first time to suffer from 'candidate's disease': an intractable belief he or she can win a particular seat despite facing a popular, long-established incumbent holding an insurmountable margin.[36] Conscious of just how easy it is for any candidate to get carried away with their prospects of success, I really needed to do a lot of homework before putting up my hand.

I knew, of course, that Gymea barber, Labor's Bill Robb, had won Miranda in 1978 and held it until his defeat by the Liberal's Ron Phillips in 1984. But beyond knowing that Phillips had held Miranda for 15 years straight, I knew little about the man, his profile or his popularity. Indeed, at the time I began thinking about putting up my hand, I really wasn't across the major issues confronting the people of Miranda and had no idea of the numbers I needed to get across the line. I wasn't even aware of the seat's geographic boundaries!

---

[36] First-time candidates do occasionally defeat long-standing incumbents with big margins at general elections — typically when there is a large Statewide 'swing' against the Government, or there is some major electorate-specific issue such as allegations of corruption against the sitting MP. Big swings against governments tend to occur more often in by-elections.

All this may seem a little odd for a political aspirant, given the fact that my wife, Jeanette, and I had lived in the Miranda electorate since 1972 and Mr Phillips had been *our* State MP for a decade and a half. But, until getting actively involved in the Labor Party in 1995, I was like most other people in the community: focusing on the everyday issues affecting their families, including their job, their kids' school and their sporting club. And like others, I only really got interested in local politics during election campaigns.[37] So what did I know about Ron Phillips MP, my local representative in Macquarie Street?

Meeting my State MP

My one and only contact with Ron Phillips had been back in the late 1980s, long before I'd ever contemplated political life. I'd gone to see him, as one of his constituents, about what I saw as a serious road safety problem at my children's school.

Kareela Public School sits at the very top of the suburb's Freya Street hill with very steep approaches on both sides. Many of its pupils crossed the street at the crest of this hill before and after School. As motorists approached the crest, the only warning they had of school children on the roadway was a red flag held out by a Year 6 pupil standing in the gutter on each side of the road! To my mind, this system was clearly unsafe. There were often 'near misses', one of which I observed on a wet afternoon. And so, as a concerned parent, I went to see my local State MP about getting traffic signals and a marked pedestrian crossing to improve road safety for the school kids.

---

[37] MPs and Party officials tend to forget that people out there in the community do not live and breathe politics as they do.

My encounter with Mr Phillips at his Miranda electorate office was disappointing to say the least. The meeting was not only far shorter than I expected; I also felt that his manner was rather condescending, and tinged with arrogance. My State MP quickly dismissed my concerns out of hand, flatly telling me that what I wanted just couldn't be done.

Ron Phillips even told me he'd been advised by experts that traffic lights and a marked pedestrian crossing on the Freya Street hill wouldn't improve safety for the school kids. Besides, he said, there'd been no serious accidents with the present system of flags! My Parliamentary representative went on to tell me that there was no point in him raising the issue with the Minister, thereby giving me the distinct impression that I was wasting his time.

I left Mr Phillips' office asking myself why I'd bothered going to see him in the first place. He didn't appear interested, didn't listen, and clearly wasn't prepared to go into bat for me and my family, let alone the hundreds of kids at Kareela Public School. As I walked down the steep flight of stairs from his office to the Kingsway footpath, I had the thought that if Mr Phillips was the only candidate for Miranda, I'd consider voting informal!

But, lo and behold, about three years later, and after my kids had left Kareela Public for high school, I saw RTA technicians installing a set of traffic signals and a marked pedestrian crossing at the top of Freya Street hill! So much for Phillips telling me it couldn't be done! It *was* done! The flags were gone, along with Mr Phillips' credibility as far as I was concerned.

Asking around

Fast forward to late 1998 and the thought of running against my local MP at the State election the following March. As I replayed in my mind that meeting I'd had with him a decade before, I began to wonder just how popular Ron Phillips really was out on there on the streets of Miranda where it really mattered.

During a call from a close friend who lived in the electorate, I confided that I was contemplating running for the seat in 1999. My friend, who had no connection with either Party, asked me what I thought of Mr Phillips. Not surprisingly, I recounted my one and only meeting with my local MP all those years ago. His response?

> "Well, at least you got to see him! Every time *I* tried to make an appointment with Mr Phillips he was too busy to see me or was in Parliament or somewhere else. I just gave up in the end."

Clearly, when it came to the way Ron Phillips dealt with his constituents and their issues, I wasn't Robinson Crusoe! There just *had to be* more of his constituents out there who'd had the same experience as me and were dissatisfied with the service they were getting from their local MP. I wasn't mistaken.

Without revealing my views or my potential aspirations, I couldn't help but ask other Shire friends and contacts I came across what they thought of Mr Phillips. They had their own stories and generally confirmed my initial gut feeling that Ron clearly wasn't the most popular man about town. As you learn in politics (often the hard way), voters don't forget what their local MPs *don't* do for them.

One of my friends even suggested that Mr Phillips didn't like having interviews with his constituents and tried to avoid these like the plague. He based that conclusion on a rumour that Ron had chosen to locate his Electorate Office on the first floor of a building in the Kingsway at the top of a very steep set of stairs to discourage seniors from coming to see him with their problems! While the MP had long since moved his Electorate Office to a building in Urunga Parade with far fewer steps, the rumour was still out there in the community many years later.

So, what did I glean from all of this talk? While several friends and contacts living in the Miranda electorate didn't know the name of their local State Member, some hadn't ever heard of Ron Phillips at all, and still others had had very little, if anything, to do with him. With some exceptions, those who had were generally dissatisfied with him. But I got the distinct impression that the dissatisfaction with Mr Phillips was not only because they felt he hadn't gone in to bat for them or wasn't delivering for their community; it was also because they "didn't see him around very much at all!"

Voter dissatisfaction with the sitting Liberal MP would provide some fertile ground for any future Labor candidate contesting the seat of Miranda. But that, of course, would not, by itself, be enough to defeat the incumbent, especially when the opposing candidate is a politically unknown with no public profile— like me!

Comparing profiles

Knocking off Ron Phillips would be no easy task. Here was a bloke with a big public profile who was no stranger to the media or controversy. He'd been the Minister for Health in the Greiner and Fahey Liberal Governments, and after Labor narrowly won the

1995 election, had been serving as the Opposition's Shadow Treasurer and Shadow Minister for the Olympics.[38]

On top of his 15 years' experience as Miranda MP, Ron Phillips also happened to be the Deputy Leader of the Liberal Party itself. In the coming 1999 poll, he would have the full support and backing of his Party machine as well as access to resources that any local Labor opponent could only dream of.

Compared to my very experienced Liberal opponent, I was not just a novice, but a complete unknown, both politically and publicly! The odds of Phillips being beaten by a first-time Labor candidate with these credentials looked to be very long indeed. Yet, while that may well have discouraged other potential candidates for Miranda, it didn't deter me. It just meant that if I was the Labor candidate, I'd have to work that much harder to win. But there was something else, it seemed to me.

It also occurred to me that having a big presence out there in media-land and being a major player in Party politics might not necessarily translate into success at the ballot box. What I believed would really count on polling day was that popularity among voters which comes from the anticipated hard work and the perceived future commitment by the candidate to the community down at the grass roots level.

A little research showed that, like most MPs, Mr Phillips was Honorary Patron of several local sporting clubs including the Miranda Magpies Soccer Club and the Sylvania Heights Community & Youth Club. He was also a Member of Miranda RSL and other community organisations in which the local Liberals

---

[38] Labor won the 1995 NSW State election by only 1 seat. Premier Bob Carr had a majority of 1 in the Legislative Assembly.

always seemed to have a strong presence, like Rotary. Even so, I really wondered, given his responsibilities, just *how* actively involved he really was in each of these organisations.

The earlier suggestion by locals that Phillips wasn't "around very much" had a ring of truth about it in late 1998. To be fair, given his earlier Health Ministry, and his later Shadow Ministries, as well as his job as Deputy Liberal Leader, he just wouldn't have had the time to deal with all the local Shire community groups and organisations, let alone attend many of their events. And, with major issues certain to emerge as the State election drew closer, it was more than likely that Ron Phillips would have even less time not only for his local community groups, but for his individual constituents and their families as well!

It seemed to me that, in Miranda, we had a local MP who wasn't nearly as focused on his electorate as he should have been and, in the pursuit other Party-political objectives over the years, had lost sight of the needs and aspirations of his constituents.

So what could I offer? At 49, I was the same age as Ron Phillips. Like him, I lived in the Miranda electorate with Jeanette, my wife of 27 years, and my family.

Both my children were born in Sutherland Hospital, and both had been raised and educated in the Shire. I was a barrister who'd previously worked in the Shire as a teacher at Port Hacking High School from 1978 to 1982 and as a Legal Aid Duty Solicitor at Sutherland Local Court for five years in the 1990s. In my 20s and 30s, I played soccer and cricket for Miranda Magpies, the Sylvania Heights and Como-Jannali Clubs and even had a season with the Sutherland Hockey Club.

I wasn't a "blow in" from outside the Shire — something the locals generally resented. And I certainly couldn't be labelled by my Liberal opponent as the candidate 'parachuted in by Sussex Street'. Nor could he point to any 'political baggage' on my part.

I saw my age and life experience, together with my long-time residency, my work in the Shire and my involvement in Shire sport as real positives. My occupation as a barrister might also impress some, as would the fact that I had written and published five successful Economics textbooks.

At the end of the day, I had what I regarded as the basic personal qualifications needed to run for the seat of Miranda and to be a good local MP. Not having Ron Phillips' public profile, political experience, Party connections or resources, one thing was abundantly clear: if I got to the election starting line I'd have to be very quick out of the blocks and run a *grass roots campaign*, focused primarily on local issues.

Factional politics: Liberal style

While I had no connection with any Labor faction, Ron Phillips was heavily involved in factional politics within the Liberal Party. As leader of Left-leaning Liberal faction called *The Group*, he was known to have played a key role in replacing sitting Cook MP, Stephen Mutch, with his own factional ally, Bruce Baird.

The removal of Mutch generated considerable division, if not palpable anger, towards Phillips among local Liberal Branch members and senior Party members— including then Prime Minister John Howard, himself a factional colleague of Mutch.[39]

I believed that Phillips' role in the preselection of Baird as the Liberal candidate for Cook was fresh enough in the minds of disgruntled local Liberal members and Mutch supporters to be a factor in the March 1999 State election for Miranda.

While some Liberal Branch members might be less than enthusiastic about helping Phillips in his coming re-election campaign, others may not help him at all. Indeed, there could even be some died-in-the-wool Mutch supporters who wouldn't even vote for Phillips, regardless of their Liberal leanings!

The margin and a puzzle solved

A key consideration for any Labor candidate thinking about running for Miranda was, of course, the margin by which the seat was held by Ron Phillips. Put another way, it was the *swing* we'd have to get to take it from him. A little research was needed here.

Quite frankly, I was pleasantly surprised at the size of the swing required to bring the seat back into the Labor fold. A State-wide redistribution of electoral boundaries after the 1995 election had reduced Phillips' margin in Miranda from 6.7% to 5.3% at the March 1999 poll. While that 1.4% fall in Phillips' margin may not appear great in the scheme of things, it moved the odds a little more in Labor's favour, and could be all the difference between winning and losing should the result come down to the wire.

---

[39] Prime Ministerial anger at the removal of Mutch by Phillips' faction is said to be the real reason why Hon. Bruce Baird never made it into John Howard's Cabinet.

So, what explained the fall in Phillips margin? The answer, quite simply, is that the boundary changes accompanying the redistribution meant that the seat of Miranda no longer included *Sylvania Waters*. At the 1999 State election, residents of that blue-ribbon Liberal suburb would instead be included in the electorate of Cronulla. Now that, I thought, was a real plus, if not a stroke of good luck, for the next Labor candidate for Miranda! But, as it turned out, luck had nothing to do with it! Let me explain.

Along with population growth and increasing urbanisation, the number of voters in each of the State's 93 electorates changes over time. Some electorates see rapid increases in resident numbers while others experience significant declines.

Now, one of the guiding principles of Australian democracy is that every vote should carry the same weight as every other vote. Called the 'one-vote, one-value principle,' it means that each electorate should contain approximately the same number of voters. To achieve this, the NSW Electoral Commission undertakes an *electoral redistribution* every 8 years.

In practical terms, an electoral redistribution means changes in the geographical boundaries of each of the State's 93 Legislative Assembly seats. As the boundaries shift, many voters will find that their homes are now located in a different State electorate. Their votes have effectively been 'redistributed' from their 'old electorate' to another, 'new' electorate.

As part of its lengthy consultation process, the Commission receives submissions on boundary changes from the general public and from each of the major Parties. Having considered these, a 'draft redistribution' is put out for comment and further submissions before settling the new seat boundaries.

I was astonished to later learn that, as part of the 1999 redistribution, the Liberal Party had actually supported the transfer of Sylvania Waters to the adjoining electorate of Cronulla! Labor had rarely, if ever, received more than 25% of the first preference votes at Sylvania Waters' booths in any previous State election. So why then would the Libs jettison the Shire suburb containing many of its most rusted-on voters from the Miranda electorate? The answer can be traced back to Ron Phillips and the power he wielded within the Liberal Party itself!

In its draft redistribution put out for public comment (maps and all), the Electoral Commission proposed retaining Sylvania Waters within the Miranda electorate and transferring the suburb of Yowie Bay from Miranda to the Cronulla electorate.

At the time, Ron Phillips lived with his family in Yowie Bay. With Ron espousing the view in Party circles that all MPs should live in their electorates, the removal of Yowie Bay from the seat of Miranda was like a red rag to a bull.[40] And so, drawing on his influence as Deputy Leader, Ron persuaded his Party to make a strong submission to the Electoral Commission which would eventually see Yowie Bay remain in his electorate of Miranda. The trade-off, of course, was Sylvania Waters!

Shipping the residents of Sylvania Waters off to the seat of Cronulla had the potential to weaken Phillips' grip on Miranda. But the move makes even less sense when one considers that, before the redistribution, Phillips' margin had fallen from 10.3% at the 1991 State election to 6.7% at the 1995 poll after a strong

---

[40] Interestingly, Dana Vale, Federal MP for Hughes from 1996 to 2010, *never* actually lived in her electorate, but in the neighbouring Federal electorate of Cook!

campaign by Labor candidate and Sutherland Shire Councillor, Paul Smith.

After the 1999 redistribution, the Liberal margin in Miranda had fallen to 5.3%, almost half of that it held at the beginning of the decade. But at least no Labor candidate could fairly claim that Ron Phillips did not live in his electorate!

3.3.   I can win this!

Call it a gut feeling or something else, but somehow, I just knew I could win Miranda! I hadn't spent hours tossing around the pros and cons of me taking on Phillips in my mind or calculating the weight I should attach to his local popularity or the margin I had to overcome given my status as a complete unknown. I didn't sit down with pen and paper and do a SWOT analysis.[41] There was really nothing objective about my conclusion at all!

While I can well understand that you being sceptical about this, the simple truth is that sitting on the train on the way home after a day in Court and not thinking about anything in particular, something inside told me I could beat Ron Phillips! Over the years, I'd learnt to listen to my gut feelings, having at times ignored them to my great regret. I'd also learnt that self-belief is a very powerful force, and from the moment I believed I could win Miranda, I never once contemplated the thought of losing.

While having dinner the same night with Jeanette I told her that I believed I could win Miranda; she didn't seem a bit surprised. There were no 'ifs or buts', no 'what abouts' and 'no whys' from her. Jeanette never once called into question my belief that I could defeat the Deputy Leader of the Liberal Party. In fact,

---

[41]   SWOT is the acronym for Strengths, Weaknesses, Opportunities and Threats.

she was just as positive about me becoming the local MP as she had been about my two previous career changes.

While we didn't canvass the issues in any detail or discuss the mechanics of any campaign, Jeanette did point out that Premier Bob Carr was very popular. Even so, we had no doubt the path to Macquarie Street would be a very tough one indeed.

We also believed that there was no way in the world that I could knock off Phillips with anything but a full-time campaign, beginning the day I hopefully secured nomination in December 1998 and ending at the close of voting on election day, 27 March 1999. Getting across the line would also mean giving up my legal practice and no income from work as a barrister for the better part of four months. If preselected, I'd have to sell my room in Chambers to help make ends meet.

Jeanette and I also knew that because the local Labor Branches and the Miranda State Electoral Council (SEC) were not exactly flush with funds, we'd have to dip into our relatively meagre savings to help fund even the most basic assault on Miranda.[42] Clearly, ours had to be an all-or nothing, grass-roots campaign run on a very limited budget. But that was a risk we were both willing to take.

---

[42]   Labor has a State Electorate Council (SEC) for each NSW electorate. These are the local administrative bodies to which local Branches send delegates and motions for debate. The SEC's role includes supporting State Labor candidates and fund raising.

3.4. Preselection for Miranda

Believing I could win Miranda was one thing. Getting preselection as the Labor candidate was something else again. But I genuinely believed I could win that as well!

Having just been through a tough preselection battle for Cook, I now knew much more about the process involved. But despite losing to Peri Young, the experience had some real positives which I believed could only help me in my quest to get the Party nod to run for Miranda.

For a start, I'd raised my profile among local Party members across the Shire. I'd gotten to know a large number of members from other Branches, many of whom I'd probably never have met otherwise. Of course, people talk among themselves and, as you learn in politics, the degree of support for you down at the local level is determined not so much by the newspaper headlines, but by the chatter among local Branch members themselves.

Secondly, many of the preselectors I'd met during my quest for Cook were also eligible to have a say in deciding the Labor candidate for Miranda. Hopefully, I'd made a good enough impression upon them to secure their vote in a preselection ballot— assuming Peri Young didn't put up her hand again.

Thirdly, the fact that I hadn't spat the dummy and had worked on Peri's Federal election campaign had not gone unnoticed by local Labor stalwarts. No one could complain that I didn't have the Party's interests at heart.

Gathering support

Having decided to seek preselection for Miranda, it was important that I talk to key local Branch members and officials to gather their views well before I lodged my nomination form.

Tony Iffland and Paul Ellercamp, my supporters for the Cook preselection, were again on board, as were Bert and Iris Rhodes, Joy and Edwina Hall, Jim and Pat Foy, Trevor Romer and my neighbour, Alan Bell. Branch Secretaries including Christine Hawkins (later candidate for Hughes) and Troy Bramston (NSW Young Labor President) were also supportive at the time.

I was pleased to secure the support of Bob Rogers, who'd just run a good grass-roots campaign in Cook. He'd agreed to be my Campaign Director should I gain preselection for Miranda!

Now that was a big plus! Telling the preselectors that Bob Rogers would manage *my* State campaign should I win the ballot (as Peri had done) would carry enormous weight with them.

Nominating

By the time Head Office called for nominations, word had gotten around that I'd be seeking preselection for Miranda. Most of those I rang for support told me they already knew I was putting up my hand again, and were happy to sign my nomination form. As usual, some who signed were keen to point out that I should not regard their signature as a "commitment to vote for me," in a ballot, "because they didn't know who else would be standing!"

On Friday the 13th of November 1998, I set off from my Liverpool Street Chambers for my second visit to Sussex Street to lodge my nomination form, together with the requisite $200 fee.

At the time, I did not know of any other potential Labor candidate; I hadn't even heard of anyone one else expressing the slightest interest in putting up their hand. But, as I learnt with the Cook preselection, I couldn't take any comfort in that. Having lodged my form, all I could do is wait until the closure of nominations at noon the following Friday, after which I'd quickly learn whether or not I'd be opposed.

Just after 12.30PM on Friday, the 20th of November 1998, I was having a coffee in Bankstown with solicitor Mark Klees after our cases at the Local Court, when my brick-like mobile phone rang.

> "Barry, it's Joy Hall. Congratulations! You were the *only* nomination!" she said, before I could get a word in.

> "Great news! Thanks Joy. Preselected unopposed! The Labor candidate for Miranda!" I said looking at my friend Mark across the table.

> Joy brought me a back to earth saying, "well, you're *not* officially our candidate just yet! The 'Admin Committee' has to endorse you first, and they don't meet until the 4th of December."

> "Well, hopefully I won't have a problem," I replied.

> "I don't think you will," Joy said quietly, adding "but you never know with that mob in Head Office!"

I don't think I could've had a more excited messenger than Joy, a senior member of Miranda Branch. I thanked her for her call and her support, and having explained what had happened to a quizzical-looking Mark, he congratulated me as well.

My first call was to Jeanette. Having given her the news, I recall saying: "Well, we're on our way to Macquarie Street!" She responded with: "I know you can do it!" That really meant a lot.

Leaving Mark, I headed back to my Chambers in the city by train. On the way, I phoned Paul Ellercamp and Bob Rogers, each of whom greeted my call with "congratulations!" Word travels fast in politics!

Paul said he had a great idea for the organisation of the Miranda campaign. With the three of us agreeing there wasn't a moment to lose, we arranged to meet at Bob's Grays Point home the following Sunday. A good start, I thought, as I walked with my blue barrister's bag over my shoulder from Museum station to my nearby Chambers where I'd pick up what would turn out to be my last brief before the State election.

Chambers for sale: arrogance or belief?

Soon after arriving, I went to see our Head of Chambers, Michael Green QC. I advised him that I intended running for State Parliament in 1999, and I'd be selling my room on the floor.

An outstanding advocate in the Court of Criminal Appeal, Michael was, to say the least, surprised. Raising the possibility that I could lose, he thought I was being hasty in selling up. While I believed otherwise, I didn't say that to him. Nobody likes the appearance of overconfidence.

Rather, I told Michael that if I was to have any chance of winning, I'd have to campaign full-time for the next four months. I'd have no time for Court work, and, not being able to take on any new briefs, I wouldn't bring in enough fees to meet my share of Chambers' rent and other outgoings. Michael understood my decision and so, before I left late that afternoon, I drafted a 'Chambers for Sale' notice to send off to the Bar Association for circulation as soon as I was endorsed.

And so, my very first act on learning of my preselection was to sell my barrister's Chambers, effectively burning my established bridge back to the legal profession if I lost the subsequent election. I knew others who would have taken a far more cautious approach, hedging their bets by sub-letting their Chambers for the three or four months of their election campaigns, just in case they lost. But not me! I never once contemplated anything but winning Miranda!

While that may seem arrogant on my part, I'd done this kind of thing twice before. Having left school in Year 10 in 1965, I gave up my job two years later to take up full-time study for my HSC going on to become a high school Economics teacher. In 1989, and without any connections in the legal profession and without any real prospect of a job in the law, I left my 17-year career in education to become a solicitor.[43]

I'd taken two major career punts earlier in my life, both of which had paid off — because I really believed in what I was doing, because I had the strong support of Jeanette, and because I simply worked my bum off in each case. For me, leaving the law to go into politics was no different!

To my mind, selling my Chambers before the election and at such an early stage had nothing to do with arrogance. This was about my deep and abiding belief that I could do it: that I could win Miranda!

---

[43] At age 39, I can tell you that it wasn't easy getting my first job as a lawyer.

3.5. Getting started: the groundwork

The endorsement decision by the Party may have been only two weeks away, but like most first-time candidates, I was chaffing at the bit to get started. I wanted to hit the ground running.

Every day was going to count, and it was important that I use that time to lay what groundwork I could for the campaign while I waited to get the official nod from Head Office. I was conscious of being a complete unknown and taking on a bloke with a high profile and 15 years in the game under his belt.

Running in a preselection is one thing; running as a candidate in a State election is quite another. When it came to the big race, I was a complete novice. Despite my enthusiasm and my deep belief that I would win Miranda, I needed the advice and the direction that comes with experience, wherever I could get it.

That first 'campaign meeting'

The first step was to meet the next Sunday at Grays Point with Paul Ellercamp and Bob Rogers, neither of whom thought my endorsement would be a problem. Paul's idea was to set up a campaign team of three, comprising two Campaign Directors and me, the candidate. As Directors, Bob and Paul would each have defined yet complimentary roles.

Bob would have the job of managing the logistics. These included setting up a campaign office, marshalling Branch members and Party supporters, organising letterbox drops, street stalls and railway station visits, and of course, fundraising events: all the basics needed to run an effective State election campaign out there on the ground.

Paul's job was to write all our campaign leaflets and advertisements as well as "media management." He described this as identifying important issues as they arose and getting our message out into our local, very widely-read newspaper, The St George & Sutherland Shire Leader, known simply as the *Leader*.

The idea of dividing up responsibilities made good sense, given Bob's experience as a Campaign Director and the high regard in which he was held by Branch members, and Paul's experience as a media adviser in Bob Hawke's office.

It was agreed that the three of us would come together after my endorsement, working side by side to map out our campaign strategy, which needed to be flexible enough to tackle all the issues as they emerged in the lead up to the March 1999 election.

The big issue

Whatever the Carr Government or Sussex Street saw as the major election issues State-wide, there was no question in our minds that our campaign in Miranda had to be run on *local issues*. So, what were the major issues for Miranda voters in November 1998, four months out from the March '99 poll?

Ellercamp had absolutely no doubt there was one clear standout: *overdevelopment*! He said that the Liberal-controlled Sutherland Shire Council had been approving high rise flats willy-nilly and residents were very worried about the impact of overdevelopment on their quality of life. Ron Phillips, he said, was not interested in doing anything about the problem at all!

Ron's failure to address residents' concerns about overdevelopment, Paul said, provided a "concrete example" of the

MP's generally poor performance, and was an issue we could raise again and again throughout our campaign.

There were, of course, other important local issues we could also run on, including the much-needed upgrade of our precious Sutherland Hospital. But for the moment, and from the word go, we all agreed that our main focus had to be on *overdevelopment*.

What about me?

Identifying the key election issues is one thing; identifying the candidate is something else again. I had to get myself known. That meant getting out there as the Labor candidate for Miranda, meeting residents and talking about the issues that mattered to them.

I couldn't, of course, do that until I was formally endorsed by the Party. But rather than sit on our hands waiting, we decided to begin work on my first piece of campaign literature. There'd be no mention of any election issue in this; it was far too early!

At Paul Ellercamp's suggestion, we decided to put together a simple, two-sided "Introductory Card" of the kind business owners use when meeting prospective customers. The front of the card would contain my photo, some brief words about my background, a campaign slogan, my contact details, the ALP logo, and the fact that I was the Labor candidate for Miranda. Given the recent redistribution, a map of the 'New Electorate of Miranda', with the major suburbs, would appear on the back of the card.

Paul offered to design the card, and arrange for it to be printed. Meanwhile, Bob Rogers was to organise a PO Box and campaign telephone number. But I had to do my bit if Paul was to have the introductory card ready to go as soon I was endorsed.

I left my first campaign meeting with Paul and Bob, having agreed to do three jobs: write a short biography, get myself a suitable photograph and come up with a meaningful campaign slogan.

In their own way, each of these had an important role to play in our quest for Macquarie Street. We'd use them on our introductory card. They'd help define, distinguish and promote me as the candidate. We'd use them time and again throughout the campaign— on our pamphlets, in our ads and on my posters (called *coreflutes*). Clearly, it was vital that I got all three 'spot on' at the very start!

A bio, a pic and a slogan

My first task was to write three or four short sentences containing the basic information I thought the voters would want to know about me: my work, my family background and, most importantly, my connection with the Sutherland Shire.

Being married and having worked, raised my kids and lived in the Shire for the past 27 years were likely to be real positives — especially in this part of the world which is often referred to as 'God's Country' by senior residents. Here, in the Shire, local families of two and three generations were commonplace.

Task number two was to get a professional photo of myself for the campaign, and I arranged to do that at *Le Tratt Studios* in Miranda the following Friday. That also happened to be my son Michael's 17th birthday, and so Jeanette and I invited him and my daughter, Sarah, along for a family portrait as well. And, since I believed I'd be leaving the law for Parliament after the election, I took along my barrister' wig and gown to get a photo for the family album.

We rolled up to the Kiora Road Studio with me clutching my blue barrister's bag in one hand and holding my new tie in the other. I'd spent considerable time at the shops choosing this particular tie: a dark blue number with white spots. Apart from blue being my favourite colour, the tie went well with my only (black) suit.

This was to be my 'campaign tie': the one I'd always be wearing whenever I met voters. I'd be wearing this tie in every photograph, including the one which would appear on my coreflutes, when I eventually got them. I figured that it was important for me to be consistent and easily identifiable, matching the way I presented myself with all my photographs.

The Studio photographer naturally asked why I was having these photographs taken. Having told him I was standing for Parliament as the Labor candidate for Miranda, he smiled and let out a little chuckle.

"That's really funny", the photographer said. "I've done Ron Phillips' election photographs for years; ever since he first got elected, in fact.

"Since 1984? Really?" I asked.

"Yes. But this time, for some reason, he's decided to get them done elsewhere, outside the Shire!"

While this may seem a little "spooky", I regarded his answer as a good omen, given Ron's 15 years in office! Besides, I'd just happened to choose a photographer who obviously knew what he was doing. Phillips' decision to jettison this capable local photographer and go out of the Shire, perhaps reflected his poor judgement: it would not go unnoticed in local business circles.[44]

My third task of coming up with a good campaign slogan proved to be a far more difficult task than the first two put together. Clearly, we needed a slogan that caught voters' attention; something meaningful; something related to the electorate; something that had within it a positive message about me; something I was comfortable with; and something that distinguished me from my Liberal opponent, Ron Phillips. And all of that in three or four words! But what?

Our slogan didn't have to be clever or even original. Chris Downey, the Liberal MP who'd held the seat of *Sutherland* from 1988 until his resignation in 1997, used the slogan 'Your Mate in the State' quite effectively and despite it being regarded by more than one voter as having sexist overtones.[45] Dana Vale, the Liberal MP for Hughes from 1996 until 2010, always used the slogan 'One of Us': three words she'd borrowed from former British Prime Minister, Margaret Thatcher which resonated very strongly with voters living in the parochial Sutherland Shire.

Having tossed around a host of possible slogans in my mind, I decided that there was no point in trying to re-invent the wheel. Surely there must be hundreds of slogans out there, devised by far more experienced political minds than mine, which had been used and reused by candidates over the years. And so, I got hold of some old ALP campaign pamphlets and went hunting through them, looking for those elusive three or four words I needed.

---

[44] The same studio photographer would later comment on the 1999 election photo actually used by Ron Phillips, saying "the shading on his face was not a good look."

[45] Chris Downey was replaced by Lorna Stone who held the seat of Sutherland until it was abolished in the 1998 redistribution.

And there it was! A slogan used by the then Labor backbencher Craig Knowles MP on a community survey leaflet in the early 1990s: *'A Local who Listens.'*[46]

Those four words said it all! They not only connected me with the Shire but carried a positive message about me. The slogan described the kind of MP I wanted to be: one who genuinely listens to the concerns of my community and acts upon them. And, having regard to my one and only meeting with Mr Phillips about the crossing at my kids' school, I also believed the slogan would distinguish me from my opponent in the minds of those voters who were unhappy with their MP's performance.

The slogan used by Knowles had a real ring to it and I had no hesitation in adopting it as my own. In doing so, I knew full well that, as the candidate and later as the MP, I'd be expected to live up to its words, and truly be *'A Local who Listens'*!

3.6. Getting a little good advice

Having done my assigned homework, I followed up Paul Ellercamp's earlier suggestion that I should make contact as soon as possible with two local Labor politicians who might give me some advice and support, starting with Senator Michael Forshaw.

I met Forshaw for the first time at his home in Yarrawarrah the following Sunday.[47] Engadine Branch member Lawrie Daly was also present.[48]

---

[46] Craig Knowles was first elected in 1990 and later became Minister for Urban Affairs and Planning and Minister for Health in the Carr Government.

[47] Michal Forshaw was Labor Senator for New South Wales from 1994 to 2011.

[48] I'd later learn that Lawrie Daly was the son of the inimitable, long-serving and very popular Federal Labor MP, Fred Daly.

Beyond knowing he was a Labor Senator who lived in the Shire, I knew absolutely nothing about Michael Forshaw, and I suspect he knew even less about me. But he *was* in Federal Parliament and, with me being a newcomer into politics, I thought that any advice he could give me would be very useful.

Having talked about my background, the Labor Party, the Liberal-dominated Shire and Phillips' public profile, the Senator made it quite clear that I had a tough job ahead of me. When I told Michael Forshaw that I believed I could win Miranda, he didn't respond. He didn't have to. I could tell by the way he looked at me and shifted in his chair, that he didn't for one moment think I'd get across the line![49] He probably thought that I was suffering from candidate's disease.

Even so, and undeterred, I asked for his advice. It was simple. "Get yourself a decent picture, get yourself a good coreflute, and get doorknocking!" Forshaw said.

Lawrie Daly agreed that if I wanted to win, I needed to do a "hell of a lot of doorknocking." That was excellent advice. I left Forshaw's home with Michael and Lawrie wishing me luck and saying they'd help me in my campaign if they could.

Overdevelopment: the strategy

The second local Labor politician to whom Ellercamp referred me was Sutherland Shire Councillor, Paul Smith. Our candidate for

---

[49]   Many years ears later, Michael Forshaw would confirm that he thought I had absolutely no chance of winning the 1999 election for Miranda.

Miranda in 1995, Paul had also stood for Cook in 1990. By the time I sought his advice, Paul had been a Councillor for eight years.[50]

A high-school teacher by occupation, Smith was a grass-roots politician who obviously knew the ropes. Astute, articulate and hard-working, with a sharp political mind, Paul had been controversial from time to time, but always when it counted. An excellent campaigner, he was both a strong voice for the Shire and real fighter for his constituents in A-Ward, the toughest of the Council's five electoral districts for Labor. To my mind, and at the time I took an interest in politics, Paul Smith was among the very best of our local Councillors.

I'd gone to Paul seeking his views and advice on what he saw as the major local issues in the forthcoming campaign. Without a moment's hesitation, Smith said that if we really wanted to win, we just had to focus on *overdevelopment*:

> "We've got open-slather development happening right across the Shire, thanks to the Libs on Council. They're not even following their own rules. They're even building bedrooms without windows!" Paul said.

> "You're kidding?" I said incredulously.

> "No! Development is out of control, people are very worried about it, and Ron Phillips couldn't care less!" Paul added.

Having confirmed what my fledgling campaign team was thinking, Paul quoted key statistics we could use to highlight the

---

[50] Paul Smith resigned from Sutherland Council in 2002 and headed off to work in England. In 2006, Paul was elected to London's Islington Council. He also became Chair of ALP Abroad, the Australian Labor Party's international wing.

rapid increase in the number of Council-approved high-rise flats across the Shire in recent years. We could even show that our local Council had approved more high-rise flats than any other Council in Sydney. Paul then outlined a strategy which we could follow to make overdevelopment a campaign-winning issue!

The strategy was simple: having raised the issue (using his facts and figures) and highlighting resident's concerns, we'd lay the blame for overdevelopment on the Liberal Shire Council — where it genuinely belonged. We'd then point out to residents that their local Liberal MP, Ron Phillips, couldn't care less and couldn't be bothered to do anything about it!

Compared to Mr Phillips, so the strategy went, I was deeply concerned about overdevelopment and its impact on Shire residents. And so, throughout the campaign I'd be calling on the Carr Labor Government to hold an Inquiry into the Sutherland Shire Council's Housing Strategy!

Until my meeting with him late in 1998, I'd had little to do with Paul personally. Yet here he was, during our first meeting, outlining the issue, giving me a very smart strategy to follow and even some great lines I could use like "open slather development!" I thought to myself: "Wow! This Smith bloke really knows what he's talking about!"

As that thought crossed my mind, Paul put the icing on the cake by offering to provide me with notes, to keep me updated and to draft pamphlets for me on the overdevelopment issue as well as other important issues that might arise during the campaign. I was delighted to have the benefit of his skills and experience. Needless to say, I'd definitely take him up on his generous offer, as soon as I was endorsed.

My visit to the Bear Pit

As I waited in a kind of political Limbo for Party endorsement, it occurred to me that I'd never actually seen inside the NSW Legislative Assembly, let alone watch State Parliament in action. That may seem a little odd for a bloke who expected to serve his future constituents as their local MP, but there it was. And so, after Court one hot November afternoon, I wandered down to Macquarie Street for a preview of what I believed would be my future workplace.

On arrival, I was ushered into an empty Public Gallery by an attendant who told me, with a grin, I could sit anywhere I liked. Here I was in the 'Mother of Australian Parliaments' expecting to see some of the robust debate for which it was well known.[51] But all I saw was a handful of MPs, sitting on green leather benches, having private conversations among themselves, and completely disinterested in a speech being delivered by one of their colleagues on some bill before the House.

That Member's speech over, a motion of some sort was put and, having been met with a 'No!' by one MP (who promptly resumed his private conversation), the Speaker called out "Division! Ring the bells!"

MPs soon began filing into the House though both doors behind the Speaker's chair and continued doing so until the bells stopped ringing and the Speaker said "lock the doors!"

The manner in which the MPs walked into the Chamber and the entire procedure itself reminded me of a scene from the 1960

---

[51] The NSW Legislative Assembly sat for the first time in 1856 and is the oldest Parliament in Australia.

movie, *The Time Machine*.[52] In its futuristic world, about 8,000 AD, 'the Eloi' (peaceful, child-like adult humans) are periodically mesmerized by loud sirens and walk, zombie-like, en masse into a building (resembling the Sphinx) through a set of huge metal doors. Waiting for them inside are the cannibalistic 'Moorlocks' (ape-like troglodytes). The Eloi continue to walk into the Sphinx until the Moorlocks have the number of humans they require for their food, and the siren suddenly stops. The massive doors shut with a bang and the Eloi who didn't make it through them snap out of their trance immediately, with no memory of how they got there, and no understanding of why they were there at all!

My analogy may seem a little cruel, but these MPs really did walk into the House like automatons, with their disinterested demeanour and their body language, clearly suggesting a kind of unwanted drudgery they had no choice but to endure.

The Members gave me the distinct impression that they didn't really want to be there; they just *had* to be there. And some of them, in fact, didn't even know *why* they were there.

Two younger looking MPs walked in just before the doors were locked by attendants and plonked themselves down on the green leather in the very back row immediately in front of me.

Oblivious to my presence, one said to the other, "What are we voting on?"

"No idea," replied the other. "I just want to get out of this joint!"

---

[52]   The 1960 movie was based on the H.G Wells classic short story of the same name and starred Australian actor, Rod Taylor.

I was astonished by both the question and the response, and I wondered what their respective constituents would have thought had they overheard this conversation.

Of course, I looked among the MPs for my local representative, Ron Phillips. And there he was, sitting in the second row, with his back to the Speaker, deep in what appeared to be a serious personal conversation with another MP, and seemingly disinterested in the proceedings themselves.

You may also be surprised to learn that my very first glimpse of Parliament in action was also the very first time I'd sighted Bob Carr or any of his Ministers in the flesh. While I'd seen them on TV, I'd never met or spoken to one of them. They too, were engaged in private conversations as two MPs walked around with ancient clipboards, counting heads and seemingly ticking off names in a kind of Parliamentary roll call.

The votes having been counted, the Speaker announced the 'result of the division' and the majority of MPs filed out, leaving five or six remaining.[53]

I must admit being disappointed with what I saw during my first visit to the Legislative Assembly in session and left after 20 minutes or so. As I walked out of the building and into Macquarie Street, I remember thinking to myself: "Is this really *the Bear Pit* they talk about? Surely, it has to be better than this!"

---

[53] The 'result of the division' is simply the number of votes by the MPs for and against the motion (the *Ayes* versus *Nos*).

3.7.   December 4th and 5th, 1998

The next major milestone in my quest for Miranda was, of course, endorsement by the ALP, and I was a little anxious about that. But I had a lot on my plate as I waited for news from Sussex Street on Friday, the 4th of December — the date allocated for the Party's Administrative Committee meeting.

Endorsement

As my last major criminal case of 1999, I'd taken on a five-day Court hearing in which I was appearing for a young man with ADHD. He'd been charged with assaulting a police sergeant and causing affray during a brawl outside a pub in the Sydney Rocks on Anzac Day. My friend, Martin Shume, a barrister I'd met just before the Bar exams, was appearing for the co-accused.

Come December 4th, around noon on the last day of the hearing, I was in Court with my very anxious client. Following what was probably my most effective cross-examination of any police officer in my legal career, I made an application to Her Honour to dismiss the charge against my client without him getting into the witness box and giving any evidence at all.

Based on all the evidence presented to that point, I submitted that the prosecution could not possibly prove its case against my client beyond reasonable doubt. This was because the police sergeant who'd allegedly been assaulted, had given evidence in the witness box which so completely contradicted his own previous written statements, that anyone with a modicum of intelligence could easily draw the inference that he was lying. In addition, none of the many bystanders called by the prosecution to give evidence could corroborate the sergeant's version of events.

As Her Honour was delivering her judgement just before the luncheon adjournment, my mobile phone rang! The ultimate sign of disrespect to a judicial officer! If looks could kill! I'd forgotten to turn off my phone after a lengthy conversation with my client before walking into Court. I now did so— and immediately apologised to the Court. Having accepted my apology, Her Honour continued on with her judgement. She not only dismissed the charges against my client but ordered the NSW Police to pay all my client's legal costs: a rare event as any criminal lawyer will tell you.

After my win, I left the Court room and, following a brief chat with my delighted client and his worried parents, I switched my phone back on to find a message from Joy Hall. I'd been endorsed by the Party! It was official: I was now the Labor candidate for Miranda! My second win of the day! The campaign could now begin, and I rang Jeanette with the good news.

Little did I know later that same day there'd be more good news which could only assist me in my campaign to become the next MP for Miranda. As they say, things often come in threes!

Macquarie Street shenanigans

December 4th, 1998 also just happened to coincide with my Chambers' Christmas Party. I'd gone home directly from Court and caught the train into the city.

By the time I arrived, our Party was well underway, and very well attended by barristers, solicitors, Crown Prosecutors and Public Defenders. Shortly after walking in the door, one of my Chambers colleagues came through the crowd towards me, glass in hand, with some unexpected news.

"Well you must be happy," he said.

"I am," I replied. "I've just been endorsed as the Labor candidate for Miranda at the State election next year."

He looked to me rather quizzically and said "haven't you heard what's been going on in Macquarie Street?"

"No, what?" I asked, genuinely puzzled.

"The Libs have just dumped Peter Collins. Word is they're going to replace him with Kerry Chikarovski! And guess who's behind it all?" he said with the grin of one pleased to be the first to reveal a great secret.

"Who?" I asked, not having the faintest idea.

"You won't believe it! Your mate in Miranda: Ron Phillips!"

"Wow!" I replied.

"That's really got to help you hasn't it?" my colleague said with a triumphant look.

"Yeah, it certainly won't hurt. Thanks for telling me," I said, as he raised his glass in toast-like fashion, downed the last of his drink and drifted off towards the bar.

I stood there for a moment, a little stunned. Apart from the fact that Peter Collins was the Leader of the NSW Opposition and of the State Parliamentary Liberal Party, I knew nothing about him. But I'd never even heard of Kerry Chikarovski.

While I was yet to comprehend all implications of this news for my coming campaign, my colleague was dead right: the news he delivered really *would* help my election campaign.

Phillips had already been instrumental in knocking off my local Federal MP, Stephen Mutch, in a preselection ballot. Now, less than six months later, he's gone and knocked off the Leader of the New South Wales Liberal Party! If there's one thing Australians loathe, it's disloyalty, and Mr Phillips seemed to have that in spades!

The enemy within

According to reports, Peter Collins received a telephone call out of the blue from his Deputy, Ron Phillips, around 2.00PM that afternoon, asking him to return to Parliament for an urgent meeting. Phillips did not disclose the nature of the meeting, saying only that it was personal and could not be conducted over the phone.

The House had risen for the term, and would not return until after the 1999 election, 112 days away. Collins had arrived at his Parliamentary office to find Ron Phillips and John Hannaford (the Liberal Leader in the Upper House) waiting for him. They took no time in telling an astonished Collins that he'd lost the support of the Liberal MPs, that he no longer had the numbers, and that he had to go!

Collins was told that internal Liberal polling showed there was no way that the Party could win the 1999 election with him as its Leader; he had to be replaced with somebody who just might do so, namely, Kerry Chikarovski. Hannaford made it clear to Collins that if he didn't resign, he'd suffer a humiliating defeat in the leadership ballot which had *already* been arranged for the following Monday. The fix was in.

It seems Collins had no inkling of what had been taking place behind his back, and his feelings of betrayal at the 11th hour by his Deputy, Ron Phillips, must have been crushing. He would later write that his "assassins had worked out my political execution with all the finesse of a Mafia hit".[54]

Not surprisingly, Peter Collins was, and would remain, very bitter. Having led the Liberal Party in Opposition for four years, he'd suddenly been dumped and replaced by another MP just three months out from the State poll, which *he* believed would see him become the next NSW Premier. According to Collins... "Journalists heard the news with disbelief, some saying it was the biggest act of political bastardry they had witnessed..."[55]

Voters aside, there just had to be Liberal Branch members in the Shire who'd take a very dim view of Ron Phillips' apparent disloyalty. While I was sure Ron Phillips didn't canvass any of their views before dispatching his Parliamentary Leader, I believed he wouldn't attract the 100% effort he might require of them during his own campaign for Miranda. For many of the loyal card-carrying Libs, Phillips clearly was "the enemy within." That could only help our Labor campaign, provided we kept reminding them of Ron's disloyalty at every opportunity.

On my birthday, Saturday, the 5th of December 1998, Peter Collins formally resigned as Leader of NSW Liberal Party.

---

[54]   Peter Collins, *The Bear Pit*, Allen and Unwin, 2000, page 302.
[55]   Ibid, page 302.

What is it about my birthdays? On the 5th of December 1972, my 23rd birthday, my political hero, Gough Whitlam, was sworn in as Prime Minister after Federal Labor's 23 years in the wilderness. He had given me my future and changed my life for the better.

Call me superstitious, but Peter Collins' resignation on my 49th birthday was, to me at least, a good omen. Apart from reinforcing my strong belief that I would win Miranda the following March, I felt for one fleeting moment that it was somehow 'meant to be'.

Conscious of candidate's disease, however, I was quick to remind myself that there was an enormous amount of work to be done if I was to make it into Parliament. I just said to myself, "Miranda, here I come!"

PART B:
A SHOESTRING CAMPAIGN

4. EARLY DAYS

4.1. Getting started...with a media event

Where to begin? For a first-time candidate with no public or Party profile, there was much to do. Clearly, there were many organisational matters with which I'd need help and direction. To be frank, I had no working knowledge of the specifics or of the many decisions to be made, given the enormity of the job ahead.

A media release?

Yet, even to a novice like me, my first task was obvious: finalise my 'Introductory Card' and get it printed so I could get out there doorknocking and get myself known!

Having provided him with my short biography, etc., Paul Ellercamp advised we also had to get my name into the Leader, saying he'd draft up something he called a "media release."[56]

Paul's brief explanation of the way in which the modern print media worked was a revelation in itself. Clearly, I could not expect to see an army of newspaper reporters in suits wearing hats labelled 'Press' rolling up at my door (accompanied by photographers) armed with pencils and notebooks, eager to take down every word I said. Those enthusiastic reporters I saw in

---

[56] With two editions each week, *The Leader* had by far the largest circulation in the Shire.

those black-and-white episodes of *Superman* I'd watched as a kid in the late 1950s no longer existed— if they ever did!

We'd just put the finishing touches to my first media release when I got an unexpected phone call from an unexpected source.

My first media event

Ian McManus MP rang me at home and introduced himself. The first State Labor MP to whom I'd ever spoken, Ian was awaiting preselection for the newly-created, adjacent seat of Heathcote, his seat of Bulli having been abolished in the 1998 redistribution.

Ian invited me to join him the next day at Sutherland Hospital for the official opening of a new $5.1 million Accident & Emergency (A & E) Unit by Premier Bob Carr and the Health Minister, Deputy Premier, Dr Andrew Refshauge. I'd never previously spoken to either Carr or Refshauge and was delighted with the invitation. Naturally I'd drop everything to be there!

Importantly, the new A & E Unit was a key local Labor achievement I could hang my hat on. And, with the Carr Government having recently announced a $79 million redevelopment of our hospital, we had a firm election commitment to which I could point as the Labor candidate for Miranda.

The long-awaited redevelopment of the Shire's only major public health facility would also provide a strong point of contrast between my opponent and me. In his former role as Health Minister, Mr Phillips wanted to privatise the Sutherland Hospital and turn the Shire's pride and joy into a centre for geriatric care.

The official opening was, the very first 'media event' I was to attend and I had absolutely no idea of what to expect. "What's my role, as the candidate?" I asked the experienced McManus.

Ian told me there was nothing for me to do or say. I just needed to turn up and follow Carr and Refshauge around with him and watch what goes on. "And bring your camera," McManus said, "you might even get a picture with Carr you can use in your campaign." Good advice, so I thought.

Meeting Bob Carr

McManus and I were waiting outside the new A & E Unit when Carr and Refshauge arrived with an entourage of staff, media advisers and, as I'd later learn, Carr's ever-watchful security officer.

Beyond a tour of the new facility, speeches and the plaque unveiling, I was surprised at how much more Carr had to do. I heard his media people use terms which were completely foreign to me: like 'meet and greet', and 'photo opportunity'. There was also a 'stand-up media conference' during which TV, radio and newspaper journalists asked Carr and Refshauge questions about everything else *but* the new A & E Unit at our precious hospital.

Like all Labor candidates, I wanted a photo with the Premier for my campaign literature— especially one taken at a big local event like this. But, while McManus had introduced me to him as our candidate for Miranda, Carr showed virtually no interest in me at all. I just couldn't get a seemingly reluctant Premier to look directly at the camera with me. Not surprisingly, the photos with Carr which I got developed later were absolutely useless.[57]

Disappointed, I later realised that after two hours of being followed around by the media, Carr must've had enough by the time I tried to get a photo with him. After all, I was just another candidate in another Liberal-held seat which Sussex Street most probably believed I had no hope of winning.

With Bob Carr facing his first election as Premier, I realised there was a bigger picture. If I wanted to be part of it, I couldn't rely on the Premier, Ministers, Head Office or anyone beyond local Branch members, supporters, my family and myself. I had to run a local campaign on local issues. I'd come back another day to get better photos at the A & E Unit for my pamphlets.

A community group

But all was not lost. Following Carr and Refshauge around during their tour of the new A & E Unit, I had the opportunity to talk with doctors, nurses, hospital staff and several patients.

In the A & E's new Children's Ward, I met three impressive members of the Southern Sydney Woodturners Guild, a local community group which had raised and donated $6,600 to buy medical equipment for the Hospital's youngest patients. Members Alan Bourne, Clive Cairns and Bert Ponder showed me the beautiful wooden toys they'd made for the kids. They told me of their ancient craft and invited me to their February meeting at 'The Cubby House' in Oyster Bay; an offer I promised to take up.

---

[57] In those days, most cameras used rolls of film. Digital cameras were very expensive and not widely used.

Here was my first encounter, as a candidate, with a Shire community group. As a political aspirant, you learn not to underestimate the importance of local community groups for many reasons, not least of which is the key role they play in spreading the word about you.

4.2. Some media of my own

The day after Carr's visit to the Hospital, I had my first encounter with the media. I was in the City negotiating the sale of my Chambers, when I received a call from the Leader. The staff said the journalist had my media release, and asked if I could come to its Hurstville Office at 3.00PM that day. Things seemed to move very fast in the newspaper world and, of course, I agreed.

After a trip in a packed train without air conditioning on a stinking hot December afternoon dressed in a suit, I spent a frustrating half-hour trying to find the newspaper's secluded office. I finally arrived in a lather of sweat looking like something the cat had dragged in.

If I was expecting to be interviewed by a reporter, I was wrong. The newspaper only wanted a photo of me! After being plonked down on a chair in a dingy little office, a photographer walked in, took three or four shots of me, and left. That was it!

On leaving, I asked when I could expect a call from the reporter. I was politely told "he's got your media release and he will only ring you if he needs to clarify something!" So much for standing in that hot train, trying to remember what was in the media release Ellercamp had sent the Leader and thinking about the kind of questions I might be asked by the waiting reporter! So much for my knowledge as to the way the media worked!

Setting the scene

On the 15ᵗʰ of December 1998, two articles, both taken from our one and only media release, appeared in the Leader. Extracts from these articles are set out in 4−1 and 4−2.

Labor takes aim

THE Labor Party will target "rampant overdevelopment" in the Sutherland shire in its bid to win the seat of Miranda at the March election.

Barry Collier, a 48-year-old barrister has been preselected unopposed for the seat which is held by Deputy Opposition Leader, Ron Phillips.

The ALP needs a swing of just over 5 per cent to win it.

Mr Collier, a father of two, has lived in the Miranda all his married life. As a barrister, he specialises in criminal law and appears almost exclusively for legal aid clients. Before joining the Bar, he worked as a legal aid duty solicitor at Sutherland Local Court.

Mr Collier said he would run on a platform "championing residents' rights against Sutherland Shire Council turning a blind eye to rampant overdevelopment."

"Development in the Shire is right out of control," he said. "It's not the Government forcing it, but the Liberal Council approving everything willy-nilly.

"Quality of life is suffering. It's frightening to think of the impact, not just of the units which are already standing, but those which have been approved and are yet to be built."

Mr Collier said the current Council had been elected on a platform of controlling development. However, their actions had been in total reverse of their election rhetoric.

Mr Collier said he would also campaign on issues of law and order, education and protecting Sutherland Hospital as a genuine community facility.

---

4 − 1: St George & Sutherland Shire Leader, 15 December 1998

My attention was immediately drawn to the first article [4 – 1], by the accompanying black and white photograph taken of me at the Leader Office. I still consider this to be the worst photo taken of me throughout the entire campaign.

I couldn't blame the newspaper for that. Had I not been such a novice, I'd have supplied the Leader with the professional studio photo taken of me several weeks before: the one I'd chosen to use on my 'Introductory Card', my coreflutes and on all our campaign literature.

Lesson learnt, I sent the Leader a copy of my studio photo for their files the very next day. Thankfully, that appalling black and white number taken at Hurstville never surfaced again.

But photograph aside, the article 'Labor takes aim', could not have provided a better start to my campaign. Firstly, in outlining my background, the article included the most fundamental detail of all: the fact I was a long-time Shire resident who actually lived in the Miranda electorate itself. While all the other personal information was important, the most basic consideration for many voters in the insular Shire was whether the candidate was a local. In that respect at least, I filled the bill – as did my opponent!

Secondly, and just as importantly, the first article clearly set the scene for what was to follow. The voters of Miranda were left in absolutely no doubt about the focus of the Labor campaign: tackling the rampant overdevelopment in the Shire under the Liberal-controlled Council.

A bold move?

In what many experienced politicians would no doubt see as a bold move, here was the Labor candidate publicly stating the central issue upon which he would fight his campaign some 3½ months out from election day. Talk about telegraphing your punches!

But Ron Phillips was clearly on notice. The battle lines having been drawn, the question now was: how would my opponent respond? While the article didn't contain any comment from Mr Phillips, I would've been very surprised if he hadn't been asked by the journalist to provide one.

Perhaps my opponent simply dismissed *overdevelopment* outright as an issue for the local Council and as one which had absolutely nothing to do with him as the State MP. Perhaps Mr Phillips felt that, as Deputy Opposition Leader, he had bigger fish to fry in supporting his new Leader and getting the Liberal Party back into Government. Whatever his reasons, the absence of any response by Ron Phillips suggested that he did not take the issue of overdevelopment, or me, seriously!

Attacking the MP's performance

The second article, focusing on Phillips's role in the downfall of Peter Collins, brought his performance as the local MP into the spotlight [4 − 2].

On the one hand, the article painted Ron Phillips as something more than a disloyal Deputy. In defending the way he broke the bad news to Collins, and effectively saying that Collins should "get a life," Ron showed himself to be rather callous, if not heartless, in the way he'd treated his respected former Leader.

Mr Phillips was clearly wrong about the community not being "overly interested in the internal plays that go on in politics." People generally are fascinated by the intrigue and happenings behind closed doors in the otherwise alien world of politics and tend to be appalled by the displays of disloyalty which surface from time to time in the public domain.

Then too, there were the died-in-the-wool Liberal voters and Branch members, who, having been reminded of Phillips' disloyalty, would never forgive him. Indeed, and as I'd later discover, when it comes to 'hating' some of their fellow Party members, the Libs leave the 'haters' in the Labor Party for dead!

But on the other hand, and while denying "he was letting down his electorate", Phillips' comments displayed all the arrogance of a powerbroker and a high-profile factional warrior who was out of touch with the people of Miranda. That could only help me.

Perhaps, like the issue of the Liberal Party leadership, Ron Phillips regarded the issue of *overdevelopment* as a "distraction!" That, too, could only help me.

Needless to say, I was delighted with both Leader articles. For many Shire locals, the paper was their first port of call for all the news, well ahead of the metropolitan dailies. Indeed, in addition to those who read each edition of the paper from cover to cover, there were those in the Shire who treated every word in the Leader as Gospel!

The message was out there! Paul Ellercamp had really done a first-class job in writing what would turn out to be his one and only media release for me during the entire campaign.

Phillips under attack over leadership coup

By MURRAY TREMBATH

LIBERAL Party "kingmaker" Ron Phillips, is under fire in his Miranda electorate over his role in the overthrow of Opposition Leader Peter Collins.

Newly endorsed ALP candidate for Miranda Barry Collier claimed residents were losing out because of Mr Phillips' "focus on numbers and factions".

"Ron Phillips appears to be more concerned with plotting the downfall of Peter Collins and (former Federal MP for Cook) Stephen Mutch than listening to the concerns of his electorate," Mr Collier said.

Mr Phillips, who leads the left-leaning faction known as The Group, denied he was letting down his electorate. "At the end of the day, the community isn't overly interested in the internal plays going on in politics," he said

Mr Phillips said that, as Deputy Opposition leader, he had a responsibility to... do what was best to improve the Coalition's chances at the March election. "I had to make a decision between my long-term loyalty to Peter Collins versus my responsibility to my team of colleagues in the Liberal Party and those people who support the Liberal Party," he said

Mr Phillips defended the way he broke the news to Mr Collins.

"I believe Peter needs to get his life back in order and then to decide what he is going to do with the rest of his life," he said.

"We don't need any distractions in the 100-odd days to the next election," he said.

4 – 2: St George & Sutherland Shire Leader, 15 December 1998

4.3. Getting out there and doorknocking

I hadn't exactly been sitting on my hands between my visit to the Leader's Hurstville office and the publication of the two articles.

By the time I picked up a copy of the paper from a footpath in Kirrawee on the 15th of December, I was already on my fourth day of doorknocking. But it wasn't with the 'Introductory Card' that Paul Ellercamp and I had worked on and finalised.

A problem—with not a moment to lose

Paul had been unexpectedly advised by the local printer, "who always did our Labor stuff," that he was closing down over Christmas and my Card wouldn't be printed until mid-January.

I just couldn't afford to spend the six weeks between my Party endorsement on the 4th of December and the 15th of January 1999 simply marking time. To me, there wasn't a moment to lose.

Despite the conventional Labor wisdom that I should not begin doorknocking until the New Year, I just had to get started. I had to get out there and doorknock as many homes as I could before election day. There was no way in the world I was going to wait until Christmas, let alone mid-January!

But what to doorknock with? I couldn't do it empty handed. I had to leave some literature at every home I visited, whether the residents were home or not!

Undeterred, and as limited as my computer skills were, I put together my own 'Introductory Pamphlet'. This was a very simple black and white version of my Card, now lying idle in our sympathetic printer's factory. I took the master to Kwik-Kopy at Sutherland where I photocopied a 1,000 on blue A4 paper at my own expense. [The master copy is shown in 4−3.]

introducing

Barry Collier
Labor for MIRANDA

Barry Collier has lived and worked in the Sutherland Shire for 27 years.

He lives in your electorate of MIRANDA. Barry is married. His two children, aged 20 and 17, were born and raised in the Shire.

Barry is a barrister by occupation. As a former Legal Aid solicitor at Sutherland Local Court, and before that as an economics teacher at Port Hacking High School, he has unique experience in the issues affecting the Shire community.

He is happy to help you with problems.

Or just to hear your concerns.

ALP

"a local who listens"

ALP MIRANDA
NSW State Election Campaign
PO Box 510 Miranda NSW 2228
Ph 9525 8309

AUSTRALIAN
LABOR
PARTY

Authorised and printed by Bob Rogers, 76 Grays Point Rd, Grays Point 2232

4 – 3: My introductory A4 blue pamphlet

The colour blue

Why blue? Apart from it being my favourite colour, I also knew it would annoy the hell out of some of the local Libs who always used blue in their literature and seemed to think they had a monopoly on the colour! Moreover, I never personally liked Labor's use of the colour red. I'd even come across seniors who saw the use of red as evidence of some link between the ALP and Communism!

Blue, by contrast, is a 'calming colour'. And who knows? Blue might suggest to some that I was not one of those so-called 'lefty Labor ratbags' but, like most people in the Shire, I was more of a conservative — which, in reality, was not far from the truth!

While it was all very well to have 1,000 A4 pamphlets to distribute, each had to first be folded. None of the local Branches had a folding machine, and so each night my wife, Jeanette, and her stepfather, Ernie Grinstead, sat at our dining table, folding my Introductory Pamphlet by hand, ready for next day's doorknocking. (As the number of pamphlets multiplied later in the campaign, Branch members helped out with this seemingly menial and mindless— but nevertheless, important— task. Even so, Jeanette and Ernie continued the folding at home after dinner every night until the eve of the election.)

Presentation basics, Day 1

On the 11th of December 1998, exactly one week after my Party endorsement, I headed out for my first stint of doorknocking, beginning with the second house around the corner from my home in Kareela. My own suburb seemed a sensible place for me to start on that very hot, humid day around 10.00AM.

First appearances count, and I'd given considerable thought to mine before hitting the streets: polished black shoes, long black pants, blue shirt, my blue spotted campaign tie, and a tasteful straw hat (that had been sitting in my wardrobe since a family cruise on the *Fairstar* a decade beforehand). I rolled my shirt sleeves up, as though I was on the job and working, or at least giving every appearance that I was ready and willing to do so.

Of course, I'd be carrying 100 of my folded Introductory Pamphlets as well as a clipboard and writing pad to note down any issues that residents raised with me, and to keep a record of the streets and the house numbers I doorknocked.

I'd also thought about what I'd do and what I'd say when I met residents at their homes for the first time. As they opened their front doors, I'd take my off my hat, introduce myself as the candidate for Miranda at the next State election, shake their hands, and tell them I was seeking their support. I'd ask if I could leave my Introductory Pamphlet with them, and finally, invite them to contact me later if I could assist them or their families.

Before going out on that first day, I also decided *not* to raise any campaign issues with residents myself. While recognising residents might raise their concerns with me, doorknocking at this early stage was definitely not about issues. It was about getting Barry Collier known as the Labor candidate for Miranda and seeking residents' support. That was it!

Besides, the last thing residents would want was some would-be politician haranguing them at their front door when they're busily preparing for Christmas! The basic idea was to do my little rehearsed spiel, wish the residents and their families a Merry Christmas & Happy New Year, then get to the next house as soon as possible. Doorknocking as I was in Kareela, of course, I'd also be sure to let residents know I lived in the same suburb!

Early reality checks

Anyone embarking on a political career is also embarking on a very steep learning curve. While doorknocking is one of most important skills to master, there are no textbooks. Others may well give you advice, but doorknocking is something that you only really 'learn by doing'.

Residents who opened their door to me on that first day were generally very polite, and in most cases, readily accepted my pamphlet. Many were surprised, if not pleased, to see a political candidate at their front door. Being doorknocked by a would-be MP was clearly something very new, even for long-time Kareela residents. (I'd never had any candidate appear at my front door in the 20 years Jeanette and I had lived in the suburb by then.)

Even so, my very first day of doorknocking brought with it three major reality checks, beginning with the questions I was asked by many householders' moments after introducing myself.

Reality #1. If you think, as I did, you'll be asked lots of questions about government policy or your stance on a particular issue or what you are promising to do if elected, you'll be dead wrong!

The questions you will be asked by many residents early on (and even up until the eve of the election) are likely to include:

"Is there an election on?"

"When's the election?"

"Do we have to vote?"

"What if I'm working all day and can't get to a booth?"

"We'll be away. How can I get a postal vote?"

"We've just moved in. What do I do to vote here?

"Do we still vote up at the School?"

"We're not all that mobile these days. Can you give us a lift to the polling booth?"

"Didn't we vote already vote for Mr Howard?"

"What's this about *Miranda?* I've never lived in Miranda; I've always lived in Kareela!"

It's not long before the penny drops. You soon realise that, while you live and breathe politics, the average householder simply doesn't.

You'll find that many residents don't know the names of their own State and Federal MPs, confuse their State and Federal electorates and have absolutely no clue as to which level of government does what. Astounded as you may be at the low level of political sophistication out there in voter-land, people are generally far more focused on their day-to-day lives than "all those goings on in Macquarie Street."

From the very beginning, it's important that you at least look like you know the ropes, by being able to answer the simple questions voters are likely to ask you. Don't go doorknocking until you know the basic mechanics of the voting system itself— including how to get on the electoral roll, postal voting requirements, absentee voting, pre-polling and local polling booth locations.

I must admit not knowing the answers to all the questions I was asked about such matters on Day 1. But I told the residents who asked that I'd get back to them as soon as I could with the answers, which I did religiously. Later, I made it my business to get hold of multiple copies of enrolment forms, and other electoral information, and take several of these with me as I went from door to door, with more in my car parked nearby if needed.

Reality #2. Like me on that first day, you'll be asked questions which go beyond 'election mechanics.' Some questions will, of course, involve Party policy; others will be based on the news on radio or TV (or these days on the mobile, internet or 'some app').

Still other questions will seek your attitude to some public figure or on some social issue. You may be asked for help on a pressing family issue or to provide legal advice. Some questions will be well out of left-field and stop you in your tracks; other questions might leave you feeling embarrassed because you feel that you really should've known the answer to them, but didn't.

It's often a question of doing a little homework beforehand. If you don't' know the answer at the front door, tell the resident you'll get back to them with it as soon as possible, and make sure you do! The majority of residents will appreciate your honesty.

Try making up the answer on the doorstep and you'll inevitably be caught out. Indeed, you'll feel very foolish as the resident answers their own question for you, and you realise that you were just being tested!

Reality #3. From an economic viewpoint, the fundamental aim of doorknocking is simple: maximise your potential vote per unit of time.

That means getting around as many homes as you can, meeting as many residents you can, and persuading as many as you can to vote for you, in the limited time you have available.

But of course, not every resident will be home when you call. What to do? What you *don't* do is leave your pamphlet in the letterbox with all the junk mail. It must go under the front door! That at least gives the resident the impression that it was *you*, the candidate, who put it there personally, and not some Party hack or a paid letter-boxer. Besides, the resident who *was* home when you called will later tell their absent next-door neighbour that it actually was *you* who turned up in person.

I'd gone out on that first day with only my Introductory Pamphlets. Each time no-one was home, I stood there writing a message on my pamphlet before signing it and slipping it under the front door.

The message read "I called in today. I'm sorry I missed you. If you have any concerns, please contact me." This was both laborious and time consuming. Every minute I spent writing that message was a minute not spent talking to a potential voter or knocking on another voter's door. And the minutes all add up!

The solution (though not my invention) was surprisingly simple. I drew up a half-page, black and white 'Sorry I Missed You' note and had 100 of these photocopied. I signed these before I went out doorknocking again the next day.[58] It meant two distinctive pieces of paper going under each unanswered door, but the time

---

[58] I later had a rubber stamp made up with the relevant words— and used this on my 'Sorry Note' to save even more time. I used *blue* stamp pad ink, of course.

I'd save by doing so over the course of the entire campaign was enormous. Lesson learnt!

An encouraging first day

I doorknocked 124 homes on that first day. While the majority of residents were content simply to take my pamphlet, a dozen more raised issues without my asking, all of which I duly noted.

But by far the major concern even at this stage was *overdevelopment*: the key issue I'd told the Leader I'd be running on at the 1999 March election! Clearly, we were on the right track.

Overall, the reception I received was encouraging. I hadn't done any doorknocking since I was a kid living in Orange in the early 1960s going from house-to-house selling mushrooms at 1/- (10 cents) a bag for pocket money. I enjoyed doorknocking back then, and I enjoyed doing it again on that that hot, humid day in Kareela, 35 years later! Enjoying doorknocking was one of those things that set me apart from other candidates I'd come across later.

A simple strategy

I'd gone out doorknocking on Day 1 without any expectations, and did so in the "comfort zone" of my own suburb.

But winning Miranda in March 1999 meant that I'd have to doorknock the entire electorate over the next three months. I decided to adopt a simple strategy: *I'll doorknock 'till I drop.* What's more, I'd have to do it *alone*. That made perfect sense to me, given I was a complete unknown with no political profile.

DOORKNOCKING BASICS FOR BEGINNERS

1. Doorknock yourself: alone, if you feel comfortable doing so. Residents prefer to meet the candidate, rather than one of his or her off-siders. There's no point having someone else doorknock for you, especially if you are a complete unknown!
2. Set a realistic doorknocking target, say 100 homes a day. That's not a lot, given some residents will not be home. Keep a record of the numbers each day and keep to your target if possible.
3. Start doorknocking about 9.30AM and finish by early evening. Don't doorknock after dark and don't go inside the house.
4. Doorknock Monday to Friday, on Saturdays from 10 am and on Sunday afternoons from 2.00PM.
5. Don't doorknock on Christmas Eve, Christmas Day, New Years' Eve, New Years' Day or on Australia Day.
6. Doorknock every suburb in the electorate, and don't forget the back streets.
7. Keep a record of the streets you've doorknocked. Mark these on a map of the electorate to make sure you have a good general coverage.
8. Note down each of the house numbers in the streets you've doorknocked, whether there's anyone home or not. You might want to follow up later on, especially with those residents who were out.
9. Make a note of the topics raised by individual householders. These will help you identify major campaign issues for the electorate as a whole, as well as for residents of particular suburbs or even streets. Get back to residents who ask for more information and, where you need to, make further inquiries.
10. If appropriate, write to the relevant State Minster, Federal Minister, Mayor or Ward Councillor on behalf of individual residents. Make sure you let the resident know that you've done so, and get back to them with any official response.

---

4 − 4: My doorknocking rules, early days

I'd already worked out how I'd present myself at the door. But if I was to get the best out of my doorknocking, I decided to devise some basic rules I would follow each time I hit the streets [4−4]. The rules I came up with were not based on advice but on common sense, my gut feelings and my early experience. Just note, however, that you need to be flexible in applying them.

Expect the unexpected

Doorknocking comes easier to some candidates than to others. Many candidates have to really push themselves to get out there for the first time. But the more you do it, the better you become! As you go from house to house, you hone your doorknocking skills, improving your presentation and developing ready-made answers to questions you know you'll be asked again and again.

You'll find the majority of householders are polite and respectful, taking your pamphlet and listening to your practised spiel. There'll be times when residents are very pleased to meet you, happy to have a quick chat and to discuss their concerns in a friendly, courteous manner. At other times you'll find it hard to end the conversation and move on to the next house.

But some home owners will be up front and tell you in no uncertain terms there's no way they'll ever vote for you, for a host of reasons, none of which have anything to do with you personally. They may just hate the Labor Leader or the Party itself; they might have always voted Liberal; they might dislike all politicians and always vote informal. You soon learn not to waste your time arguing with those who express these sentiments: there's no way known to mankind you'll change their minds.

From time to time, you will be confronted with colourful language, and even be bailed up by the family dog. There will be times you have to hold your tongue, when every fibre of your being screams out against you doing so. There may even be the odd occasion where you just have to turn on your heels and get out through that front gate as quickly as possible.

But don't be discouraged. Don't let these negatives deter you. Doorknocking is a *must!* It's not only a big vote getter; it can be very rewarding personally.

True, you just don't know the kind of reception you'll get when that front door opens. You need to be flexible and play it by ear. But you also need to be well-prepared and alert. When you go out doorknocking, you must expect the unexpected! After all, that's part and parcel of the political life you've chosen to pursue.

4.4.   A Premier call

After a morning's doorknocking on Saturday, the 19th of December, I stopped in at home to grab a quick bite. As I was about to head out again around 1.30PM, I received a phone call from Bob Carr's Private Secretary. She asked if I'd be available to take a call from the Premier at 2 o'clock. Of course, I'd be available!

An accidental candidate?

I couldn't help but wonder: why would Bob Carr, the Premier of NSW, be calling me on a hot Saturday afternoon a week out from Christmas? After all, he hadn't shown the slightest interest in me at the opening of the new A & E Unit at Sutherland Hospital!

Maybe the Party had come up with a better candidate? Perhaps they wanted somebody with a high profile to run against Ron Phillips? That's it! Sussex Street had finally worked out that it would only take a swing of 5.3% to win Miranda! Perhaps they've decided to parachute in someone they think can win it!

Let me explain. Three days before, and in an effort to get some funding from the Party, I'd had a conversation with Assistant General Secretary, Damian O'Connor. When he mentioned I needed a swing of 10% to win, I'd corrected that immediately. Head Office had not done its homework. It had to have been looking at the 1991 results for Miranda. The heavies hadn't even taken into account the 1995 result, let alone the 1998 redistribution, which had reduced the Liberal margin to 5.3%!

No attention had been given by the heavies to Miranda because they thought the seat was unwinnable! Perhaps Head Office had woken up and decided to correct its error by replacing me with a star candidate — particularly after the job Phillips did on Peter Collins? Perhaps Carr was ringing to give me the 'tap on the shoulder' before I'd really got going? Maybe I was soon to be the short-lived, 'accidental candidate for Miranda'? Such were the thoughts running through my mind as I sat on the stairs at home nervously waiting to hear from the Premier.

"Call me Bob"

The phone rang on the dot of 2.00PM. I returned Carr's greeting with "Hello, Mr Premier," to which he replied, "call me Bob."

'Bob' told me he rang because he'd heard about my doorknocking! He explained that his wife, Helena, had a good friend living in the Shire whom I'd actually doorknocked during the week. The friend had told Helena that she was impressed with me, and Helena had passed that on to Bob.

The Premier encouraged me to keep up the doorknocking despite the margin, and seemed very surprised to learn from me that the margin was only 5.3%! Carr had been very poorly briefed about Miranda by Head Office (— if he'd been briefed at all).

I told the Premier I had every intention of continuing doorknocking up until election day. Delighted by Carr's call, and feeling a sense of relief, I made a mental note that I would write to the General Secretary, John Della Bosca, early in the New Year, putting paid to the notion that I needed a swing of more than 10% to win Miranda, and seeking help with funding again.

Word-of-mouth

But there was something else. It occurred to me that if my efforts were reaching the ears of the Premier, then other people I doorknocked must be listening and talking about it to each other!

Carr's call brought home to me, perhaps more than anything could, the importance of word-of-mouth. The timing of his call also vindicated my decision to begin doorknocking before the New Year, contrary to advice from previous candidates. What better place for people to talk about 'that bloke who turned up at their door wanting their vote' than at the Christmas table, when families get together and talk about anything and everything?

After Carr's call, I went out and doorknocked for the rest of that afternoon, and continued to do so until the 23rd of December. I did so again on the 29th and 30th of December, and resumed on the 2nd January 1999.

Those I doorknocked were receptive. Some families even invited me in for a Christmas and a New Years' drink (which I respectfully declined). No one took offence at the fact I was doorknocking over the Christmas-New Year period. Perhaps it was the season, but *the vibe* was very good!

4.5.   Doorknocking stories #1, 2 and 3

Whether you're a salesperson or a would-be politician, there is simply no substitute for doorknocking, the digital age notwithstanding.

Apart from being the best way to learn all the street names in the electorate, it's also the best way to get to know your potential voters. I'm not just talking about the worries they have and the issues that concern them. I'm talking about what they do, what they think, where their kids go to school, the sporting team they follow, the Church they attend, their achievements, their hopes and dreams: you name it! In learning about the people of the electorate, you also learn something about yourself.

Every serious candidate has a swag of doorknocking stories. I'll now tell you three of mine, along with what I learnt, from my doorknocking in December 1998. I'll save more stories until later.

#1: *Being a Shire local*

I never had any doubts about the importance to voters of me being a true local: not just living in the Miranda electorate, but having a long-standing personal, work and family connection with the Shire.

My assessment was confirmed during a conversation with a spritely 85-year-old on his front porch in the suburb of Como:

"So how long have you been in the Shire, son?" he asked.

"All my married life— 27 years," I replied confidently.

"Oh, you're a newcomer then, are you?" he asked, looking me squarely in the eye.

You might think the old-timer was joking. But I can tell you he was deadly serious! Before I could get a word in, he went on, at some considerable length, to tell me of his Italian heritage and of his family history spanning three generations in the Shire.

I didn't have the heart to deprive him of the pleasure he was obviously getting in telling me about the family's past by interrupting him. While I was yet to earn my spurs as a true Shire resident in that old man's eyes, I really lived up to my chosen slogan as '*A Local who Listens*'.

Even so, I began to question just how long I could spend with one person at their front door. It wasn't because I wasn't interested; the longer the conversation went on, the less time I had at other doors and the more I fell short of my doorknocking target! Something for me to really think about.

#2: Inspirational stuff

Doorknocking can be something of an inspirational experience from time to time. Take the old fellow living on the edge of the factory area in the back streets of Kirrawee who came out of his house wearing a blue work singlet, King-Gee shorts and an ancient pair of black work boots. Even though he must have retired many years before, this looked to be his daily dress.

"What are yer, mate? Liberal or Labor?" he asked, as I began my spiel.

"Labor," I replied quickly.

"Good on yer, son," he said. "You know, nobody has knocked on my door since Gough Whitlam when he was the Member for Werriwa in the 1950's!"

Wow! I thought. Here am I doorknocking a bloke who was actually doorknocked by my own political hero, Gough Whitlam, more than 40 years before![59] Now that was real inspiration! If doorknocking was good enough for a former Labor Prime Minister, it was certainly good enough for me!

But there were also two important lessons here. Firstly, doorknocking clearly was the key to winning, and particularly winning over those who hadn't seen any candidate at their door for years, if ever! And, it was obvious, even this early in my campaign, that like those long-time residents of Kareela I'd doorknocked on Day 1, those in the neighbouring suburb of Kirrawee had probably never seen hide nor hair of their sitting MP, Mr Phillips, on their front veranda!

Secondly, my conversation with the old fellow in the blue singlet confirmed my strong view that you must doorknock the back streets. If you followed the advice I was given by a former candidate that, to save time, you should only doorknock the highways and main streets, then those in the backstreets would inevitably miss out!

For residents in the back streets who've never previously seen a candidate or MP on their front porch, your appearance is something they'll always remember. It's also something they'll tell

---

[59] Gough Whitlam became Member for the Federal seat of *Werriwa* in 1952. The electorate then took in the entire Sutherland Shire, with Mr Whitlam living with his family at Cronulla. With successive redistributions, the seat moved to Sydney's west. Along with later boundary changes, Gough Whitlam and his family moved from Cronulla to Cabramatta. The Shire has not been included in the seat of Werriwa since 1957.

their relatives, friends, workmates and even their local shopkeepers about. Your visit is effectively telling those in the backstreets who open their doors to you that, if elected, you'll go that extra mile for them too!

#3: Criss-crossing the electorate

In 1999, the electorate of Miranda included voters across a dozen suburbs, and it was clearly important that I got the message out there as widely as possible. Rather than focus on one suburb at a time, as some had suggested, I decided to doorknock the streets in two or even three different suburbs every day.

Before heading out each morning, I'd sit down with a map of the electorate and decide which streets I'd doorknock that day. That typically involved up to four adjacent streets in a particular suburb. I figured that, the more I got around, the more people would know about me and my candidacy, and the more they were likely to talk about the fact that I actually came to their door asking for their vote.

The idea was simple. After two or three hours of doorknocking my chosen group of streets in one suburb, I'd then drive across the electorate to another group of streets in another suburb and continue doorknocking there.

No doubt, I'd invariably knock on the door of a local Liberal Branch member, who'd pass the word on to Ron Phillips that I was out and about this early in the campaign. While I had no idea when (or even how) he'd respond to my movements, I thought that if I criss-crossed the electorate on a daily basis, the Libs would have absolutely no idea where I'd turn up next, and at least I'd keep them guessing.

But on one particular day, my criss-crossing of the electorate produced something truly remarkable. I began doorknocking in nearby Jannali round 10.00AM. I moved on later to spend three hours doorknocking in the suburb of Miranda before driving to Yowie Bay, arriving around 4.00PM to continue doorknocking there.

Having knocked on the flywire door of a house in a Yowie Bay street off Attunga Road, a boy aged eight or nine dressed in school uniform appeared in the hallway.

"Grandma! There's a man at the door!" he yelled.

"Just a minute," came a voice from somewhere inside.

A few seconds later, an older woman strode up the hall towards the front door. Her face looked somehow familiar.

As she opened the door to me, Grandma said, "oh, hello, Mr Collier, I met you at my house in Jannali this morning!"

Before I could respond, Grandma explained that this house in Yowie Bay was her daughter's. With her daughter working until 5.00PM, she came over from Jannali to mind her grandson after school every afternoon. Grandma nevertheless took my pamphlet, saying she'd give it to her daughter when she got home from work.

Extraordinary! With more than 40,000 voters in the Miranda electorate, what are the odds of doorknocking the same person you've never previously met *twice* on the same day at different houses in different suburbs 10 km apart?

I know I'm a touch superstitious, but this was just a little spooky. What was all this telling me? There had to be a message here somewhere! The only message I could glean from such an astonishing event was this: keep criss-crossing the electorate!

4.6. Letters to Della

As part of its 1999 campaign strategy, Head Office identified a number of 'targeted seats' These were seats, held by a margin of 5% or less, which Sussex Street believed Labor should win.

These 'targeted seats' were priorities for the Party and, as such, attracted considerable funding and other resources from Head Office. Examples included the St George seats of Kogarah and Georges River being contested by first-time candidates Cherie Burton and Kevin Greene, respectively.

At 5.3%, Miranda was only 0.3% outside Labor's targeted seat range. I'd already been alerted by Damian O'Connor and Bob Carr himself that Head Office held the erroneous view that I needed a swing of more than 10% to win.

Given the huge role Ron Phillips was likely to play in the Liberal campaign, and the need to fund my own, I faxed a letter directly to ALP General Secretary, John Della Bosca, requesting that Head Office "consider targeting *Miranda* with funds and resources to capture the seat."

Having pointed out what I saw were the obvious benefits for my campaign, I ended my faxed letter dated 2nd January 1999 noting that "... targeting Miranda must surely assist in returning a Carr Labor Government in New South Wales."

Come February, I hadn't received a response (or even an acknowledgement) from Della Bosca or anyone else in Head

Office. Thinking my fax may have gone astray in the bowels of Sussex Street, I faxed a second letter to our General Secretary.

While I had expected the courtesy of at least a reply of some sort, I am yet to receive one to this day! To me, there could only be one reason for Della Bosca's failure to respond to either of my faxes: the Party thought I had absolutely no chance of winning!

That would be confirmed later in newspaper reports where Della Bosca named the seats he believed Labor would win. Miranda was not one of them. I believed differently.

4.7. Shoestring campaigning

At some point, every candidate must face the fundamental question: "How will I fund my campaign?" However optimistic you may be, you simply can't spend money hand over fist, running up debts in the hope that these will all be met through local fundraising or from Branch bank accounts or that some sympathetic, cashed-up Good Samaritan will appear on the horizon with a sizeable donation.

There has to be planning and there has to be budgeting. Regardless of the election outcome, the harsh reality is that the campaign must be paid for, as some starry-eyed candidates have later discovered to their eternal regret!

Della Bosca's failure to classify Miranda as a 'targeted seat' corroborated something the experienced Bob Rogers told me at our first meeting: "don't expect anything from Head Office!"

We were on our own. There was no escaping the fact that the money needed for our campaign to win Miranda would have to come from local sources, and these were likely to be very limited!

Fortunately, Bob had considerable experience in campaign management, including fundraising and budgeting, and we'd need all his skills. But it was very clear right from word go that we'd have to run our entire campaign on a shoestring!

Budget basics

While ours would have to be a no-frills campaign, there were some basics we just had to have: including coreflutes, photos, Leader ads and pamphlets, all of which had to be paid for.

Later on, we'd also need thousands of How to Votes (HTVs) to hand out at pre-polling in the two weeks leading up to election day and on the big day itself. While these were always designed and printed by Head Office, we'd have to pay for them as well!

We'd also needed to set up, staff and maintain a Campaign Office somewhere in the Miranda electorate for the six weeks prior to election day. That meant paying rent, and equipping the office with desks, chairs, a phone, photocopier, fax machine and a computer, together with the consumables we'd need, like paper!

Budget finances

So where was the money for our campaign coming from? From the outset, it was clear that we would be struggling to meet even the basics from the funds immediately available locally.

The local Branches could only make a limited contribution — mainly because most their funds raised since the 1995 State election had been siphoned off to the Federal campaigns in 1996 and 1998. And, while the Miranda SEC had some funds left over from the public funding received after Paul Smith's campaign for the seat, these too, had been diminished by generous donations to local candidates for Federal and Council campaigns.[60]

As expected, I'd have to put my hand into my own pocket. I didn't mind. There was only one problem: I'd given up work as a barrister to campaign full time, and so would have no income for the next 3½ months! Jeanette and I decided to put in what we could from our limited savings as well as any proceeds from the sale of my Chambers. That would help the finances a little.

But if we were to run a successful campaign, we'd have to go beyond Branches and candidate contributions. We'd have to also rely on donations and our own fundraising activities.

Donations

Bob Rogers sought and received a donation from *the Tradies* for which we were thankful.[61] Through Bob's connections, the Randwick Labor Club also made a helpful donation. Even so, we were still staring down the barrel of a funding shortfall.

I thought I'd try seeking donations from my colleagues, past and present, in teaching and in law. But having sent off over 100 personally signed letters, hoping to raise a couple of thousand dollars, I received only one reply, accompanied by a cheque for $250, from a senior barrister I'd worked with several years before.

Perhaps, unlike me, my former colleagues didn't believe I could win; perhaps they were Liberal voters. Who knows? But

---

[60] "Public funding" aims to reimburse communication expenditures by those candidates who gain at least 4% of the first preference votes in a given seat at a NSW State election. The scheme is now administered by the NSW Electoral Commission.
[61] The Sutherland District Trade Union Club (the *Tradies*) had consistently been the greatest single supporter of Labor candidates in the Shire over the years.

needless to say, their response was very disappointing. I just hoped I was more popular with voters out there in the electorate!

So, what about seeking campaign donations from the unions? Surely, they'd support me with a donation, given the union movement's close association with the Party and the fact that the majority of our Branch members were also trade union members.

With that in mind, I wrote to John Maitland, then National Secretary of the Construction Forestry Mining and Energy Union (CFMEU). Apart from heading up one of the largest unions in Australia, Maitland actually lived in the Miranda electorate. Naturally, I thought he would take considerable interest in the seat itself. While I'd never met or spoken to Maitland (even to this day), I was optimistic about getting a campaign donation from his Union. I was wrong about that! While no donation was forthcoming, he at least acknowledged my letter.[62]

Fundraisers and a 'no-show'

Ideally, candidates are out there busily raising funds for their campaigns well before the election is called. However, for new candidates like me, standing in long-held Liberal seats we weren't expected to win, fundraising could only get under way after we were endorsed. With only three months to the big day, broken by

---

[62] In 2013, ICAC made a finding of corrupt conduct against Maitland and former Labor Minister Ian Macdonald over the awarding of a lucrative Hunter Valley coal mining licence. In 2014, Maitland was stripped of his OAM. In 2016, he was fined $3,000 and placed on a two- year good behavior bond for providing misleading evidence to ICAC. In 2017, Maitland was found guilty of being an accessory to *misconduct in public office* by McDonald and sentenced to a maximum of six years imprisonment.

Christmas and New Year, our time for fundraising time was short, and the money raised was likely to follow suit.

Bob came up with three fundraisers, none of which were expected to raise a fortune. Beginning with a 'Christmas Muster' for local Branch members ($5 a head), there followed a 'Riparian Barbie' in early February on the banks of the Hacking River at Grays Point (at $10 a head) and a 'Trivia Night' hosted by *the Tradies* with quizmaster Senator Michael Forshaw and assisted by Lawrie Daly in early March ($10 a head). Apart from the entry fee, some funds were also raised via that ubiquitous feature of every Labor gathering: the raffle.[63]

Now, it goes without saying that campaign fundraisers provide guests with the opportunity to meet, and to hear from, the candidate. But, through no fault of my own, I was an embarrassing 'no show' at one of my own fundraising events! Let me explain.

After a morning's doorknocking, I headed off to the Saturday afternoon 'Riparian Barbie' due to start at 1.00PM. On the Boulevarde in Miranda, my old Mitsubishi sedan blew a radiator hose, and was simply undriveable.

Ringing ahead to let Bob and the organisers know wasn't an option; there was no mobile phone reception beside the Hacking River at Grays Point! By the time the NRMA arrived and got me going, the function was over. I arrived well after the BBQ, and well after most of my guests had left. I felt really bad about that, and sent out an email explaining my unfortunate non-appearance and giving my apologies. Nevertheless, I felt very silly. But lesson learnt: I'll aim to arrive much earlier next time around!

---

[63]   Labor legends like "Johno" Johnson, made the ALP raffle into an art form.

I hoped to be able to redeem myself at the two traditional Labor events closer to election day: our Campaign Office Opening and our Miranda Campaign Launch. I'll return to these later.

In the meantime, it's important to remember that all these events were not just about raising funds; they were also about bringing Branch members and supporters together, enlisting their support and, ultimately, focusing their efforts on winning what would surely be a very tough election campaign ahead.

Limited funding and campaign realities

Limited funding had major implications for the way we'd have to run our campaign.

At a time when the internet was only beginning to make its mark, our small funding pot meant ruling out one of the most effective campaigning tools of all: *direct mail*. We simply couldn't afford the huge expense of personally addressed postal mail to individual voters and their families. A postal voting campaign — which could make all the difference between winning and losing — was also out of the question.

Limited funding also had implications for that major expenditure item, which all serious candidates were expected to have in those days: *A Campaign Office*. Known also as an 'Information Office,' we needed to rent premises in a highly visible location in the Miranda electorate. The cheaper the better!

Bodies on the ground

While I'd be doing all the doorknocking alone, we had to complement that with street stalls, early morning railway station visits and letterboxing across the entire electorate. We needed bodies on the ground. That included bodies to staff our Campaign Office and to hand out our How to Votes (HTVs).

Not being expected to win, we knew Head Office wouldn't be sending out hordes of Young Labor members to assist (as it did with its targeted seats). We certainly didn't have any money to pay workers to hand out our HTVs as the Liberals often did.

So far as campaign workers went, we were on our own. There was really only one source available: volunteers from the local Labor Branches, their families, our friends and supporters — and, as we shall see, they were absolutely magnificent!

Getting my dial out there

It's hard to imagine turning up to vote on election day and not seeing a multitude of coreflutes with the face, name, and Party of each of the candidates.

While there were a host of other tangible things that needed to be added to our campaign shopping cart, coreflutes were a must! Given our limited funding, I personally paid for 400 blue, simple "Barry Collier for Miranda" coreflutes showing my studio photo and ALP logo [4–5]. I can tell you these don't come cheap!

My coreflutes were destined to be screwed onto A-frames for display at street stalls, railways stations and polling places. Many would be nailed to telegraph poles on main roads and in shopping centres, as well as in other high pedestrian traffic areas.

Some coreflutes would be screwed to garden stakes. These were either given to those staunch supporters brave enough to put my dial up in their front yards or displayed on main roads and at major roundabouts during the morning and evening traffic peaks, a campaigning technique known as 'flying pickets'.

Getting the better part of 400 coreflutes onto A-frames and garden stakes was an enormous job, but one willingly undertaken in the garage of his Gymea home by retired Life Member and War veteran, Bob White. While I had to buy the garden stakes, screws and nails, as well as the coreflutes, we saved on the wooden A-frames by simply recycling the hundreds left over from previous local Labor campaigns.

You may well think that ordering 400 coreflutes is excessive, but you have to make allowances for those that never make it through the campaign to election day. Anyone who has ever worked on an election campaign for a major Party will be more than aware that a number will inevitably 'disappear', often in the middle of the night, never to be seen again!

4 – 5: Collier for Miranda coreflute,1999

Campaigning in black & white

Volunteers and coreflutes aside, there was another related question: "What kind of literature would we distribute?" It was here that our limited funding would be keenly felt.

Surprisingly perhaps, no literature would be professionally written for our local campaign. With the exception of my Introductory Card written by Paul Ellercamp and two excellent brochures written later by Paul Smith, I personally wrote all our Miranda-specific campaign literature on my very basic home computer. That included the few advertisements we'd eventually place in the Leader.

Remarkably, and as unthinkable as it is today, not one of the pamphlets distributed throughout our entire campaign was in colour, let alone glossy! Budget constraints meant that all our pamphlets were produced, first up, in black and white, regardless of their importance and regardless of whether they were to be letterboxed, handed out at street stalls and railway stations, or used by me in doorknocking.

We could only afford to have two campaign pamphlets professionally printed: our 'general issues' pamphlet with all our major commitments on roads, health, etc., and a second pamphlet devoted entirely to *overdevelopment*. Both were simple, double-sided A4 pamphlets, cheaply printed in black and white by a local supporter in the printing trade in his home garage.

There'd also be a host of other pamphlets which had to be written and distributed, and, of course, be available at our Campaign Office.

But printing every pamphlet in black and white presents obvious problems when you are handing out different brochures on different issues over a three-month period. Given our shortage of cash, we decided the best we could do was to produce black and white masters of each pamphlet and then photocopy each of these onto different coloured paper!

There was no reason why this 'colour coding' wouldn't work. After all, nobody had complained that my blue A4 Introductory Pamphlet wasn't a full-colour, glossy number. That pamphlet had generally been well received, without any comment as to the obvious lack of print quality. We believed that what really counted was our message. Besides, the cheap-looking pamphlets we were putting out there could only help confirm our status as the underdog!

Now while many of our photocopied pamphlets would invariably deal with a different issue, some would be repeated three and four times, but with a different theme or focus.

The original black-and-white version of one such pamphlet, before being photocopied onto coloured paper is shown in 4−6. While the message and layout were basically the same each time, the photograph was changed to reflect a different focus− in this case, 'hospitals and health', which, you will notice, was also one of my 'top priorities'.

Barry Collier
Labor for Miranda

Barry Collier cares about the people of the Shire. He knows it's the best address in Sydney. He wants to keep it that way. Barry is a local who listens to your concerns ... and then acts upon them.

Well qualified for the job.....

✓ Barry Collier has lived in the Shire for 27 years.

✓ Barry and his wife, Jeanette, hav two children aged 20 and 17.Botl were born, raised and educated in the Shire.

✓ Barry has university qualificatior with experience in economics, la and education.

✓ Barry taught in NSW State high schools for 17 years before entering the law in 1989.

✓ Barry has written and published HSC economics texbooks.

✓ Barry has worked in the Shire as a teacher at Port Hacking High School and Sutherland Local Court as a Legal Aid Solicitor.

✓ Barry is now a barrister specializing in criminal law.

✓ Barry has coached junior soccer, cricket and rugby. He has played soccer and cricket for Miranda, Sylvania Heights and Como-Jannali.

Barry Collier's top priorities...

- Finding solutions to the Shire's chronic over-development.
- Opposing the sale and privatisation of our electricity industry.
- Supporting the Labor Government's $79m redevelopment of the Sutherland Hospital.
- Continuing the State Government's fight against crime by supporting crackdowns on gangs, knives and drugs.
- Ensuring we, the people of Miranda, get our fair share of money for education, for youth services and for senior citizens.
- Protecting the Shire's natural environment and supporting the cleanup and restoration of its rivers, bays and beaches.
- Ensuring the Woronora Bridge & Bangor by-pass are completed on time.

Printed & authorised by Bob Rogers, PO Box 510 Miranda NSW 2228

The new electorate of Miranda includes Gymea, Gymea Bay, Grays Point, Kangaroo Pt, Kareela, Kirrawee, Oyster Bay, Yowie Bay & parts of Como, Jannali, Miranda and Sylvania.

A local who listens .....

Dear Shire Resident,
In this day and age, it's easy to be critical of politicians. Often, it appears they aren't listening: they seem to promise the world but deliver nothing.
I'm standing for Parliament on 27 March because I believe the people of Miranda need a local member who puts them first. They don't want an MP who is so involved in leadership struggles, back room party brawls and the Olympics that he has no time for them.
I believe the people of Miranda want a local who listens to their concerns- one who works hard to get the best deal for their families, for their loved ones and for themselves.
My priority is simple:
    commitment to you.
How? Through listening to you and through hard work for you.

I look forward to meeting you in the next few weeks.

Barry Collier
LABOR FOR MIRANDA

For help with any State matter, or Postal Vote Enquiries, phone Barry now on...

9525 8309

Office: 581 The Kingsway, Miranda.

4 – 6: Campaigning in black and white

Photographs

Virtually every campaign pamphlet requires a photograph, if only of the candidate. But apart from the photo taken of me at the Miranda studio there would be no professional photography at all. Our cash flow problems saw to that.

I should point out that it's common for candidates on both sides to distribute pamphlets containing photos of themselves 'discussing' key issues and achievements with (unnamed) constituents. You'll easily identify the relevant road, school, sports ground, station or other local landmark in the background.

While the constituents in the photograph always look to be 'hanging off every word' being uttered by the candidate, and give all the appearance of being members of the general public who just happened to be passing by, nothing could be further from the truth. In many cases, most of those 'constituents' are in fact Liberal or Labor Party members, their relatives, friends and supporters.

I well recall lining up a host of local Branch members to have photographs taken with me by John Goschin (a local supporter with a digital camera), at various times and various key locations over a four-hour period on a very hot and humid Saturday afternoon in early January 1999. Several were taken of me with Labor member, Martin Iffland, at Sutherland Hospital, the scene of my unusable photos taken with Premier Bob Carr the month before.

However, a number of the photos in my literature did in fact include *bona fide* members of the public. One of these appears in 4 – 6. Taken with the permission of the young woman shown, this remains, in my view, one of the best photographs taken during the entire campaign. Sometimes we got lucky!

State-wide Labor messages

It was important to remember that our campaign was ultimately directed to returning the Carr Government for a second term. That meant getting the Party's State-wide messages out to Miranda voters. Part of that message was that I'd be able to do far more for my constituents as an elected Member of the Carr Labor Government than Mr Phillips would be able to do for them in Opposition.

Out of the blue, we received a set of single-sided, A4 black-and-white pamphlets, produced by Sussex Street and spruiking the achievements, policies and future plans of the Carr Government across a variety of areas including education, law enforcement, transport, jobs and the environment. We modified each of these by adding my name to the Party slogan at the foot of the page, and then photocopying the 'new' versions onto different coloured paper. These new pamphlets now proclaimed: *Barry Collier and NSW Labor: Getting on with the Job!*

It made good sense to link my name with the achievements of the Labor Government. After all, Bob Carr *was* popular at the time! Besides, these pamphlets would prove useful in explaining Labor policies to the interested voters I met at their front doors or those who phoned with questions or turned up at our Campaign Office seeking 'information' further down the track.[64]

---

[64] The only Head Office pamphlet I didn't distribute (unless I was specifically asked for it) was the one outlining the Government's changes to *Land Tax*. I didn't attach my slogan to that one!

The Sussex Street 'tick off'?

You may be surprised to learn that none of the pamphlets we wrote and produced locally throughout our campaign were ever 'ticked off' by Head Office officials before we distributed them.

In fact, I never even saw the need to seek approval from Sussex Street for any of the material I wrote. It was clear, from the start, that Head Office didn't think we could win, and didn't seem to care anyway. So "bugger them," I thought!

In any event, time was of the essence. If the response to my faxes by Della Bosca was any guide, the State election would be well and truly over by the time some Sussex Street official bothered to get back to us with any suggestions or comments!

I just trusted my own judgement and my own ability to write appropriately targeted material. I just 'got on with the job' of getting my pamphlets out there into the hands of Miranda voters.

4.8. Doorknocking stories #4 and 5

My doorknocking resumed in earnest on the 2nd of January 1999 and continued, despite the heat and high humidity, until the eve of election day itself. This was physically demanding— and at times exhausting, in some areas.

#4: A religious experience

One of the most challenging suburbs to doorknock was Kareela, where getting up to some of the front doors would test the skills of Sir Edmund Hillary.

While at times, it was tempting to leave my pamphlet in the letterboxes of some of these houses, I always made the effort to get to the front door and meet the residents themselves. Some residents, of course, were not home but you at least got to put your pamphlets under their front doors. Those who *were* home appreciated the effort you'd made to meet them personally.

I shall never forget trudging up what seemed like 100 steps to the front door of a Kareela home perched high on a ridge, around noon on an extremely hot day. My tie was done up and my blue shirt was showing the results of my morning's work.

Having knocked on the front door, taken off my hat, and introduced myself to the senior lady who answered, she said how hot I looked. She invited me to sit at the table on her porch and offered to me a glass of water, which I gratefully accepted. The lady then sat down with me and, after thanking me for making the effort of walking up her stairs in the heat, we had a conversation I doubt few new candidates could've anticipated.

> "I'm sure you are a very nice person, Mr Collier," she began, "but I have to tell you that I can't vote for you, or for anyone else for that matter."

> "Why is that?" I asked, half-expecting her to tell me she wasn't an Australian citizen.

> "Because I am a Christian, and the Bible says that we shouldn't judge others," she replied. "In Luke 6," she continued, "Jesus himself said: 'do not judge and you will not be judged.' But by voting, I am making judgements about each of the candidates!"

> Astonished, I said, "but didn't Jesus also say 'render to Caesar the things that are Caesar's and to God things that are God's'? The government has made voting

compulsory and so we are legally obliged to vote…to render to Caesar, if you like."[65]

With a looked of surprise that I quoted the Good Book, she said "yes, Mr Collier, He did say that. But Jesus wasn't talking about voting; He was talking about paying taxes!"

Tempted as I was to say that the Jews didn't get a vote under the Romans, I held my tongue. This was one argument I was never going to win. I told this very sincere lady that I respected her beliefs, and, having downed my glass of water, wished her well, and bid her 'good afternoon.'

Walking back down her innumerable front stairs, it occurred to me that while the lady's religious beliefs meant I wouldn't be getting her vote, Ron Phillips wouldn't be getting it either!

Biblical instruction aside, my encounter with this lady also provides a good lesson for the novice doorknocker: if potential constituents tell you they are *not* going to vote for you, just accept it and move on as quickly as possible. These voters are being honest with you, and you are just wasting your time trying to persuade them otherwise. Get to the next house, ASAP!

#5: House-proud

Doorknocking later that day in Gymea, I met an older couple, one of whom was house-proud, to say the least.

Husband and wife both came to the door to greet me as I stood on their front porch, hat in hand, in the blazing westerly sun.

---

[65] *Mark*, 12:17.

The lady of the house invited me in for a drink of water. Feeling very tired and very thirsty, I accepted her invitation, against my better judgment.

Having directed me to the lounge room, and suggesting that I sit down, the lady stood reading my Introductory Pamphlet while her husband went off to the kitchen.

As he returned with a big jug of water and three glasses, his wife said: "that's a nice picture of you, Mr Collier. Can I show you some photos of our house?"

"Of course," I replied, smiling.

With that, she disappeared to another room and quickly returned carrying two large photo albums. As the lady sat down next to me in her immaculately kept lounge room, her husband quickly glanced at me with a raised eyebrow and a look that said "sorry about this, mate."

Opening the first album, the lady pointed to the first, faded black and white photo showing several big gum trees with an understory of dense scrub.

"This is our block of land before we cleared it in 1948," she said proudly.

"And this shows the bulldozer at work," she said, pointing to a second picture.

"Here's us when they started laying the foundations… and this one shows the wooden frame going up …. and look at this one; here we are …"

I could see myself sitting there for two hours while the lady showed me the complete, step-by-step pictorial history of the construction of her home—from the time the couple purchased their block of land until the final nail was driven in.

I feared she might also have several more photo albums chronicling the extensions and the cement rendering which appeared to have been completed more recently. As tactfully as I could, I looked at the clock on the wall.

"Oh, is that the time?" I said. "I'm sorry but I do have an appointment in Miranda at three thirty. I'd really like to spend more time with you but I *must* keep that appointment."

While the lady seemed disappointed, her husband looked at me with a wry grin. It was as though he'd been through all this with other unsuspecting visitors more than once before. He almost seemed pleased that I was escaping: not just for my sake but for his own as well! I'm sure he thought that I was telling a little white lie about my appointment.

"Thank you for the water and for showing me the photographs," I said to the lady, still seated with a photograph album open on her lap.

"You truly do have a lovely home which you can be proud of, and I must say how very well you maintain it", I added sincerely, as I stood up and made for the front door.

The lady followed me out to the porch. She stood there watching me until I got into my car a little down the road and drove off towards Miranda. I waved to her as I went by. Heaven help me if I'd just gone to the next house and doorknocked her neighbour!

More lessons

While Miranda wasn't part of my plans for that day, I did, in fact, drive there and doorknock there until dark. As I drove, I reflected on the lessons I learnt doorknocking that Gymea couple.

Firstly, because I was hot and thirsty, I'd broken one of my own rules: never to go inside any home I doorknocked. Apart from costing you valuable time, there is another good reason for this. There's always the possibility, however remote, of the occupant or of a neighbour making all sorts of unfounded allegations or assumptions which could put an end to your political career.

Secondly, and while I've no doubt that the lady was genuine in showing me her photographs, you can never be certain of the political affiliations and agendas of those you doorknock. It's not uncommon for Liberal Party members, and others who support your opponent, to keep you talking at their front doors for as long as humanly possible. While you are talking to them (and wasting your time), you are not talking to others who might actually vote for you! (In that respect, some voters are not unlike several Labor preselectors I'd encountered.)

I promised myself from then on, that I'd stick to my own rules and keep my visit to any one front door as short as possible. I'd say goodbye the moment I got the slightest inkling that the resident was not genuine and was deliberately wasting my time.

4.9. A bridge, a street stall and Scully

In 1998, any motorist tackling the dangerous hairpin bends on the narrow road down to the old, rickety single lane bridge across the Woronora River could not but have noticed a number of capped, half-completed concrete pylons pointing skywards above the still waters.

While the Liberal Government had begun to build a new Woronora Bridge more than four years earlier, it had only ever contracted to build the pylons to support a two-lane structure. The project had come to an abrupt halt after the Liberals lost the 1995 election. This was not merely a matter of funding; there were also concerns that the two-lane project planned by the Liberals would not meet the future traffic needs of the Sutherland Shire.

The Woronora promise

In July 1998, the Carr Government announced that it would complete the job and deliver a new, 4-lane, state-of-the-art Bridge spanning the gorge some 36 metres above the River.

As the largest, incrementally-launched bridge in the Southern Hemisphere, the new $47 million Woronora Bridge promised to be not just a marvel of modern engineering, but an iconic piece of much-needed Shire infrastructure. Once completed, the new Bridge would eliminate traffic bottlenecks and improve road safety for all local residents.

The Liberals were, of course, claiming that the new Bridge was all *their* idea. But whatever spin they'd try to put on it, the completion of the Woronora Bridge was a major election promise by the Carr Government — and something upon which all the local Labor candidates could hang their hats.

According to one insider, our candidate for Heathcote, Ian McManus MP, had a big hand in persuading Bob Carr to fully fund the new (improved) Woronora Bridge, and to get the project moving again, prior to the 1999 State election. Here's the story.

The commitment

Any MP having lunch in the Members' Dining Room at Parliament House on a sitting day could not help but see Bob Carr head out for a short walk in the half hour or so before Question Time. Ian McManus saw Carr's regular walks as his opportunity to put the case for completing the Woronora Bridge to his Premier personally — without a bevy of Bob's advisers and staffers within earshot.

Ian is said to have laced up his running shoes and taken off across the Domain in pursuit of Carr, eventually catching and haranguing the busy Premier until he reluctantly agreed to make the completion of the Woronora Bridge an election commitment.

Carr was as good as his word and, with Carl Scully's drive, commitment and passion for infrastructure, the rest, as they say, is history. But in the meantime, we first had to win the election.

First street stall

In early January 1999, Ian McManus called suggesting we do a street stall together at Jannali Shopping Centre the following Saturday morning. He told me that, as Parliamentary Secretary, he had "exclusive access" to a scale model of the new Woronora Bridge and would bring it to show the shoppers.[66]

Street stalls are part and parcel of campaigning, providing a great way of making yourself known to voters. I believed that running a street stall with an experienced MP like McManus

---

[66] *Parliamentary Secretaries* are MPs appointed by the Premier (under the NSW Constitution Act) to assist Ministers in the performance of their duties. They are, in effect, 'Assistant Ministers'.

would be a positive learning experience for me, and I just couldn't pass up an opportunity like this.

Bridge model aside, it made good sense for McManus and I to hold a street stall together, given that our electorates shared a common boundary— namely the Illawarra Railway line at Jannali. Voters of both the Miranda and Heathcote electorates shopped in Jannali and caught the train there as well. Besides, with Como-Jannali Branch members living in each electorate, we'd have no shortage of volunteers to help us.

Turning up to the street-stall, with my Introductory Pamphlet and A-frames now bearing my newly-arrived coreflutes, I met McManus and our volunteers as arranged. While I was dressed in a sports coat and blue campaign tie, I was surprised to see Ian McManus MP dressed in jeans and an open-necked shirt. Perhaps I was overdressed for a Saturday morning, but if any shopper noted the contrast, no one mentioned it.

Ian set up the model of the new $47 million Woronora Bridge in its clear Perspex case on a table against the wall of the Westpac Bank, attracting shopper's attention almost immediately.

We were salesmen with a fantastic product to sell! I was in no doubt that the Government promise to build the Woronora Bridge was a real vote getter for both of us, from the word go!

Some early intel and some early lessons

While the response from Jannali shoppers was overwhelmingly positive, several opposed the project, saying the money could be better spent elsewhere.

One lady, however, saw the new Bridge as a dangerous attraction for those in crisis or suffering depression, saying that "once built, the Woronora Bridge would become the focal point for suicide in the Shire!" Tempting as it was to dismiss her claim as alarmist, I was not so sure, particularly after she pointed out that suicide was a very real problem in the Shire and illustrated this with a recent example. While the Bridge project would go ahead, I was sensitive to her concerns, and told her I'd do what I could to help address the problem locally if I was elected.

While the Woronora Bridge was the main topic of conversation at Jannali that morning, it wasn't the only issue on the minds of shoppers. The major issue was *overdevelopment*, followed by the Sutherland Hospital, education and talk of privatising the State's electricity supplies. Valuable intelligence!

It occurred to me that, in many respects, running a street stall is not all that different from doorknocking — but with helpers. You introduce yourself, shake hands, offer your pamphlet and quickly discuss issues of concern raised with you. You invariably get the usual questions about the election date, voting and polling places, etc. And, like the lady concerned about suicides from the Woronora Bridge, you can expect the unexpected.

As with doorknocking, you'll meet some people at street stalls who are rude, if not abusive, and who hate the Labor Party, if not all politicians. You soon learn not to engage in arguing on the street with those who have an axe to grind and to quickly (but politely) terminate your conversations with these people as well as with others who are clearly just wasting your time.

For those with serious concerns and those genuinely wanting to engage in a lengthy discussion over some issue or policy, you need to have one of your helpers nearby with a clipboard ready to take down their concerns and contact details.

And, while it didn't happen during my first street stall with McManus, there was always the possibility that the Liberal candidate will turn up at the same location with a tribe of workers, some of whom will try to goad you and your volunteers into an argument over some issue. Such public bickering is to be avoided like the plague! It wastes your time and costs you votes!

Come noon, it was time to pack up and thank our volunteers. My A-frames went into my old Mitsubishi Magna, and Ian stashed the Bridge model safely into the boot of his Statesman. During our post-mortem over a coffee, we agreed that our first street stall was successful in raising Ian's local profile as well as my own.

While I really could not claim any credit for the construction of the Woronora Bridge, I had no hesitation in listing it later as one of my 'priorities' on my campaign pamphlets. If elected to Parliament, I was committed to 'Ensuring the Woronora Bridge is completed on time' [See 4 − 6].

Meeting Carl Scully

Several weeks later, Ian McManus invited me to a 'photo opportunity' with the Roads and Transport Minister, Carl Scully, and the Bridge model in a park on the western bank of the Woronora River, near the old, rickety structure. I'd never met Scully and, of course, was delighted with the invitation.

McManus also told me that the Labor candidate for Menai, Alison Megarrity (whom I'd also never met) would also be present. That didn't surprise me. The redistribution had seen to it that the Woronora River formed the new boundary between the electorates of Menai (to the west) and Heathcote (to the east). Once completed, the new Bridge would join the two.

The electorate boundaries of Miranda, however, were nowhere near the Woronora River. And so, while I'd already been promoting the project in my campaign literature, I was surprised to have been invited at all. Having said as much to Ian, he replied that the Labor candidates — Megarrity, McManus and Collier — must "must hunt together as a wolf pack", promoting the Carr Government across the Shire.[67] That made good sense to me.

Another doubting Thomas

McManus was standing by himself in the Woronora carpark when I pulled up. After a quick chat about Scully's coming visit, I wandered down to the River bank by myself to have a close-up look at the old, existing bridge. Alison Megarrity pulled up a short time later and, seeing her, I returned to the carpark, to meet her and await the Minister's arrival.

I liked Carl Scully the moment I met him. Affable and sharp as a tack, here was a Minister who'd clearly done his homework and really knew his stuff. Unpretentious, yet impressive and politically savvy, Scully made it quite clear that he was totally committed to securing a second term for Labor. In contrast to my first meeting with Bob Carr, Scully seemed genuinely interested in me and my candidacy for Miranda.

Moreover, the Minister was obviously well-versed in the needs of local candidates, spending considerable time ensuring we each got the "right photograph" for our campaign pamphlets, both individually and as a group. I was happy to be included in the photograph with Carl Scully, Alison Megarrity and Ian McManus

---

[67] I believe that Ian's terminology derived from his time as a *Wolf Cub* in the Helensburgh Scouts !

and the model of the new Bridge [4—7]. A capped, fledging pylon left by the Libs can be seen in the background.

4 – 7: With Scully, Megarrity, McManus and the Bridge model

Meeting Carl Scully for the first time was one of the highlights of my campaign. But, as is so often the case with political events, there's a postscript further down the track.

Years later, Alison Megarrity recalled our first meeting with Scully and the model down alongside the Woronora River. On arriving in the carpark and meeting McManus, she saw a bloke in the distance near the River bank (namely, me).

"Who's that over there?" asked Alison, pointing to the man down by the River.

"That's the bloody fool who thinks he can win Miranda!" Ian McManus replied.

4.10. Belief, arrogance and tall poppies

I didn't *think* I could win Miranda; I *knew* I could win Miranda. Self-belief, as I would learn, is just as powerful a weapon in the armoury of a politician as it is for anyone else prepared to work hard to achieve their goals.

Power of the mind

I've always loved books and find it difficult to walk past any bookstore without going in for a browse. After a Saturday street stall of my own, I wandered into a second-hand bookshop and came across a slim, well-thumbed volume entitled *Mind Power*.[68]

In his foreword, the author said the purpose of the book was to 'share with you a number of important techniques…in creating new realities and making your goals happen'…by 'harnessing the forces of the universe and actively participating in the creative process.'

A sceptic of so-called 'self-help books', I said to myself, "yeah, right!" as I flicked through the pages of the dusty publication. But as I closed the book, I noticed an inscription inside the front cover:

> *"Dearest Michael: I know you don't believe it. But…Try it. It works…Miki. January 22, 1993."*

Fascinated and captivated by the endorsement, I bought the book and read it from cover to cover in what little spare time I had. I was particularly taken with a Chapter entitled *Visualisation*. Here, the author argued that if you really wanted to achieve a particular

---

[68] John Kehoe, *Mind Power*, Griffin 1991 (Australian edition).

goal, you had to visualise that goal in your mind at least once a day, every day, and make it 'real' by seeing it as actually happening. A good time to do this, the author said, was just before going off to sleep. 'Why not try it?' I thought.

Each night, just before dozing off, I'd imagine a giant ballot box with my name on it. I visualised votes falling into that box, seeing myself counting them off one by one and feeling elated at being told I was the new MP for Miranda. In my mind, and as the book suggested, I'd already won the election! It wasn't just a hope I'd win; it was the *belief* that I'd actually won!

I did this every night up to and including the 26th of March 1999, the eve of election day. It couldn't hurt. In any event, the proof would be in the pudding!

A secret best kept to yourself

Even if you believe, in your heart of hearts, you really will win, you must keep it to yourself and your family. If you don't, you may well regret it.

It's not uncommon, particularly as the campaign heats up, to come across an antagonistic voter or some rusted-on member of the other Party who confronts you with: "you don't really think you're gunna win, do ya?"

Answer "yes" and you'll be called "an idiot," "a smart-arse" or even "an arrogant bastard!" Answer "of course" and you may be told "that's bullshit," "you're up yourself" or "you're kiddin' yourself mate!" Such are the milder responses, expletives deleted.

If you respond with a "yes" to that same question by a Party member who thinks you have Buckley's of winning, the rumour may soon spread through the local Branches that you're suffering from candidate's disease!

Perhaps it's a hangover from our convict past, but Australians simply love the underdog and have an aversion to 'tall poppies'. Telling even the most-polite and genuinely interested resident that you believe you'll win the election is a sure-fire way of losing the swinging voter.

When confronted by a voter with the question, "do you think you'll win?" I'd say "I'm the underdog" or "I know it's going to be tough," even though I personally believed I'd be the next MP for Miranda. If voters actually told me they believed I would win, my response was "it could be very close." That was my way of saying "I still need your vote!"

Some voters believe you have absolutely no chance of winning and will take any opportunity to tell you so, to the point of calling you "a loser" to your face. You won't change their mind. Don't argue. Just take it on the chin and move on!

News polling

These days, of course, polling is a common source of media commentary and speculation. So, what do you say to the journalist who asks you to comment on a highly favourable news poll, when you really believe you are going to win?

The best response is the old adage: "the only poll that counts is the one on election day." You might add "whatever the polls say, I think the result could be very close!"

Even if the opinion polls place you miles out in front, the reality is that you can't tell anyone (except your family) that you believe you are going to win. The moment you confirm any opinion poll predicting you will win is the moment you lose that humble underdog status and all the advantages that go with it. These include the image Australians love: that of a real fighter who's out there working hard and who is willing to have a go.

I wasn't aware of any polling being done by the Labor Party in Miranda during my campaign. Indeed, the thought never even occurred to me, probably because I was so convinced Sussex Street didn't think I had any hope of winning. But even if I had known that polling was being done in the seat, I wouldn't have asked to see the results. As I said, self-belief is a powerful thing.

4.11. Doorknocking stories #6 and 7

My 'criss-crossing' doorknocking strategy meant that I'd return to each suburb (and even more houses in the same street) again and again throughout the campaign. It proved to be a good way to pick up on new issues of concern to the residents.

#6: All politics is local ... really!

Early in the New Year, I returned to doorknocking in Kareela, not far from my own home. A very senior lady raised a very local, very specific issue with me: the absence of a Council sign on the Highway showing the direction to our own suburb itself!

Many people, including her own visitors at Christmas, she said, get lost trying to find Kareela simply because there was no mention of it on any sign on any of our major roads in the Shire. She was dead right! While I'd lived in the suburb for more than 25 years, it had never really occurred to me.

I told the lady I'd raise the problem with Labor Councillor Dawn Emerson, which I duly did. Lo and behold, a small, blue

Council directional sign with the word 'Kareela' appeared on a telegraph pole at the intersection of Bates Drive and the Princes Highway two weeks before election day.[69]

My first successful representation on behalf of a potential constituent, this episode also delivered two very valuable lessons. Firstly, while you might get elected at a State level, from time to time you will also have to go into bat for constituents on issues which involve the Federal Government and the local Council. By and large, your constituents don't give a damn who fixes their problem, so long as it's fixed!

Foolish is the candidate for State Parliament who tells voters they can't do anything about their problem because it is the responsibility of some other level of government. After all, one of the major roles of any representative is to make representations!

Secondly, this matter brought home the fundamental truth of the saying that 'all politics is local'! The lady whose Christmas visitors got lost didn't give a hoot about some new State-wide Labor policy being bandied about by Bob Carr. There were no votes in that for her. All she wanted was a directional sign to her suburb on a nearby telegraph pole: a local problem, a local solution, and a local fix for her, her family and her visitors!

I ran into that lady who wanted the sign just before election day at Kareela shops . She was grateful for my efforts, saying her visitors won't get lost anymore! "I've told all my friends about you getting the sign for us. Thank you for listening," she said.

---

[69] I'd later discover that the provision of signs on Highways was a State responsibility.

#7: 'A Local who Listens'

It was clear from the start that I had to characterise myself as a candidate, who, if elected, would not take his constituents for granted. As their new MP, I'd take their concerns seriously and put them first, ahead of all other political interests. I had to demonstrate that I truly would be 'A Local who Listens.'

Whatever voters may have thought of my slogan generally, it was only ever called into question once during the entire campaign. Even that was a positive learning experience.

I'd just finished doorknocking in a narrow, rather secluded street along the Georges River in Green Point. Walking back towards my car past the row of houses I'd visited, I heard a loud voice from behind me: "Mr Collier!" I turned to see an elderly man leaning over his front gate waving my pamphlet and my "Sorry I missed you" note.

"Have you got a minute?" he asked.

"Of course," I said, walking back towards his gate.

"It says here you're 'A Local who Listens!' pointing to my pamphlet. "Are you *really*?"

"That's right; I am," I replied confidently.

With a look reminiscent of the barrister who has just gotten the answer he wanted from the witness and is about to embark on a devastating cross-examination, the man said:

"But that means you'll only just *listen* and you won't do anything: just like the rest of them! What are you going to do for us?"

"For a start, I won't just be listening, that's for sure!" I replied. "If I'm elected, I'll be doing all those things I've promised down at the bottom of my pamphlet you've got there; things like stopping overdevelopment and building the Woronora Bridge on time," I replied.

"What if you lose? What if you don't get elected?" came the next question.

"Well, if you re-elect the Liberals, you can bet your boots that none of those things will get done! But if you elect me, I won't be sitting back taking things for granted. I'll be listening to the people's concerns and working hard for the Shire community!" I replied, looking the man squarely in the eye.

"Okay, but what are you going to do for *me*? he asked.

"What would you like me to do for *you*?" I asked, very politely.

The old man suddenly got that 'far-away look' in his eye, and, to my amazement quietly said, "I don't know."

"Well, if I get across the line first at the end of March, how about you come and see me and tell me what I can do to help you or your family?" I said gently.

"Okay, I will" he said. Looking pleased he'd had his say, he turned and trotted off into his house with my pamphlet still in his hand.

Questions and genuine listening

As a first-time candidate, you soon learn that, however prepared you are, some voter will ask you that question from left field.

But there are those other questions which, while unexpected when you began campaigning and are not always asked, tend to become somewhat predictable, if not 'standard'. The question: "what are you going to do for *me*?" falls into this category.

As you begin to identify these 'standard questions', you begin to develop 'standard answers' to each of them. True, it's generally inappropriate to respond to a question with a question. Yet, the answer I almost always received from other voters when I responded in the same way to the same question as that asked of me by the man at Green Point was: "I don't know."

Nevertheless, my chat with that elderly man sends a very clear message to every candidate: even if voters don't know what they want you to do for them personally, you must convince them you are genuine when you say you will listen to them!

You can't convince anyone that you are genuine if you are continually using clichés like "I'll take your concerns on board" but then do nothing. You must *show* voters you are genuinely listening, by doing what you can to address their individual concerns. The Kareela lady needing the sign is just one example.

Individual voters to one side, you also need to show voters you are listening to the concerns of the community you share with them. That means formulating, publicising and promoting your commitments to the electorate as a whole: your 'package of promises', which identifies your community's aspirations and seeks to address your community's major concerns.

You also show you're listening to your community by getting out and about: doorknocking, visiting railway stations, holding street stalls, talking to shopkeepers and meeting local groups including school P&Cs and local sports clubs. These days, of course, you can phone them, email them and run Facebook pages. But there is no substitute for face-to-face contact and being seen out and about publicly! (It's that word-of-mouth factor again.)

Community surveys

While it is trite to say that you won't get to talk to every single voter personally, you need to let the community know you are there and are willing to assist them and their families if needs be.

In an effort to drive home the idea that I truly was 'A Local who Listens,' I also wrote and letterboxed a host of Community Surveys — one for each individual suburb in the electorate.

My 'Sylvania Community Survey,' for example, was headed *What's important to you?* Residents were asked to rank their top five issues (from a list of 12) in order of importance and to provide me with their responses in 'the strictest confidence'. The Survey also asked respondents to note 'any other issues' important to them.

The survey wasn't my original idea, but was a fruitful way of identifying some very pressing local issues, as well as a means of making contact with individual voters and their families. I provided what assistance I could to those who, in addition to numbering the boxes, also noted their own personal concerns.

I wasn't deluged with responses to my Community Surveys. But that didn't bother me. Even if residents only read the heading on the Survey before dropping it into their garbage bin, they might get the idea that I was seriously interested in addressing their concerns. At the very least, my survey helped promote something all first-time candidates need: name recognition!

4.12. Australia Day 1999

For an unknown political aspirant wanting to gain some sort of public profile, it makes good sense to turn up wherever large crowds gather in the electorate—be it a major sporting event, football match, surf carnival, local festival, or a school fete.

You'll invariably run into two or three people you know and perhaps be introduced to their friends and family accompanying them. Others will remember you from doorknocking or recognise you from newspapers or from your campaign literature and introduce themselves. Some will ask you about particular issues; some might even seek your help. The local Liberals will invariably spot you, and report your presence to your opponent.

The big community event is also your big opportunity to be seen out and about, getting involved in your community, talking to people and introducing yourself as the candidate each time the opportunity presents itself. Those who see you or chat with you will invariably tell others they did so, and that can only help establish your connection with the community as a whole. At the risk of repeating myself, it's that word-of-mouth factor again.

Kareela Fair

January 26th, 1999 presented me with a great opportunity. Sutherland Shire Council had sponsored a large Australia Day Fair at Kareela Oval—complete with rides, entertainment, jumping castles, food stalls and evening fireworks. The proceeds of the event would be donated to The Rotary Club of Sutherland.

Off I went by myself to the Fair on that very hot public holiday afternoon, looking rather casual in long pants, short sleeve shirt (no tie) and straw hat. I also wore a badge Bob Rogers had procured from somewhere with my photo and the words "Vote 1: Barry Collier, Labor for Miranda." Apart from a few business cards, I only took my clipboard-folder and notepaper.

I didn't take any of my pamphlets along. On a day when families and friends are out together, relaxing and having fun, the last thing they want is some would-be politician bailing them up. Indeed, you are more likely to *lose* potential votes if you go around annoying people by trying to put your pamphlets in their hands at big community events like those on Australia Day!

Inspector Baz

I spent around three hours at the Fair, wandering around amid the rides, stalls, displays and the entertainment with my clipboard under my arm. I met people I knew and told them I was standing for Miranda. Some people saw my badge and stopped me for a chat, about everything from where I lived and what I did for a crust to the political issues worrying them: most notably, overdevelopment and electricity privatisation.

Several people asked me for assistance. I noted their problem and their contact details, then gave each of them my card, with the promise I'd do what I could to help them.

Every now and then, and as the crowd waxed and waned, I wandered around the perimeter of the Fair, occasionally making notes of what people had said to me. But from time to time, I noticed two men wearing Rotary Club shirts, standing together, seemingly watching me from a respectable distance. One of the men wore a blue and white striped apron, similar to that worn by butchers in the 1950s and 60's.

I couldn't understand why Rotary Club officials would be overly interested in my activities. But, given I was told that Rotary Clubs were among the last great bastions of Liberal supporters, I couldn't help thinking that they knew who I was and their motives for watching me were more political than anything else. I was wrong on both counts.

Just before leaving the Fair, I was standing a short distance from the sausage sizzle making some notes when I looked up to see the two Rotary men approaching me, looking rather serious.

As I closed my folder, the man in the butcher's apron came up to me and asked, politely, "can I ask who you are and what you are doing?"

"I'm Barry Collier. I'm the Labor candidate for Miranda at the State Election in March," I replied.

"Thank God for that," said the other Rotary man. "We thought you were the food inspector!"

Astonished as I was by that response, my first thought was one of relief: not because I thought I'd done something wrong, but because I had resisted an earlier urge to buy a sausage sandwich from this outfit!

While I didn't dare ask any question bearing upon the "food inspector," I was surprised at the image they'd formed of me as some important public official, something I'd never intended to portray at all.

But here was a classic reminder for any politician, of the importance of perception when combined with the force of circumstance— not to mention the power of the pen when combined with the clipboard!

As it turned out, I had a pleasant conversation with the two men about their local Rotary Club and the volunteer work they were doing in the Shire. They even suggested I should join up after the election! We also talked about me and my background, with one of the men noting they were yet to see their local MP, Ron Phillips, at the Fair. That was positive news for me.

But the really good news was for the Shire community. In the week which followed, there were no newspaper reports of food poisoning at the 1999 Kareela Australia Day Fair!

4.13. Keeping a promise

Promises are part and parcel of the politician's stock-in-trade, and of course, it's always important to keep them, whether you're the sitting MP or a first-time candidate.

I'm not just talking about election promises. My comment extends to every promise you make, publicly or privately, to voters right down the line. That includes promises to take their concerns to the relevant Minister as well as promises to attend their meetings and events.

I'd made one such promise to the three impressive members of the Southern Sydney Woodturner's Guild I'd met at Sutherland Hospital during my very first outing as the candidate back in December 1998.

And so, on a Saturday morning in early February 1999, I turned up at the scheduled meeting of the Guild in Oyster Bay and was astonished to find more than 100 enthusiastic members gathered inside and outside the building they affectionately called 'The Cubby House'.

Having re-introduced myself to the three officials I'd met at the hospital— Messrs. Bourne, Cairns and Ponder— I naturally asked "why the name?" They explained that the building was once an old disused Scout Hall in such a state of disrepair that it had been earmarked for demolition by the Shire Council. Needing a home, the Woodturners instead persuaded the Council to let them restore the building and use it for their activities. The Woodturners' wives said their husbands were "like excited little boys building their own cubby house," and the name stuck!

I told the three that I could only stay for half an hour. But I ended up staying for three hours — fascinated by the work on show, captivated by the infectious camaraderie between the members, and absorbed in the woodturning demonstrations taking place both inside and outside The Cubby House itself.

I shall never forget standing outside watching Bert Ponder using an ancient, foot-powered lathe to turn a piece of discarded wood into a magnificent bowl. I stood on the edge of a group of about 30 members, watching this extraordinary display of skill and listening intently to his explanation of how it was done before the invention of electric lathes. Towards the end of his talk, Mr Ponder looked up and, cigarette hanging from the corner of his mouth, telling the group, with a nod in my direction, "see that bloke over there? He's Barry Collier. He's a barrister... but he's all right!"

Wow! A personal endorsement from one of the most skilful, and most respected, local Guild members! Bert Ponder was not only a leader and an opinion-maker, but a founding member of the

Cubby House. He'd not only organised the hall's restoration; he'd acted as foreman on the job!

I have no doubt that getting the nod from Bert Ponder got me more than a few extra votes during my visit to the Cubby House that morning. In politics, as I said, it pays to keep your promises!

5. HARD SLOG

5.1. *The Beverly Hillbillies*

Running a shoestring campaign requires a little imagination as well as a little initiative. Among other things, you have to come up with new, cost-effective ways of getting your name out there. And after all, advertising certainly does not come cheap.

Helping other candidates earlier, I'd noticed some MPs and well-heeled candidates driving around in cars and vans professionally painted with their names, contact details and even their slogans. Some even paid workers to tow billboards mounted on box trailers back and forth across the electorate for weeks on end. These were luxuries we simply couldn't afford.

As a kid, I'd seen cars being driven about with signs on top, advertising everything from new shops and school fetes to bargain sales and circuses. Some also had occupants spruiking their wares and making announcements through loud-hailers as they drove through shopping centres. The penny dropped.

If we could only find a way of mounting my coreflutes on its roof, my 12-year-old Mitsubishi Magna sedan could be *my* campaign car! True, it wouldn't look particularly flash, but it would help advertise my candidacy as I drove it around.

Charlie's advertising agency

My neighbour, Charlie Low, was a good tradesman who always seemed to be welding bits of steel together and making all sorts of things for his customers in his home workshop.

I sought Charlie's help, telling him what I had in mind. He looked closely at my car's roof racks, made a couple of measurements and asked me for two coreflutes. He said he'd see what he could do and get back to me as soon as he could.

Several days later, Charlie turned up at my front door with a metal base-frame supporting a large wooden board with a coreflute screwed to each of its sides. Having bolted the contraption to my roof racks with Charlie's help, I stood back and admired his work. From the front of the old Magna, the structure looked something like a shark fin in the centre of the car's roof. Side-on, my coreflutes could be clearly seen by passing motorists or anyone standing on the footpath as I drove by.

The wooden board with the coreflutes was a little wobbly, and so, for extra support, we attached four ropes from the top of it to the roof racks [5−1]. I now had my own campaign car; one which looked not unlike something out of *The Beverly Hillbillies!*[70]

My 17-year old son, Michael, was anxious to get his licence, and that meant attaining a certain number of hours behind the wheel beside a licence-holder. From time to time, I'd let him drive me around in our campaign car to and from meetings and campaign events with his 'L-plates' on, while I gave him driving lessons.

---

[70] A US sit-com of the late 1960s & early 1970s which followed the adventures of the *Clampetts* — a poor farming family who moved from the mountains to the posh Beverly Hills after they'd struck oil on their land and became millionaires overnight.

5 – 1: With son Michael and our campaign car in Miranda

Eye-catching

My campaign car attracted considerable attention from the beginning. I well recall stopping at traffic lights in Miranda the first day I drove it around.

One pedestrian waiting to cross the Kingsway pointed at me, said something to his mate and gave me the thumbs up! Another, crossing from the other side of the road, called out "Good on ya, Bazza!" as he passed the driver's side door. Later still, a group of high school kids standing at a bus stop broke out in fits of laughter after one kid yelled out "Go Baz!"

But my campaign car wasn't designed just for driving around, hoping to be noticed as I passed by. Oh no! This was an advertising tool I could use every day and in a variety of ways.

Before going doorknocking in some suburban backstreet, I'd park my campaign car in the most visible spot I could find on the nearest main road. I'd leave it there to catch the eye of passing motorists for the two to three hours I'd be away at front doors.

Then there were always the busy shopping centre car parks. I'd park my campaign car where it could be clearly seen by motorists looking for a parking spot and by those returning to their cars with supermarket trolleys. Even those who'd forgotten where they'd parked couldn't help but notice the 'Barry Collier for Miranda' coreflutes above the roofs of other parked cars as they went searching for their own.

Not happy, Baz!

My campaign car soon became something of a talking point, attracting comments and more than a few good-natured laughs, whenever I drove it and wherever I parked it. But not everyone was happy seeing it out and about.

Whilst I was out doorknocking in Yowie Bay one afternoon, word reached me that the owner of the General Store was most upset that my campaign car had been parked for several hours in one of the many parking bays outside his popular shop.

The owner complained to a campaign worker that having my car displaying the Labor coreflutes outside his shop was "bad for business" and wanted my car moved somewhere else! Perhaps the owner assumed that most of his customers in Yowie Bay were Liberal voters. He may have also assumed (incorrectly) that the Liberal Party is the only one which cares about small business.

Whatever the shopkeeper's reasons, I believed that I had every right to park my vehicle where I did. I also believed there were residents in Yowie Bay who actually voted Labor — as well as some Liberals who might actually change their minds and vote for me. Undeterred, my campaign car remained where it was and I continued doorknocking in Yowie Bay until dark!

Can't be too careful ... or too cautious

It is an absolute certainty that in every political campaign a number of your coreflutes will simply disappear from the face of the earth, usually in the middle of the night. That is so, whether your coreflutes are attached to an A-frame, a garden stake in your front yard or even high up on a telegraph pole just under the electrical wires. It's also not uncommon for coreflutes (A-frames, stakes and all) to 'disappear' forever in broad daylight.

Knowing this, I was always concerned that the whole structure on top of my campaign car would be unbolted and removed by some overzealous Liberal campaign worker. At the very least, I half-expected the coreflutes on top of my car would be vandalised.[71]

While it was pleasing to return to my campaign car after several hours of doorknocking and find it untouched, there was always a thought that the damage would be done to it at night. And so, as I returned home each evening, I drove the car across my front lawn and into the shadow of a tree. For 'extra security' I covered the car with an old grey army blanket, making it even harder to see.

Overcautious, perhaps, but I was surprised that, unlike my coreflutes elsewhere, my precious campaign car remained untouched throughout the entire campaign. Maybe the car was left

---

[71] My Campaign Director's home and car had both been the subject of malicious damage and vandalism by unidentified persons during several previous election campaigns.

alone because my opponents thought it was laughable, and perhaps just another reason not to take me seriously!

5.2. Doorknocking stories #8 and 9

As the local postie can attest, going from house to house can be a risky business. Doorknocking is no different. As I would learn, every candidate always needs to be on the lookout for any potential risks to their personal safety as they walk through the front gate to the voter's front door.[72]

#8: Oscar

Take my visit to a house in Oyster Bay on a very hot February afternoon. The front door was propped open and the outer fly-wire door was slightly ajar. I knocked, took off my straw hat, held it in front of me and stood back on the edge of the verandah waiting for the resident to come to the door.

Almost immediately, I heard a bark from the unlit hallway inside. The fly-wire door burst open. A large dog flew out and jumped up at me. Instinctively, I put out my hand holding my hat. The dog chomped through its brim and held on, shaking its head from side to side trying to get it from me, and making the holes in the hat bigger and bigger as it did so.

From somewhere deep inside the house, a male voice yelled "Oscar!" The dog let my hat go and scurried back inside, leaving the fly-wire door jammed open against the front wall.

---

[72] Going around the house to the back yard when the front door bell remains unanswered is something to be generally avoided.

A man came to the door saying, "I'm very sorry about that. I'm really embarrassed. This sort of thing really should not happen. Please accept my sincerest apologies."

What could I say? I accepted his apology, gave him my pamphlet and asked for his vote. I'll never know whether the man voted for me or not, but I hope he felt a tinge of guilt if he didn't! And after all, there was no notice anywhere telling visitors to 'beware of the dog', and it was only my straw hat that stood between me and personal injury!

But wait! There's more ...

Undeterred, I went to the house next-door. Having knocked, I stood waiting on the porch holding my battered hat in front of me, complete with the large holes made by the dog.

A woman opened the door. Having introduced myself, she looked down at my hat and said, "Oh, I see you've met *Oscar*! He doesn't like blokes!"

A lesson well learnt about dogs and doorknocking! All too often, they don't mix. For the candidate out doorknocking, any warning of a dangerous dog on the premises means only one thing: forget it! Leave your pamphlet in the letter box!

But there's another lesson in this. The next-door neighbour knew all about *Oscar*. Had I gone to her house first, I believe she would have warned me about the dog. Next-door neighbours can be a valuable source of information, if only about each other.

#9: *The trumpet*

Doorknocking in another suburb, a resident was very interested in my occupation as a barrister. As I was about to leave, he asked me what I wanted to do in Parliament.

"I want to represent my community," I said. "If there are any problems I can assist you with, please let me know."

"Look, I really have only one problem," he replied, seriously.

"What's that?" I asked, expecting him to raise some legal issue.

"It's the bloke next door. He's always playing his trumpet and it's driving me mad! Can you just do something to stop him playing? Can you at least have a word with him?" he pleaded.

"Well, OK, if I can," I said with some hesitation.

I then doorknocked his next-door neighbour. Having introduced myself and given the resident my pamphlet, I offered to assist him, if I could, with any problems he might have.

"I suppose you've been next door," he said.

"Yes," I replied.

"Did he complain about me playing my trumpet?"

I said, "Yes."

"I don't own a bloody trumpet!" the man replied with a look of exasperation.

While I was tempted to advise him to ask his neighbour to go to a Community Justice Centre with him for mediation, I didn't do so. I hadn't raised the "trumpet issue" and he hadn't asked for my advice or assistance with it. And, rather than criticise his neighbour personally, he just seemed resigned to the fact that his neighbour was mistaken and would continue to complain about the noise from a trumpet that didn't exist anyway!

I'll never know whether these two neighbours ever resolved the trumpet issue. But I learnt a valuable lesson: don't take sides in personal disputes between next-door neighbours! You can't win. You never will. You'll only make a rod for your own back!

5.3. The Campaign Office

At a time before everyone had a mobile phone, before emails were common place, and *Facebook* was unheard of, having a *Campaign Office* was a must. There was no such thing as an 'interactive website' or a 'virtual office' somewhere in cyberspace. The candidate simply had to have an ongoing physical presence somewhere in the electorate for the six weeks before polling day.

Your Campaign Office was the place your volunteer workers met; where pamphlets were photocopied and folded for distribution; where letters were printed and faxed, and where telephone calls were made and messages taken.

The Campaign Office was also our major point of contact with the voting public. They could call in, pick up a pamphlet about some issue they were interested in, express their concerns, complain about anything (including the Party, my opponent and me), and get advice about postal voting, pre-poll voting and getting on the electoral roll.

In short, the Office served as the administrative focus for our Miranda campaign. It was essential that it be open to the public during business hours and staffed by volunteers at all times.

Location! Location!

Essential too, in my mind, was that our Campaign Office had to be in a highly visible location, with a street frontage, accessible to seniors and those with disabilities, located close to public transport—and, given our problem with finance, rent as cheap as possible! But where?

One supporter suggested that I set up my Campaign Office in the Gymea shopping strip. He told me there was a vacant shop available on a short lease and the rent was as cheap as chips! I politely rejected his suggestion, saying "but it's not Miranda!"

Taken aback by my sharp response, that supporter was at pains to remind me that previous Labor candidates for Miranda had had their campaign offices up in Gymea "and it was good enough for them!" While it was on the tip of my tongue to remind him that none of those Labor candidates with Campaign Offices up in Gymea had won Miranda since 1981, I simply said that "if I'm standing for Miranda, I want my Campaign Office to be *in* Miranda, and preferably on the Kingsway!"

My reasoning was simple. As a rule, locals equate the candidate for Miranda and the seat of Miranda with the *suburb* of Miranda. The greatest concentration of shoppers in the Shire was to be found at Miranda Fair (now Westfield Miranda), and the major arterial road through Miranda (the Kingsway) carried traffic volumes second only to those of the Princes Highway.

Miranda itself is also a major public transport hub for Shire buses and trains, and is easily accessible from all parts of the electorate for those without private cars, including seniors. It made good sense to locate my Campaign Office in Miranda and I insisted upon it. As the estate agents say, *it's location, location!*

Campaign Office, Mark I

As it turned out, my Campaign Director, Bob Rogers, found three vacant shops, side-by-side, in the Miranda shopping strip, each with a street frontage on the Kingsway, and only 30 metres or so from its major intersection with Kiora Road. The three were just a stone's throw from Miranda Fair, bus stops, pedestrian crossings, the Post Office and the very busy Miranda Station.

Each of the shops came complete with rear laneway access and a fenced, lockable private parking area, now overgrown with weeds and shrubs after a long vacancy and years of neglect.

Ironically, each of the shops was awaiting demolition ahead of the construction of Council-approved high-rise flats on the amalgamated site. The owner of the derelict shops was happy to give us a short-term lease with very cheap rent on the shop of our choice, on the condition we'd clean up before we moved out after election day. Just what the doctor ordered!

Cup of tea, anyone?

Having looked briefly at each of the vacant shops, Bob and I chose the old pizza store in middle of the three for our Campaign Office. Run down and full of dust, this had two advantages over the others: a big counter for voters' enquiries and pamphlets plus plenty of room to display our coreflutes — ideal, we thought.

After signing a two-month's lease and arranging the electricity connection, Bob collected the keys from the agent and we were set to go. As soon as we gave the old shop a thorough clean-up and vacuum, we'd have our Miranda Campaign Office up and running in no time at all. Exciting stuff!

My wife Jeanette and supporter Bert Rhodes volunteered to do the job while I was out doorknocking. They met Bob at the front door of our soon-to-be Campaign Office at 9.00AM on Day One, armed with vacuums, brooms and a multitude of cleaning products. Jeanette took along a cake, cups and everything else needed to celebrate the occasion at morning tea time.

While Jeanette and Bert got on with the cleaning, Bob headed out the backdoor and through the overgrown carpark to unlock the rear gates. He didn't make it. Bob had stumbled onto a wasp's nest, and, badly bitten for his trouble, ran quickly back inside.

While he was off seeking medical attention, Jeanette and Bert got on with the big clean-up which, by all reports, was going well. Come 11.00AM, they decided to take a break from the vacuuming and make a cup of tea. But there was no water!

Bert initially thought the water supply must have been disconnected when the old pizza shop closed down. Not so! The landlord called in a plumber who quickly discovered the problem: someone had broken in and actually stolen all the copper water pipes, presumably to sell for scrap! The transformation of the old pizza shop into our Campaign Office came to a very abrupt end before midday on Day One!

Campaign Office, Mark II

The keys to the old pizza shop were quickly returned to a very embarrassed estate agent. There followed a hurriedly arranged inspection of the long-vacant men's wear shop next door. Upon entering, the first thing we did was turn on all the taps!

Water flowing and power on, *Campaign Office Mark II* had all the features of Mark I, except for the service counter and the wasp colony. Somewhat unusually, however, this shop had two levels: a street level at the front and a lower level at the rear, accessed by a set of stairs covered with frayed carpet. A dodgy lock on the back door posed a potential security problem. No matter, we'd fix that somehow. This shop would just have to do!

We took no time in signing a new lease at 581 the Kingsway (at the same cheap rent), and, with the cleaning completed on Day two (courtesy of Jeanette and Bert), it was all systems go!

'Ramshackle' but working

Under Bob Rogers' management, the long dormant menswear shop literally burst into life like a desert after rain. Suddenly, the old place was filled with the kind of energy, enthusiasm and camaraderie among local Branch members that flows from great confidence in our Campaign Director and a belief that, with hard work, maybe—just maybe—we might win Miranda this time.

While Branch member and carpenter Maurie Bevan was doing a very basic 'fit-out' for the cost of materials alone, office equipment and consumables began arriving. The desks and chairs, a phone and fax machine, a computer and printer, trestle tables, a tea urn and paper—all of which were either donated or begged and borrowed from Branch members, supporters and friends. A black and white photocopier was a must, and this had to be leased (as cheaply as possible, of course).

Though practical, our Labor Campaign Office was, as you might have expected, far from palatial. While one journalist would later describe it as "ramshackle", Mark II served its basic purpose and was operational, even as our fitout was going on.[73]

With my coreflutes in the large front window as our only advertising, and the front door chocked open, long-time Branch Member and retired teacher Pat Foy began taking phone calls and dealing with enquiries from the public off the street: both of which she'd do exceptionally well throughout the campaign.

But of course, there were many other jobs of all kinds to do — both inside the office and outside in the electorate and, thankfully, our rosters were very quickly filled by eager and committed volunteers.

Local Labor stalwarts Thelma Deacon, Anne and Dan Long and Carole Ashworth worked in the Office every day. *Tradies'* President Graham Hill was a regular helper, while Bert Rhodes was always there working and driving around as our 'go-fer' when needed. Jeanette was a daily visitor doing clerical work and folding (something she also did each night at home).

There were always comings and goings, with committed Branch members, like Jim Foy, collecting pamphlets before heading out, maps in hand, to letterboxes in designated streets. Volunteers were picking up coreflutes to nail onto power poles or deliver to supporters for their front yards. Activity was everywhere. Something was always happening in the Campaign

---

[73] Tim Jamieson, *The Sydney Morning Herald,* 29 March 1999.

Office. Enthusiasm among the volunteers never waned. As the Rolling Stones might have sung during a visit to our Campaign Office "the joint was a 'rockin'."[74]

My visits

Compared to those of our volunteers, however, my visits to the Campaign Office were few and far between, and relatively short. The reason was simple: there were no votes to be gained there!

If you are serious about winning, you have to get out there pressing the flesh at front doors and in the streets at every opportunity. You can't just sit around the Campaign Office all day—as I'd seen some Labor candidates do throughout their (typically unsuccessful) campaigns.

I did call into the Campaign Office for brief visits every couple of days, to pick up pamphlets, meet with Bob and have both a welcome cup of tea and a chat with our volunteers.

It's important to realise that your volunteers are not merely receptionists, clerks, letter boxers or pamphlet folders. They are also the eyes and ears of your campaign out there on the ground and their work, often under difficult conditions, is absolutely vital if you are to get across the line first.

Nobody likes to feel used or taken for granted, including your volunteers. They need to feel that their views and their work count, that they are an important part of the campaign team and that you genuinely appreciate the enormous effort they are putting in, for the Party and for you personally! Take the time to listen to

---

[74] From the Rolling Stones' hit song, *Around and Around* (1964).

your volunteer workers and thank them, personally and, if the opportunity arises, publicly, for their hard work.

I know of one ALP candidate who behaved like a one-man band, taking all the credit for himself and failing to acknowledge the contribution of his volunteers. The same candidate was at a loss to understand why he had difficulty getting volunteers to help him when he stood for Office next time around!

Sharing is caring

Our Labor candidate for the adjoining seat of *Cronulla*, Scott Docherty, had a tough road ahead.

The ALP had not held the seat since the defeat of Michael Egan MP in 1984.[75] But facing a Liberal margin of 10.2% and a popular, long-serving Liberal MP in Malcolm Kerr, the prospects of a Labor victory in Cronulla were much slimmer than those in Miranda. Nevertheless, Scott Docherty had the courage to put up his hand and to mount a serious challenge. For that, he needed a campaign office.

While Labor candidates each run their own races, we do try to support each other as far as possible. And so, shortly after we opened the doors, Bob and I decided to let Scott and his volunteers use the rear, lower level of our Campaign Office as their own. After all, we had enough room in the front of the building at street level for what we needed.

So the old menswear shop at 581 the Kingsway became a dual Office for both the Miranda and the Cronulla campaigns —

---

[75]   Michael Egan served as MP for Cronulla from 1978 to 1984. He later went on to join the Upper House and become the longest serving Treasurer in NSW history.

and sharing the premises worked reasonably well so far as publicising our Labor brand went.

The Campaign Office Official Opening

Despite the fact that it had been up and running for three weeks, our Campaign Office had to have an 'Official Opening'.

Such events are part of the Labor tradition to which the Branch members and supporters always look forward. An Official Campaign Office Opening was one of those rare occasions we could meet and hear from some of our Party elite. It was also a great opportunity to get all the volunteers together as our campaign went into overdrive, a month out from polling day.

We were fortunate to have the Treasurer, Michael Egan MLC, open our (tidy) Campaign Office on 27 February. While I'd never previously met Michael, I had the honour of introducing him to the gathering.

Michael was a great choice. Raised in the Shire, Egan well knew just how tough it was for Labor to gain a foothold in any of the local seats. Egan spoke to a packed Campaign Office with the authority of someone who'd 'been there, done that'. Like everyone else in attendance, I found him both impressive and inspirational. With Michael's encouragement, we got more names on our street stall and our polling booth rosters, as well as several more letter boxers!

Under Bob Rogers' direction the Campaign Office opening was a great success. In fact, and though not salubrious, it had scrubbed up pretty well for the event. Certainly, no first-time visitor had any trouble finding our Office in busy Miranda—

thanks to something special for which neither Bob Rogers nor I could take any credit.

5.4.   A sign from above

I was fortunate to have the support of so many committed Branch members during the campaign. John McLean was one of them.

A member of the Miranda Branch, "Big John" (as we called him) was totally devoted to the Labor cause, even taking annual leave from his job to work full-time on our campaign!

No task was too much for Big John. He worked all day, every day, doing anything and everything he was asked to do by Bob Rogers or me— from his flying pickets and handing out with me at railway stations and street stalls, to letterboxing and pre-polling. But in addition to his physical strength and endurance, I'd also learn that Big John had a rather astute political mind.

Soon after we opened the Campaign Office, I dropped in to pick up some extra pamphlets. As I was putting them in my car, Big John asked if we could have a quick chat.

> "Mr Barry," he said, "I think we should put a big sign up on the roof, telling people to vote for you." (John often called me *Mr Barry*.)

> "Great idea, John," I replied, "I wish we could. But we don't have any money to pay some bloke to make up a sign and put it up there."

> "We don't have to pay anyone for it. I'll do the sign and put it up there myself!" he said confidently.

> "That's too dangerous," I said, trying to dissuade him.

"No it's not. It's OK! I've been up there already!" John said. "Just come over the road," he continued, "and I'll show you what I want to do. Please, Mr Barry!"

How could I say 'no' to that? I accompanied Big John across the Kingsway and along the footpath to a spot just outside *Carmen's*.[76] There he stopped and pointed back to the Campaign Office. "Have a look at what's on the roof!" he said to me.

There, on top of the old shop awning was a large, double-sided metal frame supported by steel wires. Obviously designed to hold advertising hoarding, the frame was angled in such a way that it could be clearly seen by motorists travelling in either direction along the busy Kingsway. The menswear shop owner must've removed his advertising but left the metal frame behind when he vacated the premises! John continued his pitch:

"The estate agent left two big white chipboards at my flats after the auction last Saturday, and we can use the back of them," John said. "All we have to do is paint the words we want on the boards and bolt them onto the frame. There's no problem getting up there. I just need money for some black paint," he explained.

"Okay," I reluctantly agreed, you can do it. But I've only got $20 on me!"

"That'll do. Thanks Mister Barry," John said.

"For God's sake, John, just be careful!" I said, emptying my wallet.

---

76 The rather imaginative name of the nightclub adjoining the Miranda Hotel. *Carmen Miranda*; get it? (The 1940s 'Brazilian Bombshell' who wore a hat festooned with fruit.)

"I will," he responded confidently. "What do you want me to write on the sign?"

"What about *Barry Collier for Miranda*?" I said as we walked back to my car and I left for more doorknocking.

Driving along the Kingsway through Miranda late the following afternoon, I couldn't help but notice — nor could anyone else help but notice — the large, hand painted sign on top of my Campaign Office awning! *Barry Collier for Miranda* it proclaimed in large black letters on a white background! [5 — 2].

To this day, I don't know how John McLean and 76-year old Bob White got those two signs up onto the creaking old awning of our Campaign Office. Nor do I want to know now, given my concerns about the risks they may have taken in doing so.

What I do know is that Big John's hand-painted sign captured the imagination of the voting public! The "amateurish sign," as one journalist called it, was one of the big talking points of the entire Miranda campaign.[77]

---

[77] Murray Trembath, *St George and Sutherland Shire Leader*, 30 March 1999.

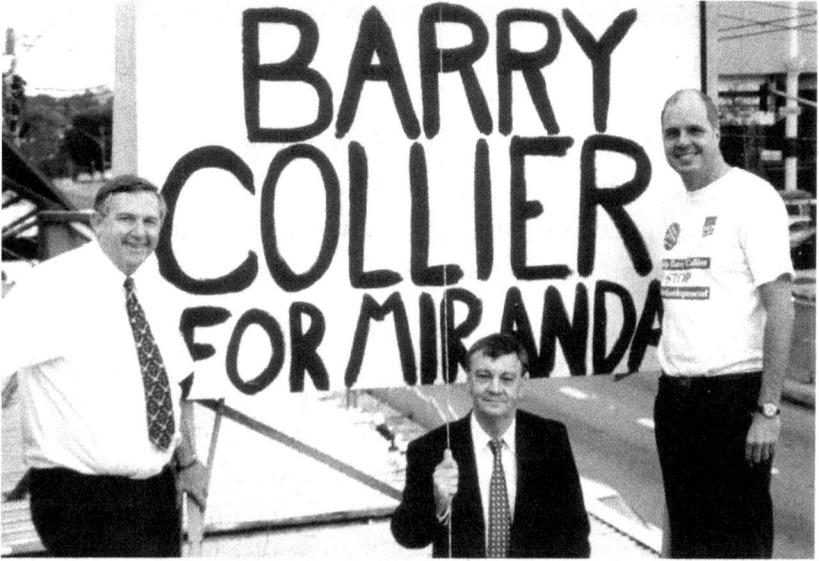

5 – 2: Up on the roof, with Bob Rogers, Big John and his sign

Campaign brilliance

The more I saw the rooftop sign, the more I liked it; and the more I thought about it, the more I recognised what a brilliant idea John McLean had come up with. People simply loved it!

In its own way, the hand-painted sign on our Campaign Office awing went hand in hand with our *Beverly Hillbillies*-like campaign car. John's sign not only helped underscore the fact that we were running a genuine grassroots campaign; it also confirmed our 'underdog status' in the eyes of many Miranda voters. John's sign was simply invaluable!

John McLean had seen and taken advantage of an opportunity which was not available at Office Mark I— namely, frames we could use for advertising on Miranda's main drag. Indeed, John's hand-painted sign was so effective that I later came to the conclusion that the thief who stole the copper pipes from the old pizza shop actually did us a favour!

I'd never even noticed the metal frames on top of the Campaign Office awning, let alone come up with the idea of using them to advertise my candidacy. And herein lies a good lesson for every candidate: listen to your campaign workers! Never underestimate their resourcefulness or their political nous, and take their suggestions seriously. However experienced or good you think you are at campaigning, you don't know it all!

5.5. Doorknocking story #10

Comments made by residents at their front doors can often give you a good idea as to how the respective Party Leaders themselves are travelling at the State level. Nothing demonstrates this better than the experience I had doorknocking in a backstreet of Miranda one Saturday afternoon.

As I walked through the rusty old wire gate and up the front steps to the flyscreen door, I could hear the loud, distinctive sound of a horse race on a radio inside. Now, there's nothing punters dislike more than being interrupted when they're listening to a race, especially when they've got a bet on one of the horses!

Having waited until the race was over and the TAB dividends announced, I pressed the doorbell. The radio was turned down and an old fellow appeared at the flywire door dressed in shorts and a sweat-stained, Bonds singlet. I quickly introduced myself and gave him my pamphlet. Knowing there'd be another race soon, I gave him a shortened version of my spiel, handed him my pamphlet and said "I won't keep you. Good luck with the gee-gees!" The old man looked pleased with that and went back inside.

I stood there making a quick note, and as I turned to walk back down the path, I overheard the following conversation through the flyscreen door:

"Who was that, love?" came a woman's loud voice.

"Oh, just some Labor bloke called Barry going for the election," the man replied.

"Good! That's who we're voting for," she said emphatically, adding "I can't stand that Chikarovski woman! There's something about her I just don't like!"

I admit being taken aback by her comments. It seemed that the lady of the house was voting for me based on nothing more than her dislike of the Opposition Leader— for some reason she couldn't put her finger on!

Even so, here were two clear lessons for every candidate. Firstly, with some voters, you can forget about policies, promises and Parties altogether. There are those who will vote for you (or not vote for you) depending solely upon whether they like you (or they don't). Call it human nature!

Secondly, that doorknocking experience at Miranda also taught me to never underestimate the power of the lady of the house. While I generally found women to be more polite at the front door and tend to ask fewer questions than their spouses, they often seemed to determine how the whole family voted!

Carr & Chikarovski: A note

As I continued doorknocking, I got the impression that, for reasons unknown, older women just did not warm to Kerry Chikarovski. And, while I believed that this was a generational thing more than anything else, some even went so far as to tell me "there's no place in politics for a woman with a family!"

But regardless of the unfavourable comments I encountered about Kerry from time to time, I never personally criticised her throughout my entire campaign. As it turns out, I wasn't alone.

Surprisingly, Bob Carr hardly ever mentioned Kerry Chikarovski by name throughout the entire 1999 State campaign. His Deputy, Andrew Refshauge, even referred to Kerry as "the woman whose name you dare not speak."[78]

The reason for all this only became clear after the election was long over. Labor research at the time showed that voters generally wanted Kerry Chikarovski to be given 'a fair go' — and that any personal criticism of the female Opposition Leader by Carr would not sit well with the electorate.

Carr's very rare mention of Kerry Chikarovski's name was also part of a broader Labor campaign strategy to deprive the new Opposition Leader of publicity, wherever possible. Not only were repeated requests by the Liberals for a TV debate between the Party Leaders refused by Sussex Street, the Labor Party held its televised Election Campaign Launch on the very same afternoon as the Liberals held theirs.

By giving Kerry Chikarovski as little 'oxygen' as possible, Labor effectively reduced her opportunities to build the strong public profile she needed to win.

---

[78] Andrew West & Rachel Morris, *Bob Carr: A Self-made Man*, Harper Collins, 2003.

Avoiding personal criticism

It really came as no surprise that, from time to time, those I doorknocked told me what they really thought of Bob Carr and Kerry Chikarovski, personally.

For the most part, these comments were negative and at times derogatory. The moment a voter uttered any such gratuitous comment about either Party Leader, I quickly changed the subject and talked about local issues. It wasn't my role to engage in what was, essentially, a kind of character assassination.

While it's often very tempting to criticise your opponent personally, beware! Doing so can be a boomerang that comes back to bite you! Voters don't like hearing you criticise your opponent's appearance or their family, their marital status, their culture, race, religion or their sexual orientation. They'll form their own opinions about the other candidates' character and background, and they really don't need to hear it from you.

So far as your opposition is concerned, the best advice for any candidate is to 'play the ball and not the man'! If you do otherwise, you may be left standing red-faced at the front door. It can also cost you votes, especially when your negative personal comments are passed on to others and even reported in the local newspaper.

I well remember having a discussion with our candidate for Heathcote, Ian McManus, about the Liberals' failure to adequately fund Sutherland Hospital when they were last in Government. Ian told me he'd make the point but wasn't going to attack his Liberal opponent, Lorna Stone MP, personally over it.

A wise move! Prior to entering Parliament after a by-election only 15 months before, Lorna had spent many years as a leading volunteer fundraiser for our much-loved Sutherland Shire Hospital, and was very well respected throughout the community. Any personal attack by McManus on her would have backfired badly. "Besides," Ian said, "Lorna's a grandmother: and people don't like you criticising grandmothers!"

5.6. A pressure group

Pressure groups are part and parcel of the political landscape. Known also as 'community action groups' and 'resident action groups,' pressure groups seek to achieve their objectives by lobbying politicians and political aspirants at all levels.

Some pressure groups are well-organised, always lobbying anyone and everyone who might help them achieve their aims. They usually ramp up their activity as the election nears.

Other pressure groups only come into existence when an election is imminent. Their leaders typically seek a firm commitment from each candidate to the group's cause and often threaten to direct their members' votes elsewhere if the candidate does not come on board.

Buderim Avenue—Box Road Community Group

Timing aside, pressure groups make their appearance for all sorts of reasons. Some are formed by residents out of what they regarded the negative impact of some existing or proposed project on themselves or on their community.

But some pressure groups come into being as a last resort after having done everything they possibly could, through official channels, to have someone in authority listen to their genuine concerns. The Kareela-based, Buderim Avenue-Box Road

Community Group fell into this category. I didn't know this group existed until a phone call out of the blue in February 1999.

Buderim Avenue resident, Gary Kedward, introduced himself as Group's Chairperson. A deep sense of frustration was evident in Mr Kedward's voice as he outlined what he said was the abject failure of Sutherland Shire Council to take any interest in the issues confronting his members.

I asked to meet him and two other affected residents – Marj Conley and Meg Andrews – the next day at the Bates Drive bridge over Oyster Creek. As a defence lawyer, I'd always found it valuable to familiarise myself with the scene of the (alleged) crime by visiting it with my client (if possible) and this was really no different.

Arriving at the Creek an hour before the appointed meeting time for a look-see myself, I walked along the western bank. As one who taught senior high school Geography classes about rivers and streams, it was more than obvious that Oyster Creek presented a potential flooding problem for nearby residents — a problem which appeared to be due primarily to years of neglect by the local Shire Council, as Mr Kedward had said.

A genuine problem

The Creek had long drained residential areas of Kareela and Kirrawee as well as parts of Jannali, Sutherland, and the nearby industrial area, into Oyster Bay. But by 1998, Oyster Creek was so overgrown and weed-infested that the naturally wide waterway had been confined to a narrow, rubbish-filled channel, utterly incapable of containing the kind of deluge which had caused extensive local flooding in 1975.

In the event of a similar torrential downpour, any flooding would be made even worse by the enormous volume of sand and silt which had accumulated at the upstream side of the very poorly-designed Council road bridge. Even the most casual observer could see that Oyster Creek was in desperate need of clearing, dredging and widening!

But, as Mr Kedward and the two Community Group Members who'd met me at the bridge explained, there was far more to it than that. As we later walked along the Creek's eastern bank together, the trio presented me with the history of their problem — something all serious pressure groups are wont to do.

Genuine frustration

In March 1998, the Sutherland Council decided to mark the land title deeds held by 22 residents living along and near Oyster Creek with the notation: "Affected by Flooding." The Council did so without any warning and without any consultation with affected land owners. Residents were, understandably, outraged.

The Council-imposed notation had devalued their properties overnight, dramatically increased their insurance premiums and made it more difficult for them to secure mortgages at reasonable rates! To rub salt into the wound, the Council had said absolutely nothing about the flooding potential in the 35 years since it first approved houses to be built along the Creek back in 1963.

The Council had also done nothing to address the potential flooding problem in the 23 years following the 1975 flood which had affected nine of the 22 houses! And, despite having the responsibility for doing so, Sutherland Shire Council had never bothered to develop a 'Plan of Management' for Oyster Creek.

Council's proposed solution to the flooding potential? Build a 1.6-metre-high levee wall along the Creek behind the houses and pump out water which came over the top of the levee when the Creek flooded! That was it! No plans to clean up or dredge the Creek. Even the crazy levee wall idea depended on the Council getting funding from somewhere other than its own coffers!

I was told that despite repeated requests, Council staff and their elected Councillors had refused to meet with affected residents. They'd also declined to discuss the residents' proposal to replace Council's notation on their title deeds with one which, on their own legal advice, more accurately reflected the risk involved: namely, that of a *one in a 100-year flood*.

These residents were not ratbags with some impossible axe to grind. They were intelligent, reasonable people who had quietly done everything possible though official avenues to get Council to come to the table. They felt completely frustrated by the apparent intransigence of Council staff and their own elected Councillors. Despite their best efforts, they'd gotten nowhere!

The public meeting

The affected residents said they'd simply had enough and "just had to go public." They had to raise their issue with candidates from both major Parties at the forthcoming State election with a view to getting a commitment from them to take up their cause — and in the hope of finally getting something done.

Ron Phillips and I turned up, by invitation, to a public meeting of the Community Group near the Creek on the corner of Buderim Avenue and Box Road, Kareela on a Saturday morning in early February. Despite invitations, none of their elected Shire Councillors turned up to meet the 40 residents who did!

Mr Kedward began by outlining residents' concerns and emphasising the lack of action by Council over the years. Ron and I were then invited to speak (sitting MP first, of course).

Mr Phillips was at pains to point out that, at the end of the day, the issues concerning Oyster Creek were strictly matters for Council. He said that after the election, he'd be "looking into it" and get his senior Council colleague, Liberal Mayor Kevin Schrieber, to address the residents' concerns. It was quite apparent that their local MP, Mr Phillips, had had no contact with the Group beyond their invitation. From what I was told, he'd certainly never met the affected residents down by the Creek.

I took a very different approach, opening my address to the gathering by mentioning my on-site meeting with Mr Kedward, Mrs Conley and Mrs Andrews and the observations I made as we walked together along the banks of the Creek. I empathised with the residents' plight, saying I was appalled at the lack of action by their elected Councillors. I promised that, if elected on March 27th, I'd be taking their concerns directly to the Minister for Lands and seeking State Government funding to develop a Plan of Management for the Creek, whichever Party won.

I came away from that meeting believing I'd scored more 'brownie points' with the residents than Mr Phillips. That had nothing to do with my oratory. It was because I had already established a connection with the Community Group and I'd presented its members with a proposal which at least gave them some hope. The gathering seemed particularly pleased that, if elected, I was prepared to override the Council and to take their concerns directly to the State Government.

On the other hand, Mr Phillips had effectively passed the buck to the Mayor of a Council which the residents and ratepayers clearly felt wasn't interested in the problem facing them and which had done nothing about it for years. Ron's solution of going back to Council was a 'nothing solution'. Their local MP may as well have told affected residents that he wasn't going to do anything about their problem at all!

Some lessons and observations

I've spent some time discussing my encounter with the Buderim Avenue-Box Road Community Group because it really taught me a thing or two about the motivations and attitudes of voters in general: things worth passing on to first time political aspirants.

Firstly, voters don't care whether their particular problem was created via the activities (or neglect) of the local, State or Federal Government; they just want it fixed and they don't care who fixes it![79] If helping a local group solve their problem means going over the local Mayor's head or taking on the local Federal MP in the media, then just do it! Whatever the outcome, you'll at least get the credit for doing so and earn a reputation for standing up for your constituents and for your community.

Secondly, and it's almost a fact of political life in New South Wales these days, that everybody hates the local Council. Nobody I met throughout the 1999 State campaign had a good word to say about Sutherland Shire Council. And it wasn't just about the major election issue of overdevelopment. Everywhere I went — whether it was doorknocking or at a street stall — I'd invariably come across somebody who'd had a 'bad experience' with the Council or had a long-standing, unresolved problem with the Council or told me

---

[79] Voters who email or write to State MPs often *cc* their correspondence to the Mayor, *all* their local Councillors and their Federal MPs. Some also include the Premier, the Minister and the Prime Minister!

they had raised an issue with their Ward Councillors who "did nothing to help them." These voters just wanted me to go into bat for them and I was happy to do so.

Thirdly, there'll always be some conflict between the State Government and the local Council. When a genuine conflict arises, don't hesitate to take on the Council if your own attempts to deal with the bureaucrats on the residents' behalf also fail. This may well put you at loggerheads with Councillors belonging to your own Party. But when it comes to fixing their problems, most residents don't give a toss about Party affiliations.

Fourthly, if you are going to turn up and address a public meeting, then at least do your homework. You want people who attend the meeting to come away believing you really understand their problem and will do something sensible to solve it for them. Roll up cold, without doing any homework and they may leave thinking you are a blithering idiot or just another politician who does nothing but mouth platitudes (or both).

Get to know the problem up front by finding out all you can about the issue and from all sides. Check out any media reports on their issue and ask the organisers for any documents they have which support their case.

Meet the group's organisers beforehand and, if the issue involves a particular physical location, visit it well ahead of the public meeting, preferably with the organisers. You'll not only get a better introduction and a better reception from the crowd, you'll at least look like you know what you are talking about and have some credibility when you put up some possible solutions.

Finally, let me sound a word of caution. It's very easy to get caught up in a pressure group's campaign and go all out for them.

But always remember, that once you take up the pressure group's cause, you are also putting your own credibility and your own reputation on the line — both in the community and in the media.

As the candidate, you may need to do some fact checking. Indeed, despite a pressure group telling you that the local MP has "done nothing" or "doesn't care," it may well be that he or she has worked on their issue for some time and has made some progress. In short, you, as a candidate, must also satisfy *yourself* independently that the pressure group's cause is genuine and that their goals are not completely unrealistic or unachievable. If you don't, then you run the risk of just becoming a mouthpiece for the group and making a complete fool of yourself!

Catching up with Ron

That public meeting of the Community Group in February 1999 was the first time I'd laid eyes my local MP, Ron Phillips, during the campaign. I'd come across Mr Phillips in the flesh only once more in the electorate during the campaign.

You may well think, as I did at the time, how extraordinary it was that I would come face to face with my opponent only twice throughout the entire election campaign for Miranda. But part of the explanation, of course, is that as the Deputy Liberal Leader, Ron Phillips MP had the added role of supporting his new Leader and working hard to get her and his Party into Government again. Naturally, that meant he'd have a host of commitments across the State, taking him away from his own seat, and lending credence to the picture we'd been painting of him as "the absent Member for Miranda."

5.7. Railway stations

Handing out pamphlets to morning commuters at railway stations is, of course, a standard campaign technique for any serious political aspirant.

The *ideal* is that you, the candidate, with the help of your volunteers, hand out your pamphlet to every weekday morning commuter you can — starting with the trickle arriving at the station just before the sparrows wake and ending as the morning peak concludes — without your opponent making an appearance at all!

In politics, 'the ideal' is not something you can ever bank on. As the campaign really heats up, there's always the chance that you and your opponent will both turn up at the same station around the same time on the same morning, with the result that commuters have pamphlets thrust at them by both sides!

Being there

Handing out at railway stations is obviously most effective when the candidate is present. That's just common sense! I made it a rule to always be there on the spot handing out my pamphlets at the station entrance with volunteers, starting around 5.00AM.

Constituents really appreciate the fact that you are there in the flesh. Being there signals that you are more than just a face on a coreflute or in a brochure. It means you are a real person who cares enough to get up, get out and meet them. That, of course, is vitally important for an unknown, first-time candidate (like me).

There may, of course be times, when your opponent doesn't turn up at the station and you have the commuters all to yourself. There may also be times when you turn up with your volunteers and your opponent sends his campaign workers but doesn't bother to put an appearance himself. On those occasions, I had several commuters take my pamphlet and, with a raised eyebrow and a nod in the direction of the Liberal campaign workers, ask me cynically, "so where's your opposition?"

Planning

Like every other campaigning strategy, handing out at railway stations is a learning experience, and should always be regarded as such every time you do it. Like every other campaign activity, too, railway visits require planning!

That means working out a campaign schedule of different stations and knowing the train timetable for each; it means identifying all the entrances to each station and working out how many volunteers and A-frames you'll need. It also means having a good idea of the commuter patronage at each station so you have enough helpers and you don't run out of pamphlets!

It pays to be at the station when the first commuters begin to arrive. Those who start work very early are often pleased to see you, because they often feel forgotten by candidates who only turn up just before the morning peak. As a rule, it's a good policy to pack the car with your A-frames and folded pamphlets the night before, set the alarm for 4.30AM and keep an eye on the weather just in case you have to call the planned station visit off.

This advice may seem simple and straightforward. But you'd be surprised how many candidates fail to pay attention to the basics, and then have the nerve to blame others unfairly for what they regard as a less than successful morning at the station.

My first station ... my first lesson

But even with the best laid plans, campaign activities at railway stations can fall well short of expectations, all for want of a little more thought. My very first morning handing out my pamphlets to morning commuters was a case in point.

In 1999, Jannali Railway Station straddled the boundary between the Miranda and Heathcote electorates, and voters living in both caught the trains there each morning. The second largest station in the Shire in terms of passenger numbers, Jannali then had only one street entrance to its city-bound platform (on the Heathcote side of the divide).

After our successful street stall together, Ian McManus suggested that we hand out at Jannali Railway Station together one morning. It seemed like a good idea at the time. After all, as a novice, I believed I could learn much about this form of campaigning from the vastly more experienced MP.[80]

As it turned out, the whole exercise was not only frustrating for both of us; it was also completely confusing for many commuters. Apart from two different coreflutes and two different pamphlets, there were two different candidates for two different electorates with two different sets of volunteers all crowded around one station entrance. The changed electorate boundaries following the redistribution had only made matters worse!

There was no way that Ian and I could know the electorate in which any individual commuter resided, and so, as each of them approached the narrow ramp down to the station platform, we

---

[80]   Ian McManus MP had won four difficult State elections straight— in two cases after his seat had been abolished via redistributions and in another after the resignation of Labor Minister Rex Jackson following a corruption scandal.

found ourselves asking "do you live in Miranda or in Heathcote?" Some knew, most didn't, and one said flatly, "what are you talking about? I live in Jannali!"

But there was no time to explain, particularly when the early trickle of commuters turned into a flood as the morning peak progressed and as departure times grew near. It got to the point where you gave a commuter your pamphlet and simply hoped you got their electorate right. Commuters rushing for a train to work were in no mood to be stopped and asked to identify the electorate in which they lived.

Interestingly, some Liberal campaign workers rolled up at Jannali around 7.00AM to set up and left very soon afterwards. I shall never know whether it was the fact that both Ian McManus and I had taken all the desirable spots or whether they saw what appeared to be organised chaos at the Station entrance (or both). If they were smart enough to go to another station, they'd have all the commuters there to themselves!

The morning's joint venture over, Ian and I decided to have our campaign managers coordinate our future visits to Jannali, so that only one of us turned up on any given morning. Next time I handed out at Jannali, I set up a large map of the electorate boundaries at the Station entrance. Lesson well and truly learnt!

Some rules and first impressions

For most first-time candidates, the greatest challenge is getting yourself known. One the quickest ways of doing that is by personally handing out your pamphlet to morning commuters at railways stations across the electorate. Like doorknocking, there are some simple rules to follow: rules as to how you look, what you say and what you do.

At the outset, it's worth remembering that handing out at railway stations provides many voters with the opportunity to make their own personal assessment of you for the very first time. For some, it may be the only time they'll meet you during the campaign—and for them, it's that brief meeting they'll talk about and remember on their way to the ballot box.

In politics, as in life, first impressions count, and you need to make a good one. For a start, you need to be well dressed and well groomed. While that sounds a bit old fashioned, it's worth remembering that commuters are going off to work looking fresh and appropriately dressed, and they expect the same of you. After all, you are there at the station presenting yourself to them as the person who wants to represent *them* in State Parliament.

I dressed as if I was going to an interview for the top job which, in my mind, I really was. I always wore a suit and tie, matching the photo on my coreflutes that we'd set up on the approaches to the station entrance and along nearby roads.

It's important, too, that the campaign workers assisting you at the stations are also neatly dressed and well presented. True, you have to remember they *are* volunteers. But it's better to have no one assisting you at all than having someone handing out for you looking like something the cat dragged in—simply because it reflects badly on you and your Party.

But being well-dressed and well-groomed is only part of the story. What do you say to the commuters? The simple answer is that you introduce yourself as you normally would, and to as many commuters as you can, beginning with "good morning", shake their hands, and tell them you are seeking their support as you hand each of them your pamphlet.

While the vast majority of commuters will shake your hand, some will not. You really can't read anything into that so far as an individual's voting intentions are concerned. But never underestimate the importance of offering your hand at the railway station to both men and women. It's not only the generally accepted way of showing you are friendly and approachable; it's also your way of saying you are genuinely interested in them. And make no mistake about it, voters will remember they met you at the station and you shook their hand.

All this sounds so simple and seems like so much common sense. But I've seen too many candidates just stand there, handing out their own brochures to commuters without introducing themselves and not asking voters for their support, let alone putting out a friendly hand.

A Como experience

Don't think for one moment that voters don't talk about the man or woman running for Parliament whom they met at the station on their way to work. It may be only a passing comment to their family, their friends or a fellow commuter, but you can bet your boots the comment is based on their perception of you – and that basically comes down to how you present yourself.

The importance of presentation was brought home to me very clearly one morning towards the end of our campaign. As I was just about to leave Como Railway Station around 9.00AM, a very well-dressed, senior lady came up to me with a rather serious look on her face.

"Mr Collier," she said politely, "I'm a member of the Liberal Party!"

"Pleased to meet you," I said, putting out my hand, anticipating criticism of the Carr Labor Government.

She shook my hand and said, "I've told my Branch members to watch out for you!"

"Oh, why is that?" I asked sincerely, but very surprised.

"Because you present yourself well. You dress well, you're obviously well-educated, you're polite and you speak well. I've told them to take you seriously!"

"Thank you for your very kind comments," was all I could think to say as her train pulled in and we said our goodbyes.

In politics, there can be no higher endorsement that a genuine one from the other side, and I have no doubt that the lady at Como was sincere in her comments. More to the point, it seemed that my general appearance and presentation were such that alarm bells were starting to ring for the Liberals in Miranda — down at the grass roots, at least!

Some don'ts

Not every commuter will be pleased to see you at their railway station. There are those who will ignore you, those who won't respond even to your 'good-morning,' those who tell you bluntly they vote Liberal and those who demand to know "what are you going to do for me?"

Some commuters will flatly refuse to take your pamphlet. If that's the case, never try to force it on them. They genuinely may not be interested; they might have work to do on the train or have worries on their mind; they could simply be dyed-in-the-wool

Libs. Occasionally, you'll come across someone who takes your pamphlet, then immediately drops into a garbage bin in front of you.

If commuters tell you they're voting Liberal, or, when you attempt to hand them your pamphlet, loudly say "no way" in the hope of getting a shocked reaction from you, stay calm. Simply tell them: "That's fine. We live in a democracy and it's your right to vote for whom you choose!"

While one or two will yell at you or even swear at you, don't engage them. Simply say "there's no need to be rude" and leave it at that. More than one passing commuter will agree with you and think the better of you for actually saying so. Those who work in customer service jobs will empathise with you; others may just think "poor bugger, having to put up with that crap!" and vote for you anyway.

The list of possible commuter responses is endless, and there will be times when all you can do is play it by ear and roll with the punches.

But during every railway station visit, there'll be two or three individuals who'll bail you up, wanting more of your precious time than you can give them in the circumstances. Some are sincere in wanting to express their views; some genuinely want to know your stance on a particular issue; some have a long-standing personal problem; and some are Liberal zealots wanting to waste your time and prevent you talking to other commuters.

There are several ways to handle these individuals: give them your business card and tell them to contact you; ask them to give their details to one of your campaign workers standing nearby with a clip-board and notepad at the ready; ask them to stand to one side and talk to them in the inevitable breaks in commuter traffic between trains; and so on.

But whatever you do, don't argue with them and don't stop greeting other commuters and handing out your pamphlets! The sincere and the genuine will be prepared to take your card or give your worker their details; the zealots will get the message; and the arrival of the next train will save you from those who are determined just to make a nuisance of themselves.

As obvious as it seems, morning commuters come to the railway station with one goal in mind: to get to work on time. You need to respect this.

If commuters are running along the Council footpath towards the station entrance as their train is about to pull in, the last thing they need is some would-be politician stepping in front of them. Get out of their way, hold your pamphlet well out in front of you with a smile, and give them the opportunity to snatch it as they pass. Many will do so! But rest assured, they won't vote for you if you are the cause of them missing their train to work!

If it's pouring with rain, don't turn up at all. Phone your volunteers and call the station visit off. The last thing that half-drenched commuters want on a wet, miserable day is to be confronted by candidates thrusting soggy pamphlets into their hands as they enter the station precincts struggling with umbrellas. Besides, your hard-working volunteers might appreciate the sleep-in!

Two practical points

Firstly, get to know the Station Managers personally. Meet each of them early in your campaign. Let them know you'll be handing out at their Station and ask them what they expect of you and your volunteers. They'll probably tell you not to obstruct access to the Station and that handing out election material on the station platform is not permitted for safety reasons.

Have the courtesy to let the Station Manager know you are there to hand out as soon as you arrive each time and when you are leaving. You may be surprised at the (unsolicited) feedback you'll get from the Manager. You might even pick up some useful information about your opponent's appearance at the same station the day before!

Secondly, don't leave a mess for the station staff to clean up! Once the morning's handing out is done, station staff face the problem of disposing of platform garbage bins, which can be full of the candidates' pamphlets.

It's often a worthwhile exercise after the event to go onto the platform, check out the garbage bins with your volunteers and even remove some of your pamphlets discarded by commuters. While this helps reduce the station staff's workload, it's also very good PR!

Checking out the bin also provides a very good indication as to just how well you've been received by the commuters that morning. The fewer the number of your pamphlets in the bin, the more successful your morning's station visit has been!

I religiously 'did the bins' with a volunteer after each station visit. While some days were better than others, we were generally pleased with what we saw — and the Station Manager was pleased with our commitment to recycling!

Persistence pays

As effective as handing out your pamphlets to commuters can be, you can't just visit any given station as a 'one-off'. Getting the full benefit out of this campaign method — translating your visits into votes, if you like— means turning up to each railway station at least three times on three different weekdays with three different brochures.

That's exactly what Bob Rogers and I decided to do at each of the five railway stations servicing the commuters of the electorate: Como, Jannali, Kirrawee, Gymea and Miranda itself. And there is no doubt that persistence pays.

Shortly before election day, I turned up at Kirrawee Railway Station for the third time during the campaign. Standing at the top of the stairs, handing out my pamphlets, one commuter came up to me and we shook hands.

"No need to give me your pamphlet today," he said.

"OK. But it's a *new* one," I replied.

"Save it, I'm voting for you anyway. I've seen you here of a morning three times now, and I haven't seen hide nor hair of Mr Phillips !" he said, as he headed off down the old station steps.

In the mind of that Kirrawee commuter, I'd made the effort to get out and meet him three times, early in the morning on his way to work. By contrast, his sitting MP was, in effect, 'a no show'.

5.8. Electricity privatisation: A case study

When it came to local issues in 1999 campaign for Miranda, there is no doubt that *overdevelopment* was by far the standout. At the same time, there was another major issue resonating with voters, not just in Miranda, but right across NSW: privatisation of the State-owned electricity industry.

Such was the importance of the debate surrounding electricity privatisation that it would feature heavily in NSW politics for the better part of the next two decades. With that in mind, we need to spend some time analysing this election issue, taking a case study approach. Let's begin with the background to this ongoing controversy from both sides of the political fence.

The background: Labor problems

In October 1997, the Annual State Labor Conference flatly rejected a proposal by Premier Bob Carr to privatise electricity in New South Wales. The Union movement saw to that, with Carr and Treasurer Michael Egan coming away from Sydney's Town Hall with their tails between their legs. With the State Parliamentary Caucus having expressed its outrage at Carr's proposal earlier in May, and some Labor MPs threatening to cross the floor, the Government's privatisation plans were quickly dropped.[81]

Carr's resounding defeat on the floor of Annual Conference was not merely a sign of disunity within the Party. According to the Liberals, the defeat was clear evidence that the Carr Labor Government was controlled by the Unions. Understandably, the

---

[81] 'Crossing the floor' means voting with the Opposition (whose Members sit on the other side of the House). This is a cardinal sin for any Labor MP, carrying with it the threat of expulsion from the Party.

Liberals strenuously argued that Union opposition to privatisation was preventing the estimated $25 billion to be gained from the sale of the State's electricity assets from being spent on hospitals, schools, roads and other much-needed infrastructure, not to mention paying off the State debt.[82]

The Liberals saw electricity privatisation as an election winner for them. They believed that the voters of NSW would have every reason to question the credibility of the Labor Leader, Bob Carr, who, after all, had painted himself into a corner.

Shortly after his 1995 election victory by only one seat, Carr got a standing ovation when he told the NSW Labor Council that as Premier, he would be a "bulwark against privatisation."[83] Yet here he was in 1997 reneging on his promise to the Unions and being publicly slapped down by his Party after seeking a mandate to sell off the State's electricity assets.

The Liberals had Bob Carr on the ropes, with both hands tied behind his back. Here was a major Labor Government policy which, arguably, could benefit the whole community, but which the Premier himself could not possibly deliver. But there was nothing stopping the Liberals from doing so!

The Liberal strategy

The Liberals' enthusiasm for privatisation was bolstered by the media, with one newspaper reporting "Opposition Leader Peter Collins will be making promises about how he will spend the

---

82   *The Sydney Morning Herald*, 31 May 1997.
83   *The Daily Telegraph*, 21 April 1995.

privatisation billions"… and noting … "Collins must already be eyeing up the Premier's suite."[84]

But any electoral advantage the Liberal Party may have had with its privatisation policy was lost after Opposition Leader Peter Collins was dumped in favour of Kerry Chikarovski, and Deputy Leader Ron Phillips took over responsibility for managing this key election issue.

In October 1998, Mr Phillips had presented Peter Collins with his strategy aimed at promoting strong voter support for the Liberal's electricity privatisation policy: give $1,000 in cash (or in shares) to every electricity customer in New South Wales! Collins flatly rejected what he said was a "brain-dead idea."[85]

Having deposed Collins, Phillips publicly resurrected his cash (or share) giveaway idea. But there were problems from the word go, with media questions such as: "will prisoners in jail get $1000?" and "would backpackers from overseas also get it?"

Bob Carr and Michael Egan, both of whom had 'kept mum' on the issue since the 1997 State Labor Conference, were quick to label the Liberal policy as "an unprecedented electoral bribe… using public assets to buy votes for Liberal politicians."[86]

Having raised more questions than it answered, and having failed the credibility test, the Liberal's privatisation policy promoted by Mr Phillips was in tatters and unravelled within days. Carr and Egan had effectively been let off the hook by my opponent, the Liberal MP for Miranda!

---

[84] *The Sun Herald*: Editorial, 5 October 1997.
[85] Peter Collins, *The Bear Pit*, Allen & Unwin, page 294.
[86] *The Sydney Morning Herald*, 15 February 1999.

The Union campaign... and Miranda

None of this was lost on the voters in Ron's own seat. Indeed, the fact that Mr Phillips was widely portrayed as the architect of the Liberals' privatisation policy was pure gold for my campaign to take Miranda from him. But I wasn't the only one who'd be campaigning on the issue.

Given their resounding victory at Labor's Annual Conference in 1997, it was only to be expected that the unions would campaign heavily against privatisation across the State. At the forefront was the Union whose members were most affected by the Liberal's plan: the Electrical Trades Union (ETU).

Led by its NSW Secretary, Bernie Riordan, the ETU was both very large and very well organised: factors which were reflected in its very strong campaign against electricity privatisation.

Along with a heavy schedule of TV, radio and newspaper advertisements, hordes of ETU members were out in the streets and shopping centres letterboxing a variety of anti-privatisation pamphlets and presenting their case to anyone they came across.

The folded, four-page ETU pamphlet I found in my letterbox at home ranks as one of the best campaign pamphlets I've ever seen. It featured a family of four with young children, sitting around a table in a darkened room lit by two candles, with an anxious mother and a very worried father holding an electricity bill from Energy Australia in his hand.

"Mummy can we put the lights on yet?" the front of the pamphlet read.

"Not if the Liberals privatise electricity," comes the mother's reply on the inside of the pamphlet, alongside a single, lit candle and a box of matches.

"Vote against privatisation. Vote 1 Labor."

Powerful stuff! Rather than emphasising potential job losses, as one might have expected, the ETU pamphlet focused on the impact of the Liberals' privatisation plans on consumers and their families, as well as on businesses. Higher electricity prices, overseas ownership, poor service and more blackouts all got a mention. This excellent pamphlet could only assist the ETU campaign, as well as my own!

But there was more to come. As election day drew nearer, insiders were telling my campaign director, Bob Rogers, that the ETU was about to ramp up its campaign by taking its message to weekday morning commuters at railway stations across the Shire.

Bob and I decided I wouldn't appear at any of those stations on the same mornings as the ETU members. After all, it was *their* campaign, and had to be seen to be such by the general public. Having me turn up at the same time as ETU members could create the perception that the union campaign was merely a cloak for the Labor campaign, and it could lose some of its impact.

There was also the likelihood that my attendance at the same time and station as the ETU members would only serve to highlight the previous conflict between the Labor Government and the union movement over the issue, attracting criticism from the more politically-savvy commuters and the local media. Besides, I'd had absolutely no input into the union campaign or the literature they were distributing.

Gymea Station and Ron

On the Friday afternoon following my first visit to Jannali Station, Bernie Riordan rang Bob Rogers, giving him advance warning that ETU members would be distributing their pamphlets to rail commuters in the Miranda electorate, starting with Gymea Station the following Wednesday morning.

The very next day, as chance would have it, Ron Phillips and I both turned up to run our Saturday morning stalls at Kareela Shops. This would be only the second, and the last, time I'd lay eyes on my opponent during the entire 1999 election campaign.

We acknowledged each other's presence with a nod and handed out our leaflets to shoppers and their families as they headed into the shops and back to their cars with their trolleys. As noon approached, the number of shoppers dwindled and as we began to pack up, Ron Phillips unexpectedly came over to me asking if we could have a chat.

Ron said that it was silly for both of us to roll up at the same station on any given morning. He suggested that our Campaign Directors come to an arrangement to ensure that we took turns at each of our five stations. His proposal made perfectly good sense to me and I agreed to get Bob Rogers to contact Ron's campaign director (an amiable fellow named Michael Douglas) to work out a Labor/Liberal roster for each station.

"In the meantime," said Mr Phillips, "I'd like you and I to decide which stations we are each doing next week."

"What did you have in mind?" I asked.

"I'd like to do Gymea next Wednesday morning," Ron said.

214

"OK. I'll do Miranda and you can do Gymea," I said, knowing full well what Ron Phillips would probably find waiting for him there.

I couldn't believe my luck! With five stations and five weekdays to choose from, my opponent chose to do Gymea on the very same morning the ETU had decided to begin its anti-privatisation campaign in the Miranda electorate! It was one of those rare, almost prophetic, moments in the election campaign when I could truly say that the planets were aligning in my favour.

From all reports, Ron Phillips turned up at Gymea Station only to be confronted by very vocal ETU members out in full force. They weren't just handing out the same general pamphlet I'd found in my letterbox. This time, cleverly, there was no mention of the Labor Party at all. Instead, the ETU postcard they were distributing specifically targeted the Liberals and Ron Phillips himself [5 – 3].

Dear Resident,

In NSW we have the cheapest electricity and the fewest blackouts in Australia.

But our affordable electricity service is at risk. The Liberals and their candidate for Miranda, Ron Phillips want to privatise electricity.

In Victoria the Liberals privatised electricity. Now Victorian households pay an average of **$85 per year** more than we do in NSW.

Plus Victoria has **double the blackouts and power failures** compared to NSW.

And how could you forget the disasterous 5 week blackout in Auckland?

PS: This election will be decided by a handful of votes. The only way to stop electricity privatisation is to vote against Ron Phillips and the Liberals.

Don't risk the Liberals' electricity privatisation.

Authorised by Bernie Riordan, Secretary ETU, 370 Pitt St. Sydney. Printed by Paravogue Printing, Smith and Gibbes Streets, Chatswood.

5 – 3: ETU anti-privatisation card, Gymea Railway Station

I was told that Mr Phillips did not make it through the normal weekday commuter rush that morning. The word was that the ETU effectively drove him and his campaign workers away from the station. I felt a little sorry for Phillips, but as you soon learn, all's fair in love and in politics.

I'll never know whether it was the ETU activity that morning or his commitments elsewhere (or both), but I never had another report of Ron being seen at *any* railway station in the Miranda electorate during the remainder of the campaign. Perhaps that explains the comment by the early morning commuter to me at Kirrawee Station about his 'absent Member for Miranda.'

My campaign: Don't privatise our power

Electricity privatisation quickly became a major election issue across NSW, including seats like Bathurst with its concentration of the State's largest power stations and industry jobs.

Locally, however, it was down to me to take what advantage I could from the growing anti-privatisation sentiment and the strong ETU campaign with its local focus on my opponent, Ron Phillips. That meant making my own anti-privatisation stance known to the voters of Miranda, very clearly and very quickly.

My first step was to write my own pamphlet, as I had done for just about every piece of Miranda-specific literature distributed throughout my campaign. The pamphlet contained a photo of Ernie, a very worried-looking senior, talking to me with a huge electricity tower clearly visible in the background.

Don't be bought off

Ron Phillips is the architect of the electricity sale. He and his Liberal mates want to sell off our power industry to pay for their costly election promises.

They say that if you vote for them they'll sell off your power industry and give you $1,000 — if the electricity bill is in your name.

You have paid electricity bills all your adult life — but you will only get the same as a back packer who is here on holiday. That's unfair.

And $1,000 is no compensation for a power worker without a job.

The Liberal's sell-off of our power industry is filled with risks we just can't afford to take. *Don't let the Liberals buy your vote.*

---

5 – 4: Extract from my anti-privatisation pamphlet

My pamphlet outlined four consequences of privatisation: higher electricity bills; blackouts and power cuts; job losses and foreign control of our power supplies. The pamphlet also included a section attacking my opponent's policy [5–4].

Now, every pamphlet needs a short heading which immediately captures the attention of the reader. I came up with: *Barry Collier, Labor for Miranda says…Don't Privatise Our Power.* The more I thought more about those four words, the more I realised I'd not only encapsulated my own position; I'd also come up with what could be a very effective campaign slogan!

Beyond my pamphlet

With the anti-privatisation campaign gathering momentum, I ordered and personally paid for 200 large red-and-white coreflutes with my new slogan [5–5].

DON'T PRIVATISE

OUR

POWER

VOTE **1**

BARRY COLLIER

FOR MIRANDA

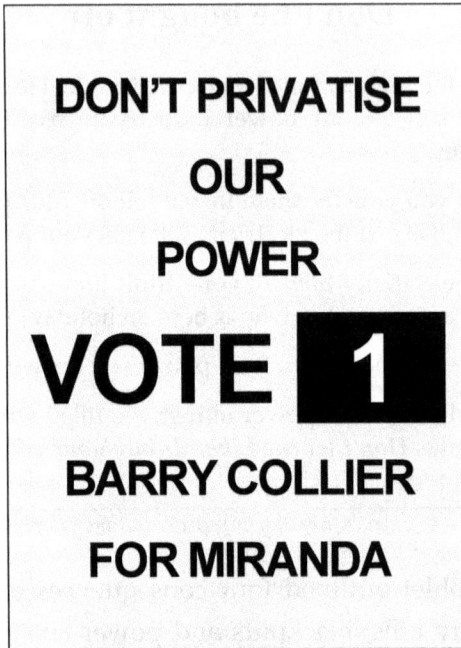

5 – 5: My anti-privatisation coreflute

While 50 of these were put on A-frames for use at railway stations, street stalls and outside pre-poll, the rest were destined to be nailed very high up on highly visible power poles on major roads and in shopping centres throughout the electorate.

I added the fact I was 'Opposing the sale and privatisation of our electricity industry' to my growing list of 'Top Priorities' appearing in the other, more general pamphlets we were letterboxing and handing out at street-stalls and railway stations.

With Ron's fingerprints all over the Liberal's electricity sell-off policy, it was important to keep the anti-privatisation pot on the boil until election day. With that in mind, I wrote and took out advertisements in the last two Leader editions before polling day, each headed up with my slogan [5 – 6].

5 – 6: My anti-privatisation Leader advertisement

In one case, my anti-privatisation ad appeared in the same edition as an article by journalist Merryn Porter quoting me as saying "A lot of people are concerned about the privatisation of the power industry".[87] Aside from reinforcing my advertisement,

---

[87]   *St George and Sutherland Shire Leader*, 23 March 1999.

that had to be one of the major understatements of my entire campaign.

5.9. Doorknocking story #11

In 1999, the seat of Miranda comprised a broad range of socio-economic groups. You didn't have to look at the statistics to see that; all you had to do was to take a 15-minute drive across the electorate. As you did, you couldn't help but notice the stark contrast between modern, multi-million-dollar waterfront homes and the 1950's two-bedroom fibros in the public housing areas.

Candidates on both sides often make the mistake of matching the apparent affluence or the apparent hardship of residents in particular areas with their voting intentions. They take it for granted that the wealthy in their electorates are always Liberal voters, while those in public housing couldn't be anything else but Labor voters. Nothing could be further from the truth.

To compound the felony, aspirants (and their campaign managers) often go further and jump to the conclusion that there is no point in doorknocking the wealthy areas if you are the Labor candidate or doorknocking the public housing areas if you represent the Liberal Party. Again, this is a big mistake!

While it may be very rare for one of the major Parties ever to win a particular polling booth, the truth is that there will always be some percentage of those attending that booth who vote Labor and some percentage who will vote Liberal.

If, by doorknocking a usually unfavourable area, the candidate actually increases his or her vote there, those 'extra votes' can make a valuable contribution to their *total*, electorate-wide vote. In a very close contest, these extra votes might ultimately determine who makes it into the Parliament.

In this respect, it's important to remember that there are real opportunities to gather votes in those parts of the electorate which, according to the statistics, always favour the opposing Party. The electorate is becoming increasingly sophisticated over time, and as it does, the proportion of 'rusted-on voters' is falling, while the proportion of 'swinging voters' is steadily rising.[88]

Kangaroo Point: Tiger territory

Perception counts for much in politics, and if appearances are anything to go by, there can be little doubt that, in 1999, Kangaroo Point was the wealthiest suburb in the Miranda electorate.

The multi-million-dollar waterfront mansions, the private jetties, boats, tennis courts, and the top of the range Mercedes parked inside the security gates all confirmed that. And if, for one minute, you thought that most voters living in Kangaroo Point voted Liberal, you'd be right!

To put it bluntly, Labor candidates in Federal, State and Local Government elections had always copped a hiding from the voters of Kangaroo Point at the ballot box. Previous Labor candidates regarded doorknocking in Kangaroo Point as a complete waste of time and had avoided doing so like the plague for many years. They were quick to advise me to do the same.

---

[88] "Rusted-on voters" are those who always vote for the same Party, regardless of the issues, and have done so for years. "Swinging voters" are those who are likely to change their voting preferences, and tend to do so regularly.

I disagreed. Kangaroo Point residents lived in the Miranda electorate. If I wanted their vote, I believed I had to make myself known to them, as I did to everyone else in every other suburb.

When I told Jeanette, that I decided to doorknock Kangaroo Point residents, her response was refreshing.

"Good!" she said. "You're not going to meet many of them catching the train to work. You need to let them know that you're a barrister: a professional person just like them. But before you go doorknocking there, why don't we letterbox that Card you got the other day?"

Great advice from my greatest supporter! Late the following Friday afternoon, Jeanette, Michael and I letterboxed Kangaroo Point with my Introductory Card (which had finally arrived from the printer). The plan was for me to then doorknock the suburb the next week, by which time we hoped the residents might have read the Card with my background on it!

Horses for courses

There is much to be said for the old adage that begins 'when in Rome'. It's also a matter of common sense that if you want to play the part, you must look the part.

Being a professional also means dressing like a professional. And so, for the first and only time during the entire campaign, I went doorknocking in a suit and tie.

For once, I wasn't driving my old Mitsubishi Magna with the coreflutes on the roof. This time, I was driving a Mercedes I'd borrowed! I really didn't think the majority of Kangaroo Point residents would be all that impressed seeing some bloke hopping out of a car which looked like something out of the *Beverly Hillbillies*, coming to their door and asking for their vote.

You're brave!

It couldn't be said that all the residents of Kangaroo Point welcomed me with open arms. But the reception was generally far better than previous Labor candidates would have me believe.

Most residents came to their door or opened their sliding gates after I buzzed their intercoms and smiled into their security cameras. While most were polite and listened to what I had to say, my doorstop (or gate-stop) was typically brief, and deliberately so. Apart from the few who raised issues about the Carr Government, I also wanted residents see me as an MP who would be sensitive to the time demands on many of them.

Among the residents I met was a high-profile businessperson who told me he was a Labor voter. He said he was "really pleased to finally see a Labor candidate" at his front door, and later sent me a note wishing me well in my campaign.

Soon after, I came across the complete antithesis: a rusted-on Liberal lady, who blew a gasket the moment I told her I was the Labor candidate. Her tirade not only served to remind me of the reasons I joined the Party to begin with, but made me even more determined to complete my doorknocking of the entire suburb.

Towards the end of my doorknocking in Kangaroo Point, I met a long-time resident at his front gate and we had a conversation which really said it all.

"You're brave coming around here!" he said, after I had introduced myself.

"Why's that?" I enquired.

"You're Labor! I'm a Liberal voter and everyone around here votes Liberal," he said.

"I'm hoping to change that," I replied.

"Well, you're not going to get my vote!" he said bluntly.

"That's fine," I answered. "We live in a democracy and that's your choice. But if I *am* elected, I'll do my best to represent you, even if you don't vote for me," I answered.

The man stood there with a somewhat surprised look on his face, but before he could respond I asked "as a matter of interest, when was last time you saw a Liberal candidate here at your gate?"

"Never," he said, confirming my suspicion that my opponent, and in fact the Liberal Party itself, had taken the voters of Kangaroo Point for granted for many years.

The lesson here, of course, is that serious candidates on both sides need to get out of their comfort zones and doorknock those areas which, on the face of it, are strongholds of the opposing Party.

While it's a mistake for, say, Labor candidates not to doorknock the 'Liberal areas', it's also a mistake for these candidates not to doorknock areas they regard as 'their own'.

Having never seen a Labor candidate at their front door, and perhaps feeling that they've been long taken for granted, a number of those who usually vote Labor may well change their vote if a

Liberal candidate takes the time and trouble to front up and ask for it. All candidates need to remember that 'swinging voter' factor when they're deciding which areas to doorknock!

5.10. Shire commitments, Labor colleagues

Promises are, of course, part and parcel of the politician's stock in trade. Governments can rise on promises made and fall on promises broken.

Individual candidates, too, can win their seats on their local commitments and lose office if they subsequently fail to deliver on their promises, for whatever reason. When it came to making major promises and delivering on major infrastructure, nobody did it better than Roads and Transport Minister, Carl Scully.

The Bangor Bypass

In mid-February 1999, I received a call from Scully's office inviting me to attend "an important media event and photo opportunity" across the Woronora River at Bangor with the Minister and our candidate for Menai, Alison Megarrity. I had absolutely no idea what this was all about, but having already met Scully by the River with the Bridge model, I readily accepted.

On arrival, I saw a very large cardboard stand emblazoned with the heading *Bangor Bypass* and an RTA logo.[89] Beneath the heading was a large, elongated aerial photograph, accompanied by a large map of the proposed Bypass route west from the Woronora Bridge (noted as 'under construction') to New Illawarra Road at Barden Ridge [5—7].

---

[89] Roads and Traffic Authority (RTA) — later renamed Roads and Maritime (RMS).

Having arrived with RTA officials, Carl Scully announced to the waiting media that the "the State Government…will build a $36 million Bangor Bypass if re-elected next month."[90]

Wow! Tacking the construction of the Bypass onto the end of the Woronora Bridge project made perfect sense. It effectively put to bed any question as to how the local roads in Menai would cope with the extra traffic generated by the new Bridge itself.

When it came to handling the media, Scully was relaxed and clearly in command. With the detailed route already planned, a timetable for the commencement of construction, an emphasis on community consultation, the provision of noise walls and the fact that the project would take an estimated 17,000 cars a day off local roads, he easily fended off questions about this being "an election stunt."

With all the bases already covered, Scully also effectively killed off any hope that Alison's opponent, Brett Thomas, may have had for making the Bypass a winning issue for the Liberals.

---

[90] *St George & Sutherland Shire Leader*, 23 February 1999, page 1.

5 – 7: Bangor Bypass Promise, with Scully and Megarrity

Colleagues and the bigger picture

But the Bypass announcement was not all about the Minister himself. Carl Scully was clearly a team player, making sure that Alison and I were involved in the publicity generated by this major infrastructure announcement.

He simply refused to pose for the Leader photographer without first ensuring Alison and I would also be in the shot. The colour photo which appeared in the paper showing the Minister, Alison and me holding the map of the Bypass route was testament to the fact that Scully usually got his way!

Looking at that photo, you could easily get the impression that, along with Alison, I played a key role in persuading the Minister to build the Bypass. One local paper not only noted that Scully had made the announcement "flanked by ALP hopefuls for

Menai and Miranda, Alison Megarrity and Barry Collier," but effectively turned the hint of my involvement in the Minister's decision to approve the project into a fact, with a very carefully worded quote:

> "Alison Megarrity and Barry Collier have been consistent advocates of a bypass to take traffic off local streets and reduce traffic snarls. Following their representations and community concern...I have concluded that there is a strong case for this project."[91]

In truth, I can't remember hearing anything about the Bangor Bypass until the day Carl Scully announced it! Indeed, driving home after the media event on that hot Friday afternoon, I wondered *why* I'd even been invited to the announcement in the first place. After all, Menai was well on the other side of the Woronora River and two electorates away from Miranda. It really *was* Alison's gig!

Reading the local papers the following Tuesday, it seemed I had been given some credit for getting the project underway, when in fact I'd had nothing to do with it at all!

Then the penny dropped! I had to look at the bigger picture. Here was a major election promise by the Carr Labor Government, which, like the Woronora Bridge, would benefit the whole of the Shire, including residents in Miranda. (As Ian McManus had said earlier, we had to hunt together!)

While full credit for the project must go to Alison Megarrity, I realised my campaign for Miranda could benefit by promising to

---

[91] *Sutherland-Menai Express*, 23 February, 1999, page 1.

"ensure that the Bangor Bypass is completed on time," and I added this to my growing list of election commitments.

While I did not actively dissuade any voter who thought the Bangor Bypass was a great project and had something to do with my advocacy, I made the point of mentioning the key role Alison Megarrity played in persuading Carl Scully and the Labor Government to build it. I also acknowledged the major role Ian McManus played in successfully lobbying for the completion of Woronora Bridge when voters mentioned that fabulous project.

At the end of the day, it really *is* all about teamwork, supporting your Party colleagues and giving credit where credit is due — and I remain grateful to Alison and Ian for including me.

And yes! It really is very common for three or four local politicians from the same Party to gather for photos with the Minister at the announcement (or completion) of a project even if they've had absolutely nothing to do with at all! After all, politics is about perception.

5.11. Shopkeepers … A captive audience

Ask any candidate how best to get their message out to the voters and they'll mention doorknocking, street stalls, letterboxing and railway stations. Few, if any, will mention talking to their local shopkeepers!

Yet, when you think about it, the local shopkeepers are more than just small business owners. Whether they are located in a large centre, a shopping strip or an isolated corner shop, storeowners are, in many ways, the pulse of the local community. And, regardless of whether they live above their shop or miles away from it, the shopkeepers know what the local issues are and what local residents are thinking— simply because they talk to their customers day-in, day-out, and up to 7 days a week.

As they serve their regular customers, these respected shopkeepers do far more than simply exchange pleasantries or pass on local gossip; they share their own views on everything from sport to politics. In short, shopkeepers are important opinion-makers within your local community, and it is vital that they have a favourable opinion of you, the candidate.

But you need to help the shopkeepers form that opinion. The best way to do that is to visit each shop, introduce yourself, have a quick chat and leave the shopkeeper with your pamphlet. Sound familiar? It should! 'Doing the shops' is really just a specialised form of doorknocking with the shopkeepers behind the counter providing a captive audience!

Doing the shops

Mention the word 'shops' in the Sutherland Shire and people think, firstly, of the very large Westfield Miranda complex which dominates the region. But there are several other centres like Sylvania Southgate and long-setablished shopping strips clustered around railway stations: notably at Jannali, Gymea, Kirrawee and even Miranda itself. Then there are the smaller local neighbourhood shopping centres (including Kareela and Grays Point), as well as the isolated corner shops.

As a candidate, you can forget about visiting the shop owners in Westfield Miranda. Good corporate citizens they may claim to be, yet Westfield prohibits local candidates canvassing for votes on their premises. Westfield security has been known to usher out candidates and their supporters who dare to walk through their precious shopping centre wearing Party T-shirts.

Westfield management even gets annoyed when candidates set up a street stall outside! Your real focus just has to be the local shops.

The shopping strips: Jannali and Gymea

When I told my friend and successful small businessman, John Goschin, that I was planning to visit all the local shopkeepers he suggested we do Jannali and Gymea (the largest strips) together. I agreed without a moment's hesitation.

After all, here was a highly experienced and very successful local businessman offering to help me canvass for votes with other business people. I had no doubt that I'd pick up more than a pointer or two from John. I wasn't disappointed when he came up with the two-man routine we'd follow inside each shop.

With John holding my business cards and me clutching a clipboard plus a few pamphlets focusing on small business, we walked together into our first shop at Jannali on a showery Monday morning around 10.00AM. The routine began with John identifying himself as a small business owner and then introducing me as "Barry Collier, the Labor candidate for the Jannali area" and handing the shopkeeper my business card.

After a firm handshake and perhaps a few quick remarks about the shop, I'd ask each shopkeeper about the issues on their mind, offer my assistance and make appropriate notes if needs be. I'd also make a point of taking one of their business cards from the counter before asking if I could leave one of my pamphlets with them. Virtually all the shopkeepers agreed, with some inviting me to leave several on the counter because "some of their regular customers might also be interested."

For most Jannali shopkeepers, the appearance of a would-be politician taking a genuine interest in them seemed to be a real first, and I was very well received. Few of them raised any issues. Those who did, typically complained about their problems with the local Council, and I promised to ask their Labor Ward Councillors to phone them (which I did).

But there were, as expected, several shopkeepers who asked "what are you going to do for small business?" Fortunately, I'd done my homework and could tell them what the Carr Government had been doing, in terms of tax relief, spending on business expansion plans, technology and funding local business enterprise centres. I'd also leave these shopkeepers with a copy of the generic, business-focused ALP pamphlet, 'Working for New South Wales' (modified with my name and contact details).

The Jannali restaurants which were closed each got one of my pamphlets under their front doors, with an invitation to contact me if I could assist them. The idea was that, even if they didn't do so, they might live in the Miranda electorate and at least be aware of my candidacy. They might also talk to their adjoining business owners about my visit or chat about the forthcoming election with their regular customers.

John and I took around four hours to do the Jannali shops. Over a cup of coffee, we agreed that we'd had a positive response from the shopkeepers and we arranged to do the Gymea shops together the following week.

With more than 100 shops, the Gymea shopping strip took virtually all day. But again, the responses were positive! And, like their counterparts in Jannali, it seemed that the shopkeepers of Gymea hadn't seen hide nor hair of their local MP for years!

I got much the same impression over the next few weeks when I did the smaller strip shopping centres of Kirrawee and Miranda by myself. If anything, the favourable responses not only put paid to both the old chestnut that 'the Liberal Party is the Party for small business,' and the 'rule of thumb' espoused by some Labor Branch members that 'all shopkeepers are Libs'.

Three observations

It's worth noting three points about these shopping strips. Firstly, each has its own 'Chamber of Commerce' or 'Business Chamber.' During my visits to the shops, I usually met members of these organisations serving behind the counter. Here was a real opportunity to get to know the local business movers and shakers and hopefully impress them by taking up their issues and even attending one of their (after-hours) meetings.

Secondly, four shopping strips in the Miranda electorate were clustered around railway stations. Having met the shopkeepers and received generally positive responses, it seemed important to keep the momentum going. After finishing handing out at the nearby railway station, we'd slip my latest pamphlet under the front door of each shop in the strip (before opening hours). The idea was that, having met me personally, the shopkeepers would now be more likely to read it or at least leave the pamphlet in the shop where one of the customers might see it.

Thirdly, when you are planning to visit the shopkeepers, it's important to keep in mind the other half of the equation: the customers themselves. With that in mind, and before doing the shops, I'd always set up six A-frames with my coreflutes in highly visible positions throughout the shopping strip (and park my campaign car near a pedestrian crossing) to let the regular shoppers know I was around.

Of course, as you go from store to store, you're going to come across regular shoppers on the footpath. As I did, I always made a point of stopping, introducing myself and giving them a pamphlet if possible. It was all about maximising my visibility and presenting myself as a local involved in his community. And rest assured, some voters like the fact that you 'shop locally!'

The neighbourhood centres and corner shops

I followed much the same process in visiting the smaller neighbourhood shopping centres like Kareela and the family-run corner shops scattered here and there throughout the electorate. Most of the shopkeepers seemed pleased that I'd called in for a quick chat and were happy to take a pamphlet (or two).

I usually combined my visits to the corner shops with my doorknocking in the surrounding streets. After two or three hours in the summer heat, calling into the shop also provided me with a welcome break and the chance to buy a drink.

From a grassroots campaigning point of view, the family-run corner shop was just as important as those in the much larger shopping strips. The corner shopkeepers usually lived in the electorate, were more than willing to have a chat in the (often longer) breaks between customers and were happy to talk about the key issues facing them and their customers. More often than not, the store owners also provided excellent intelligence about the Liberals' campaigning in their area!

Shopkeeper etiquette

Whether you're a highly experienced MP or a first-time candidate, there are some simple rules you need to follow if your visit to the local shopkeepers is to be successful.

These rules, which I've called 'shopkeeper etiquette,' are based on the fundamental principle that the shop is the shopkeeper's livelihood and, at the end of the day, it is the shopkeeper's customers who put bread on his or her table.

Even if you remember nothing from the simple set of rules I've set out in 5−8, just follow this one rule of thumb: never come between the shopkeeper and the customer!

However important you may think you are, and however interested you think the shopkeeper may be in you, your Party or your candidacy, you will always come a long second to the customer!

DOING THE SHOPS: SHOPKEEPER ETIQUETTE

1. Do your shops on the shopkeeper's lightest trading days — usually a Monday or a Tuesday. That gives the shopkeeper a real opportunity to talk to you without customers present.

2. Don't turn up as soon as the shop door opens. At that time, shopkeepers are more interested in getting ready for the day ahead than talking to you!

3. If you can, choose a rainy day to do the shops. While you can't sensibly doorknock houses in miserable wet weather, you can 'doorknock the shops'— almost all of which have street awnings! (This is all about maximising your use of campaign time.)

4. Don't go into shops that are full of customers. It's far better to come back later. There is nothing more annoying for a shopkeeper than to have some would-be politician canvassing for votes in their shop when they are trying to serve their customers!

5. If you go into a shop as a customer is about to be served, wait until that customer is on the way out the door before you approach the counter.

6. Keep the conversation short. Don't expect to spend more than three or four minutes talking with any given shopkeeper. You really only have a small window of opportunity, so work out in advance exactly what you are going to say before you enter the shop and introduce yourself.

7. If you're talking with the shopkeeper and a customer comes in, quickly wind up your conversation and give way to the customer. Sometimes the shopkeeper will ask you to stay to talk further, and, if you're lucky, might even introduce you to the customer! (The arrival of a customer can also provide you with the opportunity for a timely exit if you come across a shopkeeper who is openly hostile to you!)

8. Do your homework and be prepared. Know about your Party's budget, its record on tax, its small business programs and its policies. Find out the names of the key Chamber of Commerce officials and be prepared to meet with them if asked. It's also worth checking out the local newspaper for relevant local business stories, events and even controversies.

9. To maximise your presence, set up your A-frames in the shopping centre before you start.

10. Always follow up any issues raised by making appropriate representations if required, and always get back to the shopkeeper!

5 – 8: Shopkeeper etiquette

Rare, committed support

Whether it's a large shopping strip, the neighbourhood centre or the corner store, you know you're on something of a winner, with the shopkeeper who is happy to take half a dozen of your pamphlets and leave them on the counter for 'interested customers'.

From time to time, though very rarely, you might even come across a shop owner who is happy to go one better and actually display your coreflutes in the shop window. While you can ask, many shopkeepers will not do this, because they know that such public displays of support may mean the loss of those customers who always vote for the other mob.

Take the *Miranda Palace*, a little Chinese restaurant on the eastern edge of the shopping strip whose owners actually asked to put my coreflutes up in their front window. Several days after doing so, two aggressive Liberal campaign workers turned up demanding that my coreflutes be taken down. To their credit, the restaurant owners refused and were continually harassed by the Libs to remove my coreflutes right up until election day.

Such was the owners' support in the face of such undemocratic heavy-handedness, that Bob Rogers and I decided that we'd hold our post-campaign thank-you dinner at the *Miranda Palace*, regardless of the election outcome!

5.12. And don't forget the schools!

As a kid who left school in Year 10 and went back after two years to get his HSC — and later, as a high school teacher for 17 years — I well understand the importance of a good education and so, too, do the vast majority of parents and grandparents across the State.

Education commitments by the big Parties always play a major role in any election campaign, and it was important for me to get the Carr Government's record and commitments out to the voters in Miranda.

School visits

The most obvious way of delivering the Labor message on education, of course, was to visit the schools themselves. I visited all the public and Catholic schools in the electorate— including Port Hacking High School Miranda, where I'd taught junior and senior HSC classes 20 years earlier.

I typically combined my visit to each school with my doorknocking in the surrounding streets. I'd call in at each school's Administration Office at an appropriate time (usually after recess), introduce myself to the secretarial staff and ask to see the Principal for five minutes.

Most Principals were happy to see me and, after I pointed out my experience as a teacher, had no hesitation in discussing the needs of their schools as well as their views on education funding (mostly "off the record"). Some were so generous with their time as to give me a personally-guided tour of their school's facilities, identifying their problems first hand as we went. Several quietly commented that they hadn't seen their local State MP for a while or if they did, it was usually only ever at the school's Annual Presentation Night in December.

A few principals were, of course, unavailable to see me when I called in, but I always asked the administration staff in 'the front office' to pass on my business card and to tell the Principal they are more than welcome to telephone me. Most actually did.

But whether the Principals spoke to me or not, I always asked for the names and contact details for relevant parent groups – the P&Cs, the P&Fs and the School Councils – and later arranged to meet their officials. While Principals were often reluctant to talk about any problems "on the record" for fear of adverse publicity as well as a career-damaging scolding from the local School Inspector, the parent groups were more than willing to tell you, in no uncertain terms, about the school's needs and problems. In fact, the parent groups will *always* tell you what the Principal would *like* to tell you, but feel they can't. And of course, I'd follow up "the parents' concerns" with written representations to the Minister for Education on their behalf.

Finally, and as I learnt during my earlier career as a teacher, you should never underestimate the importance of the hard-working staff in every School's Administration Office. They are 'the front-line' in every sense.

The Office Staff know everything about the school – from the way it functions and its real issues to the problem pupils and the quality of its teachers. And rest assured, whether you get to meet the Principal or not, it will soon get around the school and out to the parents, as well as the wider community, that you, the local candidate, not only took an interest in their school but actually visited it! It's all about word-of-mouth and making first impressions count!

Afternoon pick-ups

Driving along The Boulevarde around 3.00PM in early February, I noticed a group of 15 to 20 people standing on the footpath chatting among themselves outside Gymea North Public School. Obviously, these were parents, grandparents and carers waiting to pick up kids after school.

It occurred to me that this was an excellent opportunity to talk to the parents, grandparents and carers about education where it really mattered: their kids' school itself. Here was a ready-made audience with a common interest I could meet around the same time at any local primary school on any weekday afternoon during term.

I made it a regular part of my campaign to turn up unannounced at each of the electorate's primary schools, introduce myself around and spend 10 to 15 minutes having an informal chat with those waiting for the bell to ring. Most were pleased to see me and were happy to take the Labor Education pamphlet ("Giving Our Children a Brighter Future") from me.

But there is always one in every crowd. I well remember a well-dressed grandmother seemingly holding court with several parents and protesting the fact that I had turned up.

Having spotted me talking to one of the mums, the lady in question strode over towards me with a very angry look on her face. As she did, I noticed two dads behind her look at me and roll their eyes as if to say "here she goes again".

> "You shouldn't be talking to parents about the School without the approval of the Headmaster!" she said, standing in front of me, hands on hips.
>
> "You *are* kidding aren't you?" I replied.
>
> "No! I'm not! You have no right to be doing this!" came the stern response, loud enough to stop nearby conversation.
>
> "Well, with respect, madam, I do." I said firmly. "I'm not on school property; I'm on public property and I

don't have to get the approval of the Headmaster to speak with parents or anybody else about the school or anything else for that matter!"

The mum with whom I was talking chimed in and said, "Mr Collier's right! It's up to me whether I talk to him or not…and I want to talk to him!"

With that, the now furious grandmother mumbled "how dare you call me madam!" as she stormed past me to collect her grandchild and headed off towards her car.

As she strode off, I saw wide grins appear on the faces of the two dads who'd rolled their eyes moments before. The mum to whom I was talking just shrugged her shoulders and we continued chatting about the school.

It turns out that the angry grandma wasn't a member of the school's P&C. She was just another of those outspoken parents and grandparents I'd come across during my teaching career who never contributed anything to the school or its activities, beyond their unwanted advice, unwavering opinions and complaints.

I believe I picked up a few votes that day, with one parent even offering to be in a photo with me and her children for a Labor pamphlet. And strangely enough, I thought I saw that same angry grandmother again about three weeks later: this time handing out Liberal How to Votes on election day!

6. SERIOUS STUFF

6.1. Come March and 'Candidate's Day'

As February gave way to March, we entered the so-called 'serious part' of the campaign. In accordance with official procedure, Writs would be issued by the NSW Governor commanding that a general election be held on Saturday, 27th March, 1999.[92]

Rounding the home turn, and with the finishing line in sight, our campaign activity ramped up considerably. As polling day approached, voters naturally began to take more and more interest in the State election and its outcome. The media and the Party machines saw to that, with Bob Carr and Kerry Chikarovski out selling their policies and making their promises.

Marathons and sprints

For candidates like me, the workload ramped up too! New pamphlets had to be written as new policies and issues emerged; earlier brochures had to be updated as new local promises were made; newspaper ads had to be written and submitted to meet strict deadlines; and more telephone calls to the campaign office had to be returned personally (after hours). To boot, the local journalists began wanting more comments and interviews.

There'd also be more Saturday street stalls, with two or even three being held the same day in different suburbs. Our early

---

[92] As required by the New South Wales *Constitution Act*, 1902. The Act specifies four-year Parliamentary terms and requires a general election to be held on the last Saturday in March at the end of each term.

morning station visits became more frequent, with plans to do all five in the last week of our campaign.

On top of all that, there were certain administrative tasks that had to be done, including everything from officially nominating as the Labor candidate for Miranda with the Electoral Commission to attending the official ballot draw and working out possible preferences prior to pre-poll voting getting underway.[93] There were also three major Labor Party events to attend.

Even with the extra workload, I was determined to continue my strict "doorknocking until I drop" policy. That meant my working days stretched out to 16, and at times, 18 hours. With the winning post in sight, my marathon became more of a sprint!

Candidate's Day

March would see two separate Labor campaign launches, after an official 'Candidate's Day' on the first Sunday of the month.

Labor aspirants for all 93 State seats, together with their Campaign Directors, assembled at Sydney's Radisson Hotel for what could best be described as a 'team bonding exercise' (complete with talkfest with motivational gee-up). Highlights of the Candidate's Day program included a keynote address by Premier Bob Carr and a workshop by NSW General Secretary John Della Bosca.

Along with my Campaign Director, Bob Rogers, I was excited about attending the event. Despite the fact that we'd

---

[93] The Electoral Commission of New South Wales is independent statutory body charged with the responsibility of regulating and conducting elections.

already been out there on the hustings for over two months, there was still much to learn and any tips I might pick up from the experts on the day might prove invaluable in the final weeks of our campaign.

On arrival at the hotel, Bob and I were each given a 'show bag' containing a ton of Party literature, including copies of the pamphlets currently being distributed in 'targeted seats' by first-time candidates, Kevin Greene (Georges River) and Cherie Burton (Kogarah). Given that all of my pamphlets were only A4 black and white photocopies, I couldn't help feeling just a little envious when I saw Greene's glossy, professionally-produced and folded, full-colour brochures.

Initially, I also reflected that, had Della Bosca given *Miranda* the targeted seat status I'd twice requested earlier, my brochures, too, would have looked far more up-market. But I soon dismissed the notion.

Distributing glossy, colour brochures would be completely at odds with our clear underdog status and the no-frills, shoestring campaign we were running against my high profile, well-funded opponent. The hand-painted signs, the 'ramshackle' Campaign office, and the *Beverly Hillbillies*-style campaign car all seemed to be resonating well with the voters, so perhaps it was to our advantage that Miranda was *not* a targeted seat after all. Besides, if the Party was known to be pouring buckets of money into Miranda (as they were into Georges River and Kogarah), Mr Phillips would have been taking me more seriously than he seemed to be doing. That is not something I would have wanted, and so I decided not to raise the issue of money with John Della Bosca, if I ever got to speak to him.

Della's wisdom

I clapped eyes on our General Secretary for the very first time at the opening session, but didn't get to speak to him at all during Candidate's Day. In fact, and as strange as it seems, I never once spoke to Della Bosca during the entire State election campaign!

I did, however, attend Della Bosca's trumpeted session entitled "Campaign Techniques," in which he spent considerable time espousing what he called the 'vomit principle'. This is the idea that it's not good enough for you, the candidate, to tell the voters what you have done for them or what you are going to do for them, once only. You must tell them, and keep telling them, again and again, over and over, until they are physically sick of hearing it. It's only then that your message has finally sunk in!

That's all very well, I thought, for Bob Carr, his Ministers, the repetitive radio and TV ads, and even our candidates in the targeted seats. But for those unknown, under-resourced Labor candidates like me, contesting seats Head Office believes are unwinnable, you really only get *one chance* to talk to voters before election day. Whether that's at their front doors, at a street stall or at a train station, you have to be convincing first-time round!

Della Bosca's grass roots wisdom aside, the highlight of Candidate's Day program was to be the address by the Premier.

That elusive photo ...

Bob Carr's speech was as well crafted, as perfectly delivered and as inspirational as ever. But it ran a long second behind the invitation to all candidates to have an individual, officially-approved photograph with the Premier afterwards.

The photographs could be used, we were told, in our campaign literature. Not surprisingly, all the candidates had turned up appropriately dressed for the session.

We were directed to line up in alphabetical order according to our seats, and we each took it in turns to be photographed with the accommodating Premier. While I was delighted to be finally getting a formal pic with Bob Carr after my failure to do so during his visit to Sutherland Hospital, I was again disappointed with the result when it arrived in the post a week later.

My photograph showed a beaming Barry Collier standing beside a Premier who not only looked completely bored and disinterested, but appeared to have a bad smell under his nose. There was absolutely no way I could use this photo in any of my campaign pamphlets!

I was asked by one of our workers "why aren't there any photographs of you and the Premier together in any of the stuff we're handing out?" I made the excuse that Carr was so busy with the media and travelling NSW that he had no time to pose with candidates for photos. In truth, I could never get the Premier to stand still for long enough for me to get a decent photo with him. Besides, I believed he wasn't really interested anyway!

An unknown ... still

Part of the attraction of Candidates Day was the prospect of meeting other Labor aspirants and getting better known within the Party itself.

By early March 1999, and strange as it may seem, I only knew the local Labor candidates, all of whom were contesting Shire seats. Beyond having Michael Egan open our Campaign Office, meeting Scully twice and briefly talking to Carr and Refshauge at Sutherland Hospital, I'd never previously spoken to any other serving State Labor MP. Neither had I'd attended the NSW Party's Annual Conference at the Sydney Town Hall.

Apart from my individual photo and brief biography appearing in a Labor booklet entitled 'Profiles of Candidates,' I was still completely unknown in Party circles by the time of the Radisson get-together. Being without strong Party connections, I felt like something of an outsider throughout Candidate's Day, and I'm sure that other first-time candidates in seats regarded by Head Office as unwinnable felt much the same.

I left Candidates Day the same way I arrived: as an unknown. But that didn't matter. I'd been on my own from the start anyway, and the next day I'd get back out there doing my own thing: going from door-to-door in my blue shirt, sleeves rolled up, blue spotted tie and straw hat.

6.2. Doorknocking stories #12 and 13

When it comes to doorknocking, the sitting MP has clear advantages over every first-time candidate.

The advantage of incumbency is the first and most obvious. Sitting MPs seeking re-election at the end of their four-year terms have had every opportunity to meet many individual voters and deal officially with their concerns. They've also had the time to develop extensive, up-to-date, personal files and databases covering all their contacts and their interactions with individual constituents, community groups and local business owners.

Secondly, both major Parties provide each of their sitting MPs with sophisticated internal computer systems which enable them to identify and track every individual constituent on the electoral roll, according to a host of criteria — including the issues of concern to them and the MP's every interaction with them.

These systems are regularly updated to include newly-enrolled constituents in each electorate. And with the touch of a button, the sitting MP can produce the full list of the names and details of every voter living at any given address in any given street — by odd and even house numbers, if needs be. Some would say it's the perfect doorknocking tool.

The first-time candidate, on the other hand, has no such advantages. The Electoral Commission does, however, provide each candidate with a copy of the electoral roll for the seat they are contesting.[94] In 1999, the Miranda electoral roll was a bound book compiled by the Commission and distributed to candidates after nominations had closed about two weeks before polling day and about three months after I began doorknocking![95]

#12: Doorknocking blind

While the incumbent has the potential to walk up to any given door armed with a wealth of knowledge about those who live there, the first-time, unknown candidate has no such luxury. You never know who is going to open the front door to you. For want of a better expression, the first-timer is 'doorknocking blind.'

I mostly came across men and women I'd never previously met, some of whom were well-known local public figures. On several occasions, however, I encountered individuals with whom

---

[94] The 'electoral roll' is simply an alphabetical listing of the names and addresses of all residents living in a particular electorate who are eligible to vote.

[95] These days, candidates are given the relevant electoral roll on a computer disc.

I'd previously worked or played sport, former students I'd taught many years before, former clients I'd represented in the criminal courts, acquaintances with whom I'd long lost contact and even 'friends of friends' I knew nothing about.

But I was really taken aback when a lady who opened her door to me identified herself as Mrs Thomas, the wife of Brett Thomas, the Liberal candidate for *Menai*, who was standing against my Labor colleague, Alison Megarrity. While I knew Brett, a local lawyer, from my days working as a Legal Aid Duty Solicitor at Sutherland Local Court, I had absolutely no idea he lived in the Miranda electorate, let alone at that particular address. I told Mrs Thomas as much. She was polite and most gracious to the point of offering me a glass of water, which I gratefully accepted.

I didn't offer her my pamphlet or make any comment about the election. To do either of these things would have been both inappropriate and disrespectful. Having a spouse running for public office puts enormous extra pressure on their wife (or husband), and it's an unwritten rule that candidates and sitting MPs should always show respect for their opponents' partners!

#13: Some cheeky doorknocking

Having said goodbye to Mrs Thomas, I continued to doorknock. As I did, the thought occurred to me: what if I did some doorknocking near Ron Phillips' home next time I was in his suburb? What sort of reception would I get from residents living nearby?

While that would be seen as a little "cheeky" on my part, I thought it would be a good way to test the water and see how well I was travelling against my opponent in his own suburb.

Several days later, I doorknocked several streets near Mr Phillips' home—but no closer than 400 metres. I used the same spiel I'd used at every other front door and, as usual, was particularly careful not to mention my opponent's name.

While I'd half-expected to meet with some hostility, or even be shunned by some of Ron's neighbours in the area, I was pleasantly surprised at just how well I was received. Residents generally took my pamphlet politely, and surprisingly, only one person, mentioned my opponent.

"Ron Phillips is my local MP," the senior lady began, "and he lives up the road."

"Oh", I said, with a look bespeaking incredulity.

"I've lived in this house for 20 years", she continued, "and he's never even spoken to me much less come to my door! At least you turn up to say 'hello'," she said with a tone of discontentment.

To be fair, I didn't believe her local MP had been living in that suburb for 20 years. Even so, the lady's comment suggested that my opponent wasn't even well known in his own suburb! I left the suburb feeling a certain vindication that we were correct in labelling Ron Phillips as 'the absent Member for Miranda!'

6.3. My Sussex Street summons

Criss-crossing the electorate in my old Mitsubishi Magna seemed to be paying dividends so far as word-of-mouth was concerned. The more I doorknocked, the more residents told me that their relatives and friends had already met me at their own homes in other suburbs. I was pleased to hear that the comments they had passed on about me were generally positive.

Driving between suburbs, I stopped off at our Campaign Office around noon to collect some more pamphlets, not to mention having a short break on a very hot Friday afternoon in early March. Despite the heat and the lack of air-conditioning, our "ramshackle" office was a hive of activity. As usual, I made a point of first having a quick chat with our very enthusiastic local volunteers, including my wife, Jeanette, who was folding brochures with Anne Long and other Branch members.

But no sooner had I walked in, when Campaign Director Bob Rogers took me aside with a rather serious look on his face:

"We just had a call from Mark Arbib," Bob said.

"Who's that?" I replied in all honesty.

"The Party's Assistant General Secretary! He wants you and me to come into Head Office and talk to him about our campaign!" Bob replied in a low voice.

"Why? Is there a problem?" I asked, surprised.

"I have no idea! Arbib wouldn't say," replied Bob. "He just said he wants to see us next Monday morning. He said we can bring in a trusted Branch member with us if we wanted!"

"OK, we'll talk later," I said. "I'd like Bert Rhodes to go with us."

"Good choice," Bob replied, "we can all catch the train in together".

I left our Campaign Office armed with more pamphlets and more than a little puzzled about being called into Sussex Street. Why the hell would some Head Office honcho I'd never met want to talk to me this far into our campaign? They'd never bothered about Miranda before this, and I still hadn't heard from Della Bosca! This Sussex Street summons was a bit odd, I thought.

But like the well-behaved schoolboy who'd been called to the Principal's office, I asked myself, 'what have I done wrong?' Whilst knowing it wouldn't be long before I'd find out, I was angry at the thought that I'd be better off out there doorknocking rather than wasting half a day travelling in and out of town to see this bloke Arbib!

Head Office with Arbib, Bob and Bert

Arriving on the 9th floor of the Sussex Street building, Bob, Bert and I were shown into a modern, well-appointed boardroom, complete with large photographs of Labor heroes (including Whitlam, Hawke and Keating). The contrast with our run-down Campaign Office back in Miranda could not have been starker!

Mark Arbib turned up and got straight down to business, saying he wanted to talk to us about canvassing for votes. He said that while we were "doing a pretty good job" of getting out and doorknocking, "we could do better."

Arbib told us that the Party had been looking at trialling the latest technology to contact more voters, more efficiently and to engage them more effectively. With that in mind, Head Office had hired a telemarketing company to help selected Labor candidates personally seek votes over the telephone.

The Assistant General Secretary went on to briefly explain how it all worked and what he saw as key benefit: namely, giving me the ability to touch base with far more voters than I could by traditional doorknocking. Other Labor candidates, Arbib said, had found this style of campaigning very helpful and the Party had decided to offer it to our Miranda campaign. That would require me coming into town each day and spending time on the phone at a call centre.

While I personally entertained a few doubts, both Bob and Bert thought it was a good idea. We agreed that I'd at least give the telephone canvassing a go, starting the following Monday morning, after doing an early railway station.

Naiveté

Call it naiveté or something else on my part, but I didn't ask Arbib the most obvious question of all: "why had Head Office suddenly decided to spend money on Miranda? Why now?"

To any experienced political campaigner, there could only be one answer. Yet, for some reason that eludes me to this day, I didn't even think about asking the question at my meeting with Arbib, let alone seeking an answer! Perhaps it was my unshakeable, privately-held belief that I would win and my determination not to be distracted by anything along the way.

It wasn't until well after the election that Bob Rogers told me why we'd been summoned to Sussex Street. Arbib had given Bob the reason before we all went into town, on the strict understanding that he wouldn't tell *me* on pain of death!

Barry Collier calling!

After a long train trip into the city and what seemed an even longer walk from Central Station, I arrived at what appeared to be an old factory building in the backstreets of Ultimo. If I was expecting to find the name of the telemarketing outfit anywhere on the building, I was wrong. There was nothing on the brick front wall except the street number matching the address I'd been given by Arbib. If this is where the telephone canvassing was being done by ALP candidates, I thought, then it is certainly meant to be a very well-kept secret.

On entering the building, I saw an elderly man of Asian appearance sitting behind a cheap, makeshift reception desk. Having introduced myself, he said: "Ah, we are expecting you, Mr Collier," he said in broken English. "Come!" 'This'll be good,' I thought to myself.

I followed the man around a series of screens and stopped dead in my tracks. I just couldn't believe what I was seeing: a very large, open space with what appeared to be more than 100 people sitting, row upon row, focused on their own individual computer screens and talking into microphones attached to their headsets! Wow! Looking at the building from the outside, no one could believe the activity going on inside! The scenario was like something out of a *Get Smart* script![96]

The elderly receptionist then introduced me to a very well-dressed and very well-spoken young woman:

> "We are ready for you, Mr Collier," she said. "Please accompany me to your workstation."

---

[96] The popular 1960s US Television comedy series featuring bumbling Secret Agent 86, Maxwell Smart, and his sidekick Agent 99.

"Are all these people working on the Labor campaign?" I asked, as we walked along a row of enthusiastic telemarketers.

"Many are," she said, "but most of the workers here are doing other things like selling products, marketing insurance and raising money for charities! The Labor people are in that section over there," she said, pointing to a large area in one corner.

I could see half a dozen Labor candidates I'd spotted during our 'bonding day' at the Radisson Hotel, including Cherie Burton vying for Kogarah and the Hon Gabrielle Harrison, Sports Minister and sitting Parramatta MP.

Arriving at my workstation, and seated comfortably at my computer with headset on, I was given a carefully-worded script to record and then taken through the procedure I was to follow.

Pressing a given key, a computer program telephoned a seemingly random household in the Miranda electorate. My screen displayed the address and names of the occupants as well as all relevant information known about them, including their ages and likely voting preferences. If my call was answered, I'd introduce myself, briefly discuss election issues and my local commitments, offer my assistance and ask for their support on polling day. If my call was picked up by an answering machine, the computer would leave the short message I'd recorded earlier.

Despite several voters asking how I got their telephone numbers, and one or two complaining about my call being an invasion of privacy, the telephone canvassing seemed to work quite well. Clearly, there were advantages to be had from this type of campaigning, and I wasn't alone in thinking that.

During the lunch break on that first day I had a chat with other Labor candidates at the call centre, including Cherie Burton, who, interestingly enough, was not doing all the telephone canvassing of Kogarah voters herself. Sitting either side of her at their own computer stations were four of Burton's campaign workers with much the same script calling homes "on Cherie's behalf." But that wasn't all. A group of students, fluent in Chinese, were there being paid by Head Office to call Kogarah homes in which English was likely to be the second language.

And, while Cherie and all her offsiders were working the phones, Young Labor members were out doorknocking for her in Kogarah. Sussex Street was clearly spending a small fortune on its 'targeted seats'. That much was not lost on other candidates at the call centre, most of whom, like me, were on their own.

A backward step?

After a week of this 'cold-calling', I'd grown very tired of staring at a computer screen and talking to a disembodied voice 25 km away in the Miranda electorate. I found myself missing the face-to-face doorknocking contact I'd been doing for three months.

While it seemed that I was reaching more voters by phone than by doorknocking, there were some clear drawbacks to the call centre approach. The most obvious was the absence of the personal appearance and that all-important handshake.

'What's more impressive?' I thought: the voice of some bloke you've never met on the telephone asking for your vote, or some bloke who has just trudged up 50 steps on a stinking hot day to your front door to seek your support in person? Call me 'old fashioned', but to me the answer was a no-brainer!

One benefit of the call centre, however, was the fact that I could get a message to voters who weren't home. But then, I couldn't leave my pamphlet under their front doors if I was at a call centre in Ultimo. The potential for positive word-of-mouth to those who *weren't* home from their neighbours who *were* home was also limited when my only contact was a telephone message.

Then there were the swings and roundabouts. Each call centre visit meant a two-hour round trip by train plus a walk to and from Central Station. This was time I could spend doorknocking and being seen out and about in the electorate. And, rather than talking to only one person on the phone at a time, I'd often meet two or three members of the same household at the front door.

Besides, having actively portrayed Ron Phillips as the 'absent member for Miranda', the best way to distinguish myself from him was to be seen out in the electorate on a daily basis.

I decided to give the call centre away. Arbib saw that as a backward step, but I was determined to return to 'real' doorknocking, which I did the following day.

6.4. Candidates, donkeys and preferences

Three weeks out from polling day, campaigning by the major Parties shifted up another gear. Advertisements, articles, opinion pieces and election promises began occupying more and more space in the newspapers; interviews with Party Leaders began appearing on TV and radio with monotonous regularity; talkback radio began to go into over-drive prompted by the shock-jocks.

Minor Parties, like The Greens and One Nation, also began publicising their policies. 'Third party campaigners,' like the ETU and the Nurses Association, were also flexing their muscles.[97]

We were now at the 'pointy end' of the campaign. Along with the growing public awareness that a State election was being held on 27th March, we'd see a flurry of official activity by the NSW Electoral Commission which would set the scene for a gruelling, final two weeks of campaigning and the big day itself. The first step was the appointment of a Returning Officer for each of the 93 electorates comprising the NSW Legislative Assembly.

Nominations

Writs issued for the State Election set out a number of formal procedural steps which are subject to strict deadlines. And, as history has shown, failure to meet any of these deadlines can prove fatal to one's own political aspirations.[98]

From the candidate's viewpoint, the most important first step is his or her 'Official Nomination for Public Office.' We were advised by the Returning Officer (RO) for Miranda, Mr Robert (Bob) Rimoldi, that nominations closed at 12 noon on the 11th of March. At 2.30PM the same day, a ballot would be held by Mr Rimoldi at his Kingsway Office to determine the *order* in which the candidates' names would appear on the official voting paper.

---

[97] These are groups and organisations which spend money campaigning on particular issues or promoting their own agendas throughout the election period, but don't actually field any candidates.

[98] In 1973, NSW Minister for Health Harry Jago famously failed to be re-elected to the safe Liberal Seat of Gordon because he forgot to lodge his nomination form before the deadline!

I personally lodged my nomination papers on March 9th and personally paid the $250 nomination fee I'd managed to scrape together from my own funds.

The candidates

In NSW politics, it's not uncommon for candidates to come out of the woodwork at the last minute — turning up just before noon to lodge their nomination forms.

Apart from my Liberal opponent, Ron Phillips, and possibly someone from the Greens, I had no firm idea if any other Party would field a candidate. Then too, there was always the possibility that an individual who is not a member of any political Party – 'the Independent '– might also run.

While any eligible adult could nominate as a candidate for Parliament without being a member of a political Party, several of our more seasoned campaigners warned me that was all too common for the local Libs to run "dummy Independents." These are political unknowns with absolutely no chance of winning the seat and whose sole purpose in nominating is to divert votes away from Labor to the Liberals!

At the close of nominations, there were six candidates for Miranda, each of whom represented a political Party: Australians Against Further Immigration (AAFI), Australian Democrats, The Greens, Pauline Hanson's One Nation, Liberal and Labor. Bob and I were thankful that no "Independents" had nominated.

The next procedural step was the ballot draw to decide the order of the candidates' names on the voting paper for Miranda.

Under our preferential voting system, this order can be crucial to the entire election outcome, especially if the voting between the major Parties is very close. The possibility of an unfavourable ballot draw produced a very anxious 2½ hour wait for my superstitious Irish Campaign Director, Bob ('Paddy') Rogers, and me.

Ballot draws and donkeys

Jeanette, and our son Michael, joined Bob Rogers and I in our Campaign Office shortly before we left to attend the ballot draw. As we were about to leave, one of our volunteers rushed in with the news that he'd "just seen Pauline Hanson in Miranda Fair!" Now that really *was* a surprise!

Pauline Hanson arrived at the ballot draw to be presented with a bunch of flowers by her One Nation candidate, 20-year-old Max Remy. Of the six candidates who'd nominated, there was one notable absentee: my Liberal opponent. (Though represented by his Campaign Manager, I was surprised by Ron's 'no show'.)

But now, with the candidates, managers and supporters all sitting together, the Returning Officer conducted the draw. Each candidate's name was placed in its own small plastic canister which was then sealed and placed in an official cardboard ballot box (which one of the candidates had assured all and sundry was empty). The box, with all the canisters inside, was then shaken vigorously and held high by an Electoral Office staff member. Bob Rimoldi then pulled the canisters out, one by one, announcing the candidate's name as he did so.

Now, no candidate wants to fall victim to 'the donkey vote.' This is the name given to the votes by constituents who are (typically) disinterested in the election outcome and simply number their voting paper from the top to the bottom: that is, 1,2,3,4, etc., down the voting paper following the order in which the candidates' names appear. And so, with Jeanette and Michael sitting either side of me, I held their hand for luck, hoping like hell that my name would come out of the box ahead of Phillips'.

First out was the Greens candidate, Kerry Nettle.[99] The next canister drawn was mine! Number 2 on the voting paper! Wow! I'd be next after the Greens and above Ron Phillips! As between the two major Parties, I'd at least capture the donkey vote! I was one step closer to winning!

The Returning Officer continued on with the ballot draw. The last canister out of the box was that of my main opponent, Ron Phillips himself! It really *was* the 'luck of the draw'!

The ballot draw could not have been better for me, and its importance for the seat of Miranda was not lost on the local newspaper [6 – 1].

Libs get donkey vote in 4 seats

THE Liberal Party has gained a valuable advantage over the ALP on ballot papers in four key seats in St George and the Shire.

Liberal candidates will be placed higher than their Labor opponents in the highly marginal seats of Kogarah, Georges River, Heathcote and Menai.

This will give the Liberals the "donkey vote" from voters who number their paper from the top down.

Labor had some joy in the seat of Miranda, where its candidate, Barry Collier, will be placed second on the ballot paper with Liberal incumbent, Ron Phillips, in the last spot.

6 – 1: St George & Sutherland Shire Leader, 16 March 1999

---

[99] Kerry Nettle later served as Senator in the Federal Parliament (2002-2008).

A matter of preference: the system

Knowing the official order of candidates' names on the voting paper was one thing. Bob Rogers and I now had to decide, as a matter of urgency, if and how, we would direct our preferences amongst the five other candidates.

In NSW, we have an 'optional preferential voting' system for the Legislative Assembly.[100] Voters have a choice. If your vote is to count, you must, at the very least, put the number '1' in the box next to your favoured (or first-choice) candidate. For an individual candidate, the total number of first-choice votes across the electorate is referred to as their 'primary vote'.

But voters also have the 'option' of showing further preferences for other candidates by placing the number '2' in the box next to their second choice, the number '3' next to their third choice, and so on. Voters don't have to number every box: they can number as many (or as few) boxes as they wish. The numbers '2, 3, 4', etc., are referred to as their 'preferences'.

To be elected under the optional preferential voting system, a candidate must receive an 'absolute majority' of more than 50% of the valid votes. If a candidate's *primary vote* results in an 'absolute majority,' he or she is automatically elected. No further counting is necessary to determine the winning candidate.

If no candidate gains an absolute majority on the primary votes, the candidate with the least number of 1st preference votes is 'excluded'. Votes for this candidate are "distributed" among the remaining candidates according to the 2nd preferences shown on the ballot papers of those who voted for the excluded candidate.

---

[100] The NSW Electoral Commission provides an explanation of this on its website.

This process of exclusions is repeated until one candidate has an absolute majority. The voting figures for the final two candidates left after all preferences have been distributed are referred to as *two-party-preferred* (or 2PP).

My choices

In Miranda, and to my mind at least, there was no doubt that the election result would be decided on the two-party-preferred vote. Clearly, I needed the preferences of other candidates to win.

Bob and I had some pretty quick thinking to do. We only had two hours after the ballot draw to decide the order of preferences as we wanted them to appear on our 'How to Vote Labor' pamphlets (HTVs). Our choices had to be faxed to Head Office by 5.00PM if we were to have them approved, printed and ready to hand out at the commencement of pre-poll voting in three days' time.

Now, it's common for two political Parties to make 'preference deals'. That generally means each agreeing to put the other as their 2nd preference on their HTVs, or at least preference the other before a third Party. It may also involve an agreement to put another particular Party last on their respective HTVs!

Before nominations closed, Bob had agreed with the Greens to preference their candidate ahead of the Liberal, Ron Phillips. That made sense. It didn't lock us in before we knew all the Parties nominating and their order on the official voting paper.

The HTV paper Bob and I came up with is shown in 6 − 2. It was Labor Party policy to put One Nation last at No. 6, and we had no problem putting Australians against Further Immigration second last at No. 5. In keeping with Bob's earlier discussions with the Greens, the Liberal candidate was placed at No. 4. The real problem was which of the remaining Parties — the Australian Democrats or the Greens — should we place at No. 2 and No. 3?

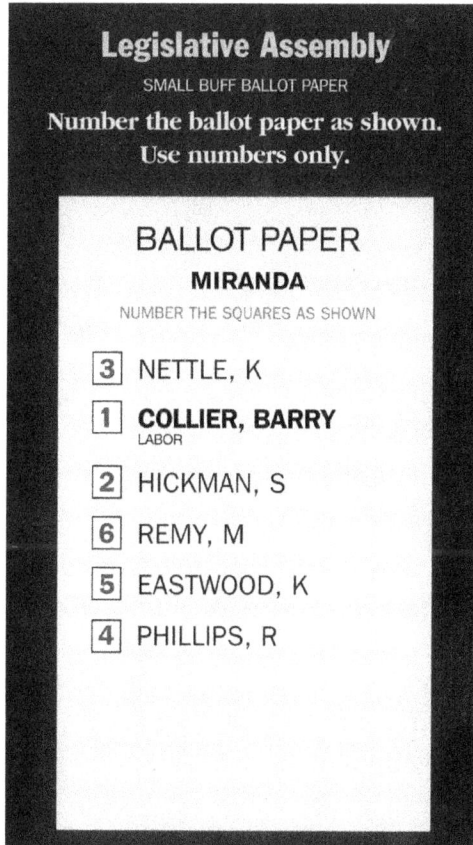

Legislative Assembly

SMALL BUFF BALLOT PAPER

Number the ballot paper as shown.
Use numbers only.

BALLOT PAPER

MIRANDA

NUMBER THE SQUARES AS SHOWN

3	NETTLE, K
1	**COLLIER, BARRY** LABOR
2	HICKMAN, S
6	REMY, M
5	EASTWOOD, K
4	PHILLIPS, R

6 – 2: Labor How to Vote, Miranda 1999

Labor and the Democrats had similar philosophies and had traditionally preferenced each other. But the Greens were becoming increasingly popular. While they were likely to get more first preference votes than the Democrats, they were also likely to preference us second.

But the big problem with Greens voters, Bob had said, is that their votes tend to 'exhaust' early. Greens voters are notorious for ignoring their Party's HTVs and not recording a 2nd preference for another candidate! Being next after the Greens on the official voting paper, I'd probably be the 2nd choice for those Greens who *did* preference other candidates, even if it was a donkey vote!

We decided to put the Democrats at No. 2 and the Greens at No. 3, ahead of the Liberals. Head Office approved our choices. Our HTVs would be ready for collection at 3.00PM in Sussex Street the following Sunday, after the Labor State Campaign Launch.

6.5. Two campaign launches

There was much more to do than submitting nomination forms and deciding preferences in that crucial third week out from election day. It was also the time for two official campaign launches: one for the local Labor candidate and one for the State Labor Party as a whole.

Going down the Miranda Road

For Branch members, volunteers, supporters and candidates themselves, the official launch of their local Labor campaign is always a major highlight of the last few weeks before polling day.

Coming as it does just after nominations close and before pre-polling commences, the local launch is more than just a key campaign milestone: it's also a signal to everyone involved that 'make or break time' has finally arrived!

The local campaign is usually launched by a serving Minister or by some well-known, widely-respected Party identity at a formal dinner, which, not surprisingly, doubles as a fundraiser.

My campaign for Miranda was officially launched by Attorney General, the Hon. Jeff Shaw, QC, MLC during a very well attended dinner at *the Tradies*. As a barrister myself, it was an enormous privilege to have the State's distinguished first law officer do the honours, encouraging all in attendance to make every effort to help me return Miranda to Labor after 15 years.

The Attorney's speech was the last of three. The first, by my Campaign Director Bob Rogers, outlined the campaign so far, and exhorted ALP Members and supporters to add their names to the pre-poll and booth rosters, and to help out whenever and wherever they could — be it letterboxing, street stalls and railway stations, or assisting in our Campaign Office. And of course, he encouraged all present to dig deep when buying raffle tickets!

As the candidate, my speech had to be different. With the Branch members, workers and supporters together, the official launch of the Miranda campaign was my opportunity to sincerely thank all of them for their hard work and dedication to date.

But my speech was also the last opportunity I'd have to encourage them all to go that extra mile in the final two weeks ahead, when their continued commitment to our Miranda campaign may well mean the difference between winning back the seat for Labor and leaving it in Liberal hands. It was also a time to thank my family, including my wife Jeanette, who'd worked just as hard as everyone else.

As I sat down to write my most important speech of the entire campaign, it occurred to me that I really needed some kind of theme or rallying cry or some kind of vision we could all share. I thought about my preselection, my first day out doorknocking and the long journey we'd all been on together.

I thought, too, about the victory I always believed we'd have at the end of our campaign; a victory for everyone involved in the campaign; a victory we would all share and celebrate together with my swearing in as the new MP for Miranda at Parliament House, Macquarie Street, Sydney. How to marry these two ideas: the journey and the shared victory?

I had an image of all of us — Branch members, volunteers, supporters and family — walking together from our Campaign Office on the Kingsway down nearby Miranda Road to the notorious Five Ways and continuing on our long journey into Macquarie Street Sydney and the Parliament itself.

Throughout my speech at the launch, I invited everyone present to "come with me down the Miranda Road into Macquarie Street." I urged everyone to bring their families and friends and "join us as we walk together, arm in arm, down the Miranda Road into State Parliament." I called on all the guests to "continue working together as we go on our journey down the Miranda Road to reclaim our seat in the Legislative Assembly for Labor and Bob Carr."

The image with its underlying theme appeared to resonate with the guests and, judging from the applause, was very well received. Indeed, years later there are those who still remember my "Miranda Road speech" at our local campaign launch in 1999.

Here is the lesson for every political aspirant: think about your speeches, make them relevant and make them memorable!

State campaign launch

Bob Rogers was fortunate to secure two tickets to the State Campaign Launch at the Joan Sutherland Performing Arts Centre in Penrith the following Sunday. On arrival, my savvy Campaign Director quickly grabbed two seats next to an aisle, saying, "I'm told Carr will walk this way to the stage. If you sit here, you might just be lucky enough to greet him."

As odd as it may seem, I thought to myself, "I'll do more than just greet him: I'll shake Carr's hand, and I'll go on to win this bloody election!" But, of course, Carr would be the final speaker and I'd have to wait until after all the preliminaries before his highly anticipated appearance.

The crowd having been revved up by John Della Bosca and Penrith MP, Minister Faye Lo Po, in walked Carr to rapturous cheering, feet stamping and thunderous applause — down our aisle just as Bob Rogers had said. As the Premier approached us, I stepped out into the aisle and shook his hand vigorously. Carr looked at me without any hint of recognition. But that was understandable, given his focus on the major speech he was about to deliver to the Party faithful.

Carr was well known for his measured and magnificent oratory, and he didn't disappoint. In what can only be described as a positive and powerful performance, he carefully laid out Labor's first term record, addressed the key issues and clearly articulated his Government's policies for its second term, without attacking Opposition Leader Kerry Chikarovski (or mentioning her name).

Carr certainly rallied the troops. I have no doubt that all Party members left Penrith with an extra dose of enthusiasm for their own local campaigns. I'm also sure those watching the launch on TV in the NSW country regions felt exactly the same.

The Party would now go into overdrive State-wide, doing 'whatever it takes' to ensure the return of the Carr Government. This was no time to relax. For Bob Rogers and me, it was straight to Sussex Street to collect our 'How to Vote Labor' pamphlets and do those last-minute preparations for the next phase of our campaign, beginning in less than 24 hours: the pre-poll!

6.6. Pre-polling, Miranda style

Voters in NSW are permitted to pre-poll: that is, vote in person before election day in certain circumstances. These include the voter being out of the State on election day or being unable to get to a polling booth that day because of work commitments, or holding religious beliefs which prohibit them from voting.

Pre-polling in Miranda took place at the Returning Office on the Kingsway under the watchful eye of the RO, Mr Bob Rimoldi. Pre-poll voting ran over the final two weeks prior to the election on Saturday 27 March, from 8.00AM to 6.00PM from Monday 15 March to Friday 26 March and included Saturday 9.00AM to 5.00PM and an extra two hours on Thursday nights for late-night shoppers.

The pre-poll booth had to be manned at all times, and I was fortunate enough to have a team of enthusiastic campaign workers willing to hand out my How to Votes to the 'early voters.' While there were no gaps in our pre-poll roster, Jim Foy was always on-hand to ensure a smooth changeover from one team to the next, and to cover for any unexpected absences.

Like election day itself, voters arriving at pre-polling would be confronted with a plethora of coreflutes on A-fames. These had to be put in place each day before the pre-poll booth opened and removed as soon as the booth closed. Here again, I was fortunate to have Big John McLean doing the setting up and the removal of my A-frames, as required by the Returning Officer, not to mention the Sutherland Shire Council![101]

Pre-polling and balanced campaigning

With less than two weeks to go before State election day, one of the key questions confronting each candidate is: how much of my time should I spend at the pre-poll?

The best answer is the one which finds the right balance between greeting constituents as they come to vote at the pre-poll and continuing to doorknock out in the electorate.

According to the experienced Bob Rogers, pre-poll voting tends to be very slow in the morning, pick up around lunchtime, slacken off in the afternoon and pick up again in the last hour before the pre-poll closes. He said there were often times when only a couple of votes would be cast at the pre-poll booth in one or two hours. But, if I spent that same one or two hours out in the electorate, I could doorknock between 10 and 20 homes! That being so, we agreed that it was better for me to continue doorknocking and call into the pre-poll at the times it was likely to be busy.

This proved to be the correct strategy. Of the total 40,434 votes in Miranda at the 1999 election, only 1,193 (less than 3%) were cast over the two weeks of pre-poll![102] There were clearly

---

[101] Each candidate received a letter from the Council's General Manager advising that his staff had been instructed to remove any campaign posters left on Council property!

[102] The percentage is much higher today. The NSW Electoral Commission now actively encourages pre-poll voting.

more votes to be gained by doorknocking than by standing around at pre-poll waiting for a trickle of voters to turn up.

The importance of being 'Barry'

Each time I did turn up to pre-poll, I'd follow a very simple routine. I'd first say 'hello' to all campaign workers present (regardless of their Party), and then have a quiet chat with our Labor campaign workers as to how 'things were going' before handing out for a while myself.

As voters arrived, I'd introduce myself, shake their hand, and ask for their support as I gave each of them my HTV. This approach was generally well received, and if anything was very good practice for the big day itself!

During one visit, very early in the pre-poll period, I arrived to hear one of our campaign workers simply say "ALP" as he handed my How to Vote to an elector on her way into the booth. It occurred to me that this approach said nothing at all about the candidate. There was no candidate called "ALP" on the voting paper, and the last name I wanted voters to hear (and remember) as they approached the ballot box itself was mine!

I quietly suggested to our worker that, as he handed my How to Vote to the next voter, he should say: "Barry Collier for Miranda", instead of just "ALP."

He looked a little stunned, responding with "but we've always done it that way!"

"Precisely," I said. "We need to take a different approach and let them know exactly *who* the Labor candidate is! We want my name to be the first in the minds of the punters as they put numbers in the boxes on the voting paper."

"Okay, if that's what you want," he replied, with a look that said I was betraying the Party or at least involving him in some act of heresy or treason.

"Yes", I said, "that way I think we'll get more votes for the ALP here in the blue-ribbon Liberal Shire."

On returning to our Campaign Office, I instructed Bob to tell all the campaign workers that we wanted them to say "Barry Collier for Miranda" or just "Barry Collier" as they handed out at the pre-poll. We agreed that's what we'd also be telling all our volunteers to say to voters at every booth on election day.

One Nation's Max Remy

If I attended the pre-poll expecting to see all other candidates from the major Parties handing out their HTVs in person, I was wrong – with one exception. The One Nation Candidate, Max Remy, was there, by himself, every time. Indeed, our workers told me he was there in his fold-up chair outside the booth, all day, every day.

On one of my very early visits to the pre-poll, my volunteer campaign worker told me she needed to leave unexpectedly and I took her place for an hour, handing out alongside Mr Remy.

I noticed his HTV pamphlet showed the number 1 in the box alongside his name, but the other five boxes were empty. In short, he was recommending that voters do not preference any other candidate but him. The votes of those who strictly followed his One Nation HTV would exhaust! That was his choice, and was perhaps understandable, given that Labor, the Liberals and the Greens had put his Party last on their own HTVs!

Political etiquette

Now, there's a kind of 'political etiquette' that candidates are courteous to each other and demonstrate a modicum of respect for one another when they meet publicly during the campaign, especially outside polling booths.

Clearly, it's not a good look for them to be seen as being at each other's throats when the voters arrive. The talk between opposing candidates outside polling booths typically takes place between the voter arrivals, and, far from involving key issues or philosophical differences, is typically innocuous and mundane.

Max Remy's How to Vote was not something I discussed with him. Rather, and during what seemed to be an interminable wait between voters arriving at the booth, we had a long, general chat about his background, his career plans, how he got interested in politics, and so on.

Regardless of his politics, he appeared to be a polite, well-spoken local young man in his early 20s. Remy departed from the general chit-chat between us only once: when he volunteered that he had no time for my Liberal Opponent, Ron Phillips. He didn't give his reasons and I resisted the urge to ask why. Who knows? His reasons weren't going to affect any preference vote by One Nation supporters for me or anyone else — or so I thought.

One Nation preferences?

On visiting the pre-poll two days later, I was astonished to see Max Remy sitting in his fold-up chair with a pile of his HTVs on his lap, numbering the empty boxes 2 to 6 with a black felt-tipped pen! He was now manually allocating preferences on his HTVs before handing them out to the pre-poll voters. From what I could see, Remy was putting 2 in the box next to my name.

Spotting this, a Liberal worker complained to Remy saying it was against the rules, whereupon the One Nation candidate told him bluntly to take his gripe to the Returning Officer! I did not get involved in the argument. Neither did I complain!

I do not know whether or not a complaint was lodged. But I do know that Remy continued on with his practice of filling in the boxes, turning up later with One Nation HTVs actually printed with his preferences in time for the big day on 27 March.

An official 'housekeeping' lesson

With the pre-poll at his Kingsway Office, candidates and campaign workers alike came into regular contact with the Miranda Returning Officer (RO), Mr Bob Rimoldi.

The RO is officially responsible for the conduct of the entire election process at the local level, everything from the calling of nominations through to the declaration of the poll after all the counting has been finalised. Our highly experienced RO made it very clear from the start that he expected all the candidates, as well as their campaign directors and workers, to follow the rules and to abide by all his directions, without exception.

Now it often happens that candidates and campaign workers deliberately ignore the rules and the RO's directions. More often than not, it's usually a part of some mindless, misguided attempt by zealots to gain some kind of 'advantage' over their Party's rival. But they certainly picked the wrong bloke if they thought they could get away with that when Mr Rimoldi was in charge!

Around 9.00AM on a rapidly warming day during the first week of pre-poll, I called in to our Campaign Office on the Kingsway after handing out at nearby Miranda Station. I was standing at the front counter with Pat Foy, when Mr Rimoldi strode in through the front door with beads of sweat on his forehead, looking very serious, if not a touch angry!

"Have you got a pair of scissors I can borrow?" he asked, before I could utter a word. Pat quickly found a pair of scissors and gave them to Mr Rimoldi, whereupon he turned sharply on his heels and strode swiftly out of our Office.

Pat and I looked at each other rather stunned, as if to say, "What was that all about?" We had our answer about five minutes later when our RO came back in holding our scissors and four of Ron Phillips' coreflutes, some with strings attached.

He said, "I told them, like I told you, not to display election posters on the fence near the pedestrian crossing! I warned the Liberals to take theirs down, but they ignored me! Now, they can collect these posters from me after the election!

"Thanks for the scissors," he said, as he put them down on the counter and left our Office with the Liberal coreflutes.

This was a first! None of our campaign workers, including some with over 40 years' experience, had ever heard of a Returning Officer actually coming into a candidate's campaign office! But this extraordinary event is easily explained.

The RO had received numerous complaints from the public about the coreflutes tied to the metal safety fencing on the median strip immediately adjacent to the major pedestrian crossing near our Campaign Office. There was no doubt that, placed where they were, these coreflutes obscured the vision of motorists and pedestrians alike, presenting a danger to those crossing the road. My campaign team had not put up any Labor coreflutes there for just that reason.

While all the coreflutes tied to the fence belonged to the Liberals, Mr Rimoldi had personally told *all* campaign managers to remove any posters belonging to them and not to put any more up there during the election campaign. Several days after his warning, a voter complained to him about the posters on the safety fence. With that, Mr Rimoldi immediately walked from his Office along the Kingsway to see for himself. He borrowed our scissors, cut the offending coreflutes down and confiscated them until after the election! Fair enough, I thought.

Here is a very simple lesson for every candidate: don't upset your Returning Officer by not following his (or her) instructions to the letter, and especially by disobeying his directions!

6.7. Doorknocking story #14: The Litmus test

Having spent much of the day doorknocking and the last hour at the pre-poll, I called into the Campaign Office for a quick catch-up with Bob Rogers and a break before heading out onto the streets again. Shortly after I arrived, Paul Smith turned up.

"How's it going out there?" Paul asked.

"The feeling's good," I replied, adding, "it all seems pretty positive out there for us," I said.

"Has the Party been doing any polling? Paul asked.

"Not that we know of. I don't think so, though," I answered.

"Well, there is *one* way to find out, apart from polling, that is! Have you doorknocked Honeysuckle Street in Jannali?" came Paul Smith's surprising question.

"Not yet, why?" I asked.

"Bill Robb said he could always tell whether he was going to win or lose by the reception he got down in Honeysuckle Street.[103] It was his 'litmus test'.

"First time he ran and won in 1979, Bill said he got a good response; when he ran and lost to Phillips in 1984, he said the feeling down in Honeysuckle Street was just terrible!

"So why don't you go and doorknock there?" Paul advised.

And that's exactly what I did. I doorknocked every house in the Street late the next day, at a time I figured most families would be home (including dad from work). The response - *the vibe,* if you like — was extraordinarily positive.

If Bill Robb's analysis was still true to form, then I was home and hosed. But I have never been one for taking things for granted, and besides, there was no polling taking place in the seat (that I knew of at least).

I didn't report back to Paul and I didn't say anything about the positive *vibe* in Honeysuckle Street to anyone else. I certainly didn't want any of our campaign workers getting overconfident or thinking I had the dreaded candidate's disease.

---

[103] Bill Robb was the Labor member for Miranda from 1978 until he was defeated by Ron Phillips in 1984.

7.   THE HOME TURN

7.1. Overdevelopment

While electricity privatisation was far and away the major campaign issue State-wide, there can be no doubt that the major local issue for the voters of Miranda was *overdevelopment*! We'd focused on this issue at the very beginning and would continue to do so until election day. In fact, it would be fair to say, that we threw everything at overdevelopment, including the kitchen sink.

A campaign case study

Having identified overdevelopment as the major issue for voters in Miranda, our strategy was deceptively simple — and I repeat it here for the sake of completeness.

We laid the blame for the 'rampant overdevelopment' where it truly belonged: The Liberal-controlled Sutherland Shire Council which was approving flats that did not comply with its own codes. We then attacked my Liberal opponent, Mr Phillips, saying he'd done nothing about the problem of "the open slather development" taking place. As the State MP responsible for Miranda, he'd simply failed his constituents by not pulling the Liberal Councillors into line, given he was in a position to do so.

All very well, you may say! It's very easy to attack your opponent for his failure to address the major problem confronting constituents; it's far better if you can back up your arguments with key facts. We could do that.

But beyond the nodding acceptance by the general public of your criticism as valid, you quickly lose credibility if you can't provide the voter with a realistic solution, or at least a workable policy alternative. So, what were Barry Collier and Labor going to do about the problem of overdevelopment in the Shire?

We had an answer! We knew exactly what we were going to do if I was elected! We'd get a State Government Inquiry underway into the Shire Council's Housing Strategy. We made this clear very early in the campaign and drove the message home towards its very end, with help from an unexpected source!

As I look back today, I am convinced that Labor's overdevelopment strategy and its implementation during the 1999 Miranda campaign, provides a classic case study of issues management for every political aspirant. It's appropriate to explain that here, as the campaign neared its end.

The front man

Before we begin our case study, I have an admission to make. As a first-time candidate with no experience, I had no idea how to structure a campaign around such a key issue— and it would be wrong of me to claim the credit for devising the basic strategy we would follow.

The credit goes to (then) Labor Shire Councillor, Paul Smith who'd later write what I consider to be the defining pamphlet of the entire 1999 campaign. Apart from writing other leaflets which incorporated the Labor stance on overdevelopment, my role as the candidate, of course, was to sell the message at every opportunity. I was lead salesperson: the front man, if you like.

In the beginning was the media

In my media debut on the 15th of December 1998, I left the voters of Miranda in no doubt that Labor would target overdevelopment in our bid to win the seat. I went so far as to say I would run on a platform "championing residents' rights against Sutherland Shire Council turning a blind eye to rampant overdevelopment."[104]

With my cards very clearly on the table 3½ months out from the election, I expected a rapid-fire response from my very experienced Liberal opponent — in the form of either an attack on me or a strident defence of his Liberal colleagues on the Council. At the very least, I could foresee a statement refuting my claims and laying the blame for overdevelopment in the Shire on the Carr Government's planning policies.

But there was no response to my first media report in the Leader from the 15-year Parliamentary veteran. Nor was there any response from the Liberal Mayor, Councillor Kevin Schreiber!

Another chance

You may think that the local Liberals chose not to respond to that first Leader article in the belief that, because it was so close to Christmas, residents were unlikely to be interested.

You might also have thought, as I initially did, that the Liberals were 'keeping their powder dry' until the timing was 'right' later in the campaign. But neither explanation rings true.

---

[104] See 4—1: *St George & Sutherland Shire Leader*, 15 December 1998.

In my Leader letter of 2 February 1999 responding to readers, I specifically called for answers from Mr Phillips and the Council to key questions about overdevelopment [7−1].

Council blamed

THE rampant overdevelopment...has nothing to do with the present State government. It is the product of a Shire Council which disregards its own Housing Strategy and fails to apply its own regulations consistently.

As the only consent authority for medium density, dual occupancy and flats...it is the Council which decides the number, mix, and quality of new dwellings throughout the Shire. Yet it has flagrantly disregarded its own housing strategy.

This set annual targets of 1,000 new dwellings in 1997 and 1998, with a mix of 30% flats and 70% other kinds of development ... But the council report reveals that it approved more than double its targets (2344 in 1997 and an estimated 2250 in 1998) and that 60% of these approvals were flats.

Disturbingly, a survey of Council statistics shows that more than 80% of new dwelling approvals do not comply with its own codes (under its Local Environment Plan).

(A named reader) points to the issue of overdevelopment being raised in the Leader in May 1998, but what has the council done about it since? What has the local MP, Mr Phillips, done about it? Why is the Council ignoring its own plans, reports and rules?

Why, as (another reader) asks, does the council appear to have one set of rules for developers and another for ratepayers?

The voters of the Shire *are* asking these questions!

The council knows it. Mr Phillips knows it.

So what about some answers?

BARRY COLLIER
Labor candidate for Miranda

---

7 − 1: St George & Sutherland Shire Leader, 2 February 1999

Here was a second chance for the Liberals to attack my stance on overdevelopment, and to argue theirs. But again, and contrary to my expectations, there was no response! For whatever reason, Ron Phillips and the Liberal Council had now, on two occasions, effectively declined to dispute what I had been publicly stating, from the very beginning, was the central issue of the entire Labor campaign in Miranda. Astonishingly, they'd left my claims about overdevelopment and who was responsible for it completely unchallenged!

This was not a case where 'silence is golden'. Far from it! Like any lawyer worth his salt, I regarded the failure by Mr Phillips and the Liberal Councillors to respond to my claims about overdevelopment in the media on two occasions as an admission on their part; one which gave me the green light to continue attacking them on the issue — something I'd continue to do with gusto out there on the ground in the electorate!

Armed with relevant statistics provided by Paul Smith, and copies of my letter to the Leader, I could honestly respond to any voter who disputed my claims about overdevelopment with:

> "If you think I'm wrong about who's responsible for all the overdevelopment you see going on in the Shire, then why hasn't your Liberal State MP, Mr Ron Phillips, or the Liberal Council, come out and said so?"

There really was no answer to that!

Ron responds ... finally

Three weeks out from election day, and almost three months after I nailed my colours to the mast, Mr Phillips publicly responded to my claims about overdevelopment for the first time in a Leader article on 9 March 1999 [7 – 2]. It's really worth analysing.

Overdevelopment sparks a row

STATE MP for Miranda Ron Phillips has urged the State Government to approve changes to Sutherland Shire Council's Local Environment Plan (LEP) to combat overdevelopment.

The Liberal candidate, seeking a re-election, assured that a Coalition government, if elected, would work with Sutherland Shire Council for a realistic plan that allowed for development in accordance with the leafy character of the Shire.

Mr Phillips said that the council's amended LEP was approved by the Minister only after the Government's State Environmental Planning Policy (SEPP) 53 was introduced which allowed overcrowding in certain areas.

"We have to get rid of SEPP 53, which forces councils to have higher density blocks," he said.

The Minister for Urban Affairs and Planning spokeswoman said SEPP 53 did not apply to Sutherland Shire Council because it had its own residential strategy. "We do not tell Sutherland Shire Council what to do. We haven't had any input into what they do down there," she said.

Barry Collier, who will contest the Miranda seat, said Mr Phillips' comments on overdevelopment were a smokescreen to take the heat off his Liberal colleagues on Sutherland Council

Mr Collier said it was the council, as the consent authority, which was responsible for overdevelopment in the Shire, not the State Government.

"The real issues are: why has the Council approved 1383 home units in 1997 and 1400 units in 1998 – five times the number allowed by its own Housing Strategy?

"And why don't 81 per cent of these approvals comply with the council's own codes?"

7 – 2: St George & Sutherland Shire Leader, 9 March 1999

In the very first paragraph, my opponent effectively admitted that overdevelopment was a very real problem. In the second, he implied that such development which *had* taken place was not in keeping with the ("leafy") character of the Shire.

Next, and in an attempt to exonerate his Liberal Council colleagues from responsibility for overdevelopment, Mr Phillips blamed State Labor Government planning policies. He quotes something most voters had never heard of—namely, SEPP 53— and was immediately slapped down by a Ministry spokeswoman who also confirmed that Shire overdevelopment was the product of Council decision-making.

That, in turn, provided me with the perfect opportunity to suggest that Ron Phillips was protecting the Liberal Council from valid criticism, and to publicly ask again, the same questions I'd asked in my earlier letter to the paper and which had remained unanswered by the Liberals for nearly three months!

At the end of the day, Ron Phillips' response in the local paper was something of a 'gift' to us in our campaign against overdevelopment—the key issue upon which we had focussed in our determined effort to return his seat of Miranda to Labor!

Some media lessons

These days, the media is not confined to newsprint as it was in Miranda in 1999. Yet, regardless of the multiple communication channels now available, there are three key lessons every political aspirant would do well to learn from Ron Phillips' handling of the overdevelopment issue in the local media.

Firstly, candidates need to respond as quickly and as decisively as possible to their opponents' media announcements involving key issues and major election commitments.

As Deputy Liberal Leader, Mr Phillips had the media contacts, the professional staff, the know-how and the resources to respond to my statements on overdevelopment swiftly. But, despite being in a far more powerful position than me, he didn't do so for three months. When he did, his response was pretty weak.

By early March, the groundswell of public opinion we'd generated on the issue of overdevelopment was showing every sign of becoming a tsunami which would swamp Mr Phillips and the Liberals on election day!

The rule of thumb is simple: don't give your opponent's claims any 'oxygen' by delaying your response. The longer you leave it, the more oxygen you give your opponent's claims and the more likely it is that you won't be able to put out the fire. In short, you may well be politically burnt by what follows!

Secondly, always take the issues your opponent raises in the media very seriously. The political graveyard is full of former high-profile MPs, and even Party Leaders, who didn't do so.

While we can speculate on all the reasons why he didn't bother to respond to me for three months, Mr Phillips' delay in doing so was clear evidence that he did not take me seriously. Maybe the explanation lies in the fact that he was being challenged by a political unknown with no public profile. At the same time, I believe that he probably ignored the advice of his own Liberal campaign team, at a time when those at the grass-roots must have known that overdevelopment was by far the major local issue.

Finally, and while the news media plays an important role in election campaigns, candidates often make the mistake of relying much too heavily upon it to get their message out to voters.

If Mr Phillips thought for one moment that the issue of overdevelopment would simply 'go away' or I'd give up on it after a couple of Leader articles or letters, he was badly mistaken! Indeed, our Labor campaign team used every opportunity and every campaign tool to drive our anti-overdevelopment message home to voters, from December 1998 until the polls closed.

Doorknocking story #15: Everyone hates the Council

From my very first day of doorknocking in December 1998, it was abundantly clear that overdevelopment was the major local issue on the minds of residents. As I went from house to house with my pamphlets, I'd end my rehearsed spiel by saying "if I can help you or your family with anything, please let me know."

Most residents simply said "OK, thanks" and went back inside. But others took the opportunity to express their concerns, and in some cases, their sheer anger, about "all the development going on in the Shire." The residents' comments typically began with:

"What about all these flats going up?"

"The developers are ruining the place!"

"I'm worried about what's happening to our Shire!"

"What are you going to do about all this overdevelopment?"

These were my cues. I did more than just agree with the resident that overdevelopment was a very real problem. I confirmed their concerns by quoting the relevant statistics I was given for flats and went on to explain that the Liberal Council was responsible for all the high-rise development they saw going on. I'd then add that 81% of flats approved by Council didn't comply with its own rules; it had even approved flats without bedroom windows!

All too often, the moment I mentioned "the Council", the floodgates opened. Countless residents were quick to respond with a host of unsubstantiated accusations and allegations, ranging from "you can't trust the Council" to "someone at the Council is on the take," or "someone up at Sutherland is getting their palm greased." Then there were some who just alleged that "the Council is corrupt and should be sacked!"[105]

I avoided commenting on (or agreeing) with such statements. In keeping with our strategy, my response was simply to say:

"Look, we really need to stop all this overdevelopment! As soon as the election's over, we need to get an *official inquiry* going into what this Liberal Council's been doing!" Adding,

"I can't understand why our local State MP for Miranda, Mr Ron Phillips, hasn't been pulling his Liberal mates on the Council into line."

These statements were usually well received by those residents who were worried about overdevelopment— even more so by

---

[105] I encouraged every resident who made allegations of corruption to take what evidence they had directly to ICAC.

residents who complained they'd had a 'bad experience' with Sutherland Council.

But the more doorknocking I did, the more I came round to the general view that 'everyone hates the Council'. While that will be seen by some as a gross exaggeration, suffice to say that, armed with supporting statistics and pamphlets, it was relatively easy to get across the idea that the Liberal-controlled Council was responsible for the all overdevelopment going on in the Shire.

Overdevelopment literature: the defining pamphlet

Not surprisingly, 'overdevelopment' occupied a prominent position in our literature from January 1999 onwards.

Each of our simple photocopied A4 pamphlets, like that shown in 4−6 included a list of 'Barry Collier's Top Priorities'. First on that list was "finding solutions to the Shire's chronic overdevelopment."

Later, in the first of our two professionally printed, black and white pamphlets we repeated and expanded on each of these priorities (in roads, health, etc.) Letterboxed across the entire Miranda electorate by volunteers, this general 'promises pamphlet' again listed my top priority as 'stopping rampant overdevelopment.' This pamphlet included a photograph of two worried seniors accompanied by yours truly looking up at units under construction in Willock Avenue, Miranda with the caption:

'Barry Collier says: "Let's stop overdevelopment in the Shire." Why has this happened? We need an Inquiry!'

But it was our second, professionally printed, black and white pamphlet, entitled 'Help Barry Collier's Stop Overdevelopment' which really said it all.

Written entirely by Labor's Paul Smith, and devoted entirely to the issue of overdevelopment, the pamphlet clearly set out what politicians often refer to as the "killer facts."

The pamphlet's front fold and inside page are shown in 7−3 and 7−4 respectively. Apart from my usual slogan, etc., the other page contains a short letter signed by me, expressing my deep concerns about overdevelopment and questioning why our local MP, Mr Ron Phillips, has been 'strangely quiet' on the issue.

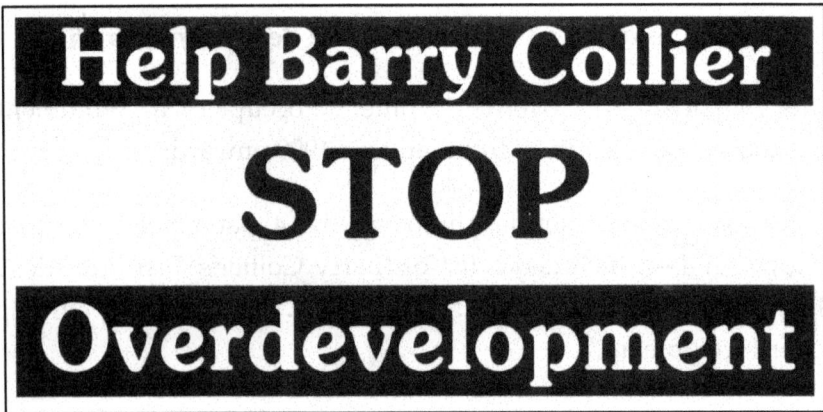

Help Barry Collier
STOP
Overdevelopment

7 − 3: The defining overdevelopment pamphlet (front fold)

One only has to look at the graphic in 7−4 and read the factually-based questions posed, to see why this pamphlet sent a very powerful message to both the Liberals and the voters. In fact, without hesitation, I regard this as the defining pamphlet of our 1999 campaign for Miranda.

Overdevelopment

Our Shire is being ruined by the Liberal controlled Council's open slather approach to development. It is well documented that they were supported in the September 1995 election by developers who objected to the previous Labor Council's "restrictive" approach to development. The Liberal controlled Council have approved more flats than any other Council in Sydney. Its own survey shows that 81% of flats don't even comply with Council's own rules.

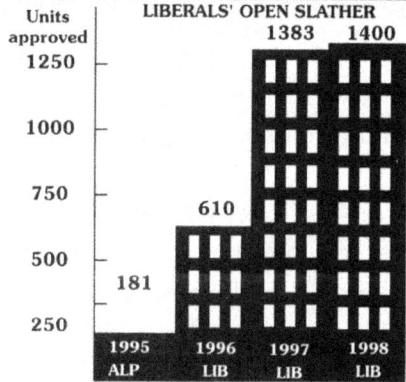

LIBERALS' OPEN SLATHER

Units approved	1995 ALP	1996 LIB	1997 LIB	1998 LIB
	181	610	1383	1400

Source: Council Report EHC 184

We need an inquiry!

Some Questions the Liberal Councillors need to answer

1. **Why** did 81% of flats approved fail to comply to Council's own rules? *(Source: Council Survey 1998)*

2. **Why** did the Liberals approve units in Willock Ave. Miranda without bedroom windows? *(Source: Council Minutes 3.10.95)*

3. **Why**, when Council's own Housing Strategy allowed for only 275 units in 1997, did they approve 1383 - five times as many? Then pass another 1400 in 1998? *(Source: Council Report EHC 184 22/2.99)*

4. **Why** did Liberal Councillors try to introduce Multi Unit Development, which would have allowed flats in all Shire residential areas? *(Source: Council Minutes 8/11/97)*

5. **Why** did they vote against telling the public the legal facts about this change? *(Source: Council Minutes 6/7.98)*

Barry Collier knows residents are concerned about overdevelopment.

INVESTIGATIONS HAVE ALREADY FOUND:

Two inquiries into specific incidents have already made unprecedented findings:

- **Justice Holland suspended Liberal Councillor Jill Deering for 2 months for failing to declare pecuniary interests as required by law. At the time she was Deputy Mayor and Chair of the Committee which dealt with developments. No other Councillor has ever been suspended in Council's history. (Source: Findings of the Pecuniary Interest Tribunal, Justice Holland)**

- **The Liberal Councillors' plan to sell a park opposite Wanda Beach to developers, before local residents could challenge their decision in the Court of Appeal was investigated by the Dept of Local Government. This resulted, for the first time ever, in a Council being ordered not to sell a park until the residents have had their day in court. (Source: Dept of Local Government Report 1998)**

7 – 4: The defining overdevelopment pamphlet (inside)

Beyond the pamphlet

Of course, not everyone who catches the train or goes to the local shops does so when candidates are handing out their pamphlets. And not every pamphlet which is letterboxed makes it through the front door —especially if it arrives around the same time as the regular mountain of junk mail.

Clearly, we needed something more to keep our key issue front and centre in the minds of Miranda voters until the close of polling. So, I designed and personally paid for 400 red coreflutes with a very simple message [7−5].

7−5: Overdevelopment Coreflute

These were nailed to telegraph poles on main roads, near railway stations and at shopping centres, and attached to garden stakes in supporters' front yards. Labor Life Member, Bob White was once again enlisted to attach 150 of the coreflutes to A-frames for use at street stalls, at pre-poll and of course, on election day itself. John McLean also used a host of these for his early morning and late afternoon "flying pickets" on the Kingsway, the Boulevarde and the Princes Highway.

We also had to remind voters of our anti-overdevelopment stance via advertising in the Leader. The problem, which had plagued us throughout the campaign, was, of course, money. Even so, we are able to pay for two simple, black and white 'stop overdevelopment' ads I designed and wrote for the last two weeks of the campaign [7−6].

7 – 6: Overdevelopment Leader advertisement, 18 March 1999

Somehow, Bob Rogers had also managed to get a small number of cheap white T-shirts printed with 'Help Barry Collier Stop Overdevelopment' and 'Vote 1 Barry Collier' (in blue, of course). We'd use these at the pre-poll and on election day itself.

Politics is like marketing: for your message to be effective, you must be consistent across all forms of publicity you decide to use — and that's exactly what we did.

7.2. Enter Mr Knowles

Political campaigns often present surprises, and a major surprise came my way in a call from Bob Rogers as I was walking between houses on the second last Monday before the election day.

> "Keep it to yourself," Bob said, "but we've got a special visitor coming to the Campaign Office tomorrow afternoon at 3 o'clock!"

> "Special visitor? Who?" I responded.

> "The Planning Minister, Craig Knowles," whispered Bob.

> "Why?" I asked, more than a little surprised.

> "He wants to talk to you about overdevelopment! See you tomorrow here at three. And remember: it's all hush, hush!" came another whispered response.

> "OK. See you tomorrow at three," I said.

Strange, I thought, I'd never previously met Mr Knowles and knew absolutely nothing about him. I'd never spoken to his staff or asked for him to visit us, and I had no idea who had. Despite our focus on overdevelopment, Bob and I had never discussed the possibility of a visit by the Planning Minister himself!

I didn't clap my hands or jump for joy as a more experienced candidate might have done. We'd been on our own since our campaign began without much help from Sussex Street, and so the thought of a visit by a Minister to Miranda itself had never even crossed my mind. Naively, I said to myself: 'Oh, well, that's good. The word has finally reached the Government that overdevelopment is a big issue down here!'

I just got on with my doorknocking, and didn't give Mr Knowles' visit another thought. I'd find out later who had arranged my appointment with him.

The Minister appears

Come 3.00PM on Tuesday, 16 March, Minister Craig Knowles arrived at our Campaign Office to be greeted by me, Bob Rogers, Paul Smith, Scott Docherty, Jim Foy, John McLean and Leader journalist, Murray Trembath (whom I'd also never met).

Introductions over, we all walked with the Minister the short distance to Willock Avenue, Miranda. This location just happened to be the scene of my photo with the worried seniors in our pamphlet. But by the time of Knowles' visit, Willock Avenue had become synonymous with overdevelopment in the Shire.

As we walked along the narrow Willock Avenue, with its unbroken row of three and four storey units, Knowles told the journalist that his visit was "not an election stunt" but followed "community outrage" about overdevelopment.

The Minister quoted relevant facts and figures, noting that in 1997 the Council had approved five times as many developments as were required under its own housing strategy.

"Sutherland Shire is a beautiful part of the world - it's a great shame to see this sort of development here. You don't see this sort of concrete streetscape on new developments anywhere else in Sydney," Mr Knowles said.[106]

The Minister added real meat to our campaign by going beyond the mere promise of a Government Inquiry to actually announce its terms of reference! And, in response to the Liberals blaming the Carr Government for overdevelopment in the Shire, Knowles pointed out:

> "I'm here to say 'I am staring you fellows down—I am going to look at your activities in your jurisdictions, and see how you are carrying out your affairs'. "[107]

Minister Knowles made the government's views on overdevelopment abundantly clear to the journalist and supporters outside the flats being built in Willock Avenue, Miranda [7–7].

---

[106] *St George & Sutherland Shire Leader*, 18 March 1999, pages 1 & 2.
[107] Ibid, page 2.

7 – 7: With Knowles, Murray Trembath & Scott Docherty

Gold!

Two days later, on 18 March, the front-page of the Leader said it all [7 – 8].

7 – 8: *The Leader, front page, 18 March 1999*

This was pure gold! Its timing, during the first week of pre-polling and less than two weeks out from election day could not have been better!

Here was public recognition that overdevelopment was a very real problem and that our call for an Inquiry now had official Government backing. In effect, we now had an election promise by the Carr Labor Government to take the Liberal Council to task about overdevelopment—something we had long been saying the sitting MP had not bothered to do.

Knowles' visit to Willock Avenue was also clear evidence that the Government was listening to *me*, the Labor candidate for Miranda and would do so in the future, should I be elected. The Leader article boosted my credibility—as a candidate, as a very real alternative to Ron Phillips, and as one who could get things done!

While the Minister's reported comments and observations mirrored those of our campaign pamphlets, there was also another bonus. I had the good fortune to have my own overdevelopment advertisement [7 — 6] in the *same* edition of the Leader — purely by accident and with no knowledge of Minister Knowles' impending appearance at the time I lodged it with the paper. An amazing coincidence by any standard!

(I couldn't help but comment on the *other* story on the Leader's front page. Perhaps the Minister's visit was prophetic: signalling an aftershock in the form of a 'political earthquake' in the Sutherland Shire on 27 March!)

One mystery solved

Knowles' planned visit was not only kept from me, but was one of the best kept secrets of our entire campaign. And, while I was, of course, grateful for the Minister's timely appearance, the mystery remained: who had arranged it?

I'd later discover that it was Paul Smith. Yep! The same Paul Smith who'd written my overdevelopment pamphlet had also personally briefed Knowles' office and arranged the visit, including our walk with Minister along 'the Street of Shame.'

When I really thought about it, who else could it have been but Paul? He had been actively fighting overdevelopment by the Council, and had vast experience, enormous political nous, and a proven track record as a fearless campaigner for all his constituents in Council's A Ward.

A modest man who always put Labor first, Paul Smith never once sought the credit he truly deserved for what was perhaps the most significant event of the entire Miranda campaign— not to mention all the overdevelopment literature he wrote for us. I was fortunate to have Paul's advice and input, and I remain grateful for his tremendous contribution to our 1999 campaign.

Direct mail?

If I thought Craig Knowles' involvement in my campaign ended with his visit, I was proven wrong the very next week.

Three days out from election day a letter from the Planning Minister appeared unexpectedly in every letterbox in the Miranda electorate. Signed, personally addressed and produced, it said, 'without using taxpayers' funds', the letter focused entirely on overdevelopment across the Shire.

After citing the appropriate statistics, the Minister's letter of 23 March 1999 clearly sheeted the responsibility for Shire overdevelopment home to both the Liberal Council and the sitting Liberal MP. Its five dot-points included:

- *'Sutherland Council is dominated by the Liberal Party and their developer mates...'; and*

- *'Liberal Candidate, Ron Phillips, has allowed Sutherland Council to get away with this overdevelopment. He supports Council's actions.'*

Craig Knowles' signed, direct mail letter to the voters of Miranda ended with:

> *"Barry Collier and the Carr Government have called on Sutherland Council to review their residential strategy to ensure that all development is sensitive to local needs."* And:

> *"P.S. Barry Collier, Labor candidate Miranda, has been fighting hard to ensure your views about overdevelopment are heard."*

The letter came completely out of the blue. I could scarcely believe it! A ministerial visit followed by one of the most effective (and most expensive) campaigning techniques of the day: direct mail to every household in Miranda! This was something we never expected, and could never have hoped for, or paid for — given our small (and by then almost exhausted) bucket of money.

Now, an experienced candidate would have concluded that, for the Party to spend the kind of money required for direct mail in a non-held seat like Miranda, its own polling must be showing that we were either getting close to knocking off Phillips or at least rapidly closing the gap. But, no! Not me!

As odd, and as naïve as it may seem, I didn't even consider the possibility that the Party had been doing any polling in Miranda. Certainly Bob Rogers had never mentioned ALP polling in the seat. Besides, given Della Bosca's lack of response to my plea for assistance three months beforehand, I'd always assumed that we were on our own so far as Sussex Street was concerned.

Grateful as I was to Craig Knowles, I never even turned my mind to what must have been obvious to every seasoned campaigner or long-term Party member: that Head Office was behind both the Minister's visit and his direct mail — somewhere!

Beyond my inexperience, I can only put my failure to join the dots down to my unshakeable belief, from the very start, that I would win Miranda — and so I never once allowed myself to become complacent and simply refused to let anything distract me. That was particularly so in the final two weeks of the campaign, when I just didn't have time to scratch myself let alone think about Labor Party polling or the source of any direct mail.

It's all in the timing

For any first-time political aspirant, one of the key lessons of our case study is the importance of timing. And, from the perspective of our campaign, the timing of Knowles' visit to Miranda and his direct mail were impeccable!

True, the Minister's visit in the second last week of our campaign came after we'd been campaigning on overdevelopment for three months. But this was the very time, with pre-poll underway and election day soon to follow, that voters were really beginning to focus on the political issues important to them and their families.

The front page of the Leader trumpeting the Minister's promise of an official Government Inquiry into Council's Housing Strategy no doubt had helped focus the voters' attention on overdevelopment in the Shire. I also believed that the prospect of such an Inquiry was a very attractive proposition to any voter who'd ever had a problem with Sutherland Shire Council — and from my doorknocking, I can tell you that there were many!

The direct mail was timed to appear in household letterboxes after the Leader had finalised its very last edition before the election. That left the Liberals with no time to respond in the popular local newspaper, let alone print and distribute any pamphlet taking the Knowles' letter to task. It is often said that in politics, "timing is everything" — and our case study provides a classic example of that!

7.3. Infrastructure and other commitments

While overdevelopment was the major local issue and electricity privatisation the major issue State-wide, there were other issues of particular concern to voters in Miranda.

Chief among these were the major local infrastructure projects which the Liberals had either failed to deliver or ignored completely. I have already mentioned the $47 million Woronora Bridge and the $36 million Bangor Bypass. But there were two other infrastructure commitments which were very much on the minds of Shire residents, involving health and the environment.

The Sutherland Hospital redevelopment

Sutherland Hospital officially opened its doors in 1958, after the community lobbied the State government for 16 years and actually raised the funds needed to build it! Not surprisingly, Shire residents love their Hospital, and, with more than 90% of its patients living locally, have a deep and abiding commitment to it.

But Mr Phillips's record left much to be desired so far as this iconic local Hospital and public health were concerned. Prior to the election of the Labor government in 1995, the last major upgrade of Sutherland Hospital took place in 1984, the year Ron was first elected to State Parliament. During his time as Minister for Health in the Fahey Liberal Government, nothing was spent on new capital works at the hospital. What's more, Mr Phillips had sought to sell off hospital land and to privatise its services, just as he had done on the mid-north coast.[108]

The privatisation of Port Macquarie Public Hospital over strong community opposition on Mr Phillips' watch had proven to be an unmitigated disaster – with calls in 1998 for the Carr Government to buy the facility back from the corporate sector.[109]

The Labor Government's $79 million commitment to redevelop The Sutherland Hospital was very well received by Shire voters and we naturally campaigned heavily upon the benefits of the project to the community at large. Whilst accentuating the positives, we had no hesitation in reminding voters that our commitment stood in sharp contrast to the failure of their sitting MP to secure funding for the project.

Our general issues pamphlet carried a brief outline of Labor's Hospital redevelopment project, accompanied by the photograph of me talking to a mother with two young children outside the Hospital's Emergency Department with the caption

---

[108] *The St George & and Sutherland Shire Leader*, 31 March 1992 and 12 August 1993.
[109] The NSW Labor Government did so in 2005.

"Barry Collier cares about the future of our Hospital."[110] But having noted his record as the last Liberal Minister for Health, voters were simply told: "We can't afford to let Ron Phillips and the Liberals get their hands on our Hospital again."

Three weeks out from election day, and in response to a letter in the Leader by the Liberal Candidate for Heathcote, Lorna Stone MP, I reminded voters of the opening of the Hospital's new Emergency Department under Labor three months earlier and of our firm commitment to the Hospital redevelopment.[111] Quoting Leader sources, I then contrasted these with Mr Phillips' poor record and unfulfilled promises, for example:

> "Mr Phillips... said that work on the new emergency wing would commence before the end of 1993, financed by public fundraising (Leader, 9/11/93). No reference to government finance."

Given his high-profile as the former Health Minister, I was surprised that there was no response to my letter from Ron Phillips himself. I do know, however, that my letter in the Leader struck a chord with older residents who remembered all the hard work that went into public fundraising and persuading the government of the day to build our Hospital in the first place.

Cronulla Tertiary Sewage Treatment Plant

The Shire prides itself on its beaches. But by the mid-1990s, these were the most heavily polluted in Sydney. Swimmers were getting sick from swimming in the filth pouring out of a nearby cliff face sewage outfall.[112] Indeed, many residents had been building

---

[110] We re-used the same photo which appears in 4–6.
[111] *Labor's record, St George and Sutherland Shire Leader*, 4 March 1999.
[112] *St George and Sutherland Shire Leader*, 6 October, 2017.

backyard pools — because a family day at the beach was a sure-fire recipe for their kids bringing home ear and other infections.

Community concerns over beach pollution culminated in the February 1995 "POO March" with more than 1,000 placard-waving protesters marching behind a makeshift coffin at Cronulla Beach, chanting "what are we going to do? Stop the poo!" The so-called POO March (P.O.O. being the acronym for *Pollution Out of the Ocean*) had put the issue on the political agenda shortly before the 1995 State election.

In January 1999, the Carr Government signed a $90 million contract to design, build and operate a world-class Tertiary Sewage Treatment Plant at Cronulla — the first of its kind in New South Wales. Labor's firm promise of delivering cleaner Shire beaches was a very welcome infrastructure commitment and certainly one we were sure to let the voters know about.

The supporting cast

Beyond the major issues and infrastructure projects, there was, of course, a raft of general Labor policy and expenditure commitments across all areas of government: everything from law and order to transport and from education to small business.

While I included these State-wide commitments in our pamphlets I did so, as best I could, with a *local focus*. Shire voters were far more interested in knowing what these general Labor commitments meant for *them*, rather than for someone living elsewhere. And so, when the Government began trumpeting its achievements in law and order (including record spending on frontline police, cracking down on gangs and longer prison sentences), I met with the Shire Police Commanders. They told me the new laws were working and crime rates in the Shire were significantly lower as a result. Good news for my campaign!

With the approval of Superintendent Henry Karpik, I was even able to get a photo showing me talking with two police officers outside Sutherland Court House for my 'general issues' pamphlet!

Now, while many State-wide policies and commitments share less of the limelight during the campaign, they can, and do, play an important role in the voting decisions of individuals and families whose lives are affected by them. You just can't ignore them.

Voters who are not 'rusted-on' to any Party, may well agree with all your major commitments, but vote for your opponent, because they do not agree with your Party's policy on one particular issue. As a candidate, you need to remember that while a certain issue may be insignificant to you in the overall scheme of things, it may be very close to some voter's heart. The rule, quite simply, is that *every* issue is important!

7.4. Newspaper ads, flies and loyalty

We'd worked very hard to get our message out to voters through letterboxing, street stalls and railway stations, not to mention my visits to thousands of front doors. But two weeks out from election day, there was one obvious avenue we hadn't gone down: advertising in the Leader.

Local rag, local ads

With voters being bombarded by the media and pre-polling underway, it made good sense for us to "put some ads in the local rag" during the last two weeks of the campaign.

While you may think that leaving newspaper ads to the last two weeks was all to do with our carefully planned strategy, that's only part of the picture. The other part was that our campaign funding cupboard was looking increasingly like Old Mother Hubbard's!

Sure, they say it pays to advertise; but advertising in the Leader did not come cheap! There was no way we could pay anyone to design our ads — and costly coloured ads were out of the question. It was down to me personally to design and write a number of simple black and white ads for each of the last four editions of the paper over the last two weeks of the campaign.

First up, we decided to do an ad featuring me as the kind of MP the people of Miranda needed: an advertisement contrasting me with the incumbent, Ron Phillips, without mentioning his name and without attacking him personally [7 — 9].

We'd follow this with other ads on our two major issues — electricity privatisation and overdevelopment in the same format.[113]

---

[113] See 5 — 6: My anti-privatisation Leader advertisement and 7 — 6: Overdevelopment Leader advertisement, 18 March 1999, respectively.

Miranda needs a Local MP who takes the time to listen to YOU and works to get you the best results. On March 27...

VOTE **1** Barry COLLIER

Labor for Miranda

"A local who listens"

For advice and postal voting r assistance:
Phone Barry Collier on 9525 8309
Or call in to **Barry's Campaign Office at
581 The Kingsway, Miranda.**
Post: PO Box 510 Miranda. 2228
e-mail: barrycollier99@hotmail.com

Authorised by Bob Rogers, PO Box 510 Miranda NSW 2228

7 – 9: Our first Leader ad – the MP Miranda needs

But Bob and I decided we also needed a larger ad listing all my major commitments in both editions of the Leader in the last week of the campaign, and so I set about writing one. But there was a problem. Yep, you guessed it; money!

While we had enough to pay for the earlier series of ads, finding enough money for our "commitments ad" was clearly going to be a problem. Even so, we were optimistic we'd be able to get around that when the time came.

But as the poet Robert Burns would have it, some unforeseen difficulty often emerges despite the "best laid schemes o' Mice and Men."[114] In our case, there were two flies in the ointment we weren't expecting but would have to deal with, and very quickly.

Two flies in the ointment

Under the NSW Labor Constitution, each State electorate has its own local administrative body—in our case, the Miranda State Electoral Council (SEC).

While the SEC provides a forum for local Branch delegates to raise and debate State issues, its key function is to support the endorsed Labor candidates for the seat through campaign activities and fundraising.

In 1999, the President of Miranda SEC was Paul Ellercamp, the man who wrote my first media release and Introductory Pamphlet in December 1998 — before promptly disappearing from our campaign in early January 1999. The SEC Secretary was Troy Bramston, who, as it turned out, had his own political agenda.

Early in the second last week of the campaign, Paul called an urgent SEC meeting at *the Tradies* on the very same night Bob and I had arranged a meeting at our Campaign Office with volunteers to finalise our all-important election day booth rosters.

I had no doubt which was the more important and went to the Campaign Office. During our meeting Bob Rogers received an angry phone call from Paul demanding that we attend the SEC

---

[114] From Burns' poem: *To a Mouse* (1785).

meeting. I refused and Bob decided to go and represent me while I continued working on the rosters.

Bob came back an hour later with the news that both Ellercamp and Bramston were livid at my lack of attendance. But worse still, the SEC had decided that it would not provide any more of its funds to support our election campaign!

This was simply outrageous, given the SEC's functions, the hard work we'd already done on a shoestring and something our volunteers and supporters had been reporting: the very positive *vibe* for us and our campaign out there on the ground.

Ellercamp and Bramston had apparently decided that we weren't going to win and spending any more SEC funds trying to defeat Phillips would just be throwing good money away. They had taken the view, it seems, that the SEC should keep what it had left in its coffers for the *next* Labor campaign for Miranda in 2003! At the time there was also some speculation that Bramston, who'd been working on Ian McManus' Heathcote campaign, wanted to be the next candidate for Miranda and was positioning himself for the job! [115]

With the President of the SEC effectively withdrawing his support when the finishing line was clearly in view, I could not help but feel a sense of betrayal. Paul well knew that, after the election and regardless of its outcome, the SEC would receive public funding which would more than compensate for our planned advertising expenditure. Even so, the prospect of getting

---

[115] Troy Bramston stood for preselection as a candidate for Sutherland Council in September 1999. He was famously beaten for top-spot on the Labor ticket on a draw out of the hat after he tied for votes with another candidate, Councillor Phil Blight.

those two 'commitments ads' in the Leader in the last week was looking particularly bleak.

'Bugger Ellercamp!' I thought. Having come this far, I wasn't about to give up that easily! These commitment ads could be the difference between winning and losing. I'd already written them, and they were ready to go. So why not see if we could pay for our Leader ads *after* the election?

With Bob having paid for the previous week's ads upfront, we'd at least established some financial relationship with the Leader already. Miranda businesses which advertised in the Leader had 30-day credit accounts, so why not us?

After a very brief discussion, Bert Rhodes and I went to the Leader's Miranda office – which just happened to be located above Ron Phillips's own office in Urunga Parade. We took our ads, and asked the clerk at the front desk if we could arrange to pay for them after the election.

Despite our well-rehearsed arguments, the answer was a flat "No!" We were told bluntly that the paper wouldn't extend credit to us; we had to pay upfront, or the advertisements wouldn't be accepted for publication at all. With the deadline for advertising copy just an hour away, it was either pay up now, or forget it!

Loyalty ... with a capital 'L'

I was virtually broke, our campaign was on its last financial legs, and as I stood at the Leader counter with Bert, the future for our commitment ads looked absolutely hopeless. My face must have said it all.

Bert Rhodes looked at me and suddenly reached into his back pocket. He opened his wallet, took out his credit card, slapped it down on the counter, said firmly to the clerk "There! Take the money out of that!"

I don't know who was more astonished: the clerk whose jaw had suddenly dropped open or me!

If ever there was an example of *A True Believer* in action it must surely have been Bert Rhodes! Here was a stunning display of loyalty and commitment, and one I shall certainly never forget. Bert was the man up the ladder I'd met at his home during my preselection quest for the Federal seat of Cook. And here he was, long retired and on the pension, digging into his life savings at a crucial time for the Labor Party and for me. That was true loyalty.

Our commitment ad, published in the last two editions of the Leader, thanks to Bert Rhodes, appears in 7−10.

I like Chinese ...

On a lighter note, Bob was approached by a salesman from The Chinese News Weekly to put an election ad in his newspaper during the last week of the campaign−for the price of a song.

Why not put our important commitments ad in the paper? Having sent off our ad to the paper, we soon received a proof copy. The only words I could make out were "Barry Collier" and "Miranda". Soon after, I took a call from the paper's staff:

"What do you think of our advertisement, Mr Collier? Do you like it?" he asked politely.

"I don't know," I replied.

"Why not?" he asked, seriously.

"I can't read it! It's all Chinese to me!" (I couldn't resist.)

He laughed, and assured me the proof was an accurate translation. I was happy with that.

My commitments ad turned up in the Chinese language newspaper alongside a similar one for Gabrielle Harrison – and amongst a ton of similar campaign ads for other candidates! It pays to advertise, so they say.

ADVERTISEMENT

Barry Collier
Labor for MIRANDA

My commitments to YOU...

✓ stopping the overdevelopment of our Shire.

✓ opposing the sell-off and privatisation of our electricity industry.

✓ supporting Labor's $79 million redevelopment of our Sutherland Hospital.

✓ continuing the crackdown on crime and the fight against drugs in the Shire.

✓ cleaning up and restoring our Shire's rivers, bays and beaches.

✓ getting our fair share of money for education, youth services and senior citizens in our Shire.

✓ increasing employment opportunities for youth in our Shire through Labor's *Jobs for the Future Plan.*

✓ completing the Woronora Bridge and Bangor By-pass on time.

BARRY COLLIER...
'a local who listens'

VOTE **1**
Barry Collier

(Authorised by Bob Rogers, PO Box 510 Miranda)

7 – 10: *Our final Leader ad - My commitments*

7.5.   Where *is* 'The Absent Member for Miranda'?

From the very start of our campaign, we sought to characterise Ron Phillips as "the absent Member for Miranda." The clear implication was that the people living in the seat had a Liberal MP who wasn't around and had no time for them — simply because his whole focus was elsewhere.

Ron on notice

Our argument, simply put, was that Mr Phillips had taken his constituents for granted and wasn't listening to them and their families. I'd said as much in the Leader on the 15th of December 1998, within a week of my endorsement as his opponent.

By then, Mr Phillips's would have gotten word that I'd been out doorknocking with my simple blue Introductory Pamphlet, and one or two of his supporters may have even provided him with a copy. The message to voters was simple: I was a local who would listen to them and was happy to help with their problems.

While "Mr Phillips...denied he was letting down his electorate" in the Leader, he was effectively on notice that, from Day 1, we'd be portraying him as the 'absent member for Miranda,' throughout the campaign and we were serious about doing so.[116]

Early campaign literature

Newspaper reports aside, I also had to characterise myself as a future MP who would not take his constituents for granted. I'd

---

[116]   See 4 − 2: *Phillips under attack over Leadership coup.*

listen to them, and, unlike the current Member, I'd put them first, ahead of all other political interests.

In a series of one-page pamphlets beginning in January 1999, I used my slogan as the heading for a column in which I sought to draw a clear distinction between my opponent and me; between the kind of MP the people of Miranda didn't want, and myself as to the kind of MP they *did* want:

> "I'm standing for Parliament on 27 March because I believe the people of Miranda need a local member who puts them first, who listens to them.
>
> "They don't want an MP who is so involved in leadership struggles, backroom party brawls and the Olympics that he has no time for them.
>
> "I believe the people of Miranda want a local who listens — one who works hard to get the best deal for their families, for their loved ones and for themselves. My priority is simple: commitment to you."[117]

These pamphlets did not specifically name Mr Phillips or the Liberal Party. Why run the risk of giving my opponent or his Party any 'oxygen' when I didn't need to? Besides, the whole purpose of the column was simply to present myself as a better alternative to the sitting MP — not to attack him personally.

---

[117] Extract from 4−6. (Hon Ron Phillips MP was also the Shadow Minister for the Olympics.)

The writing on the wall

Whatever the messages our pamphlets and my doorknocking were sending to my opponent early on, they were clearly falling on deaf ears.

If the Leader's front-page story of 11 February 1999 was true, then Mr Phillips clearly wasn't listening to the Miranda voters. The writing was on the wall [7−11].

While I had absolutely no idea that polling was taking place by either Party in Miranda, my opponent's response to the opinion poll was astonishing. It appeared to me that, despite the fact I'd been out there campaigning and despite an opinion poll showing he could lose his own seat, Mr Phillips was waiting "to enter the hot part of the campaign" before he got out on the hustings.

Phillips Rejects Horror Story

BY MURRAY TREMBATH

DEPUTY Opposition Leader Ron Phillips has played down an opinion poll which indicates he would lose his seat of Miranda as part of a Labor landside win.

Mr Phillips was one of the key figures when Kerry Chikarovski replaced Peter Collins as Opposition Leader.

The poll says the move backfired. It shows the Carr Government stretching its lead over the Coalition, and… on a two-party preferred basis…Mr Phillips' seat would fall to ALP candidate Barry Collier with a swing of 5.3 per cent.

Mr Phillips said the poll should be treated cautiously. "Our internal polling shows that we are marginally behind in a number of key seats, but that we are in there with a good chance to win the next election.

"We are yet to enter the hot part of the campaign, and I'm convinced that when people start to focus on the election campaign, and when all the messages are out there, that the election result will be very tight."

Seat lost says poll

Mr Phillips said he did not take his seat of Miranda for granted and would be campaigning hard to hold it.

Asked if it had been a mistake to dump Mr Collins, he said, "It was the overwhelming desire and position of the Parliamentary Liberal Party that they needed a change of leader.

"I'm confident they are fully supporting Kerry because they believe she will give them the best result."

7 – 11: St George & Sutherland Shire Leader, 11 February 1999

Mr Phillips ' response also sought to justify his role in removing Peter Collins from the top job and focused on selling Kerry Chikarovski as the new Liberal leader. That could only help our campaign by confirming what we had been saying all along: that Ron Phillips' interests lay elsewhere, and not in his own electorate of Miranda.

We saw Phillips' denial that he had taken his seat for granted as significant. Perhaps our strategy of portraying him as 'the absent Member for Miranda' was starting to bite.

Whether he'd actually be "campaigning hard" to hold his seat was another matter. We could only assume that meant we'd be seeing much more of Mr Phillips (or at least hearing much more about him) during the remaining six weeks of the campaign than we had to date. No doubt, time would tell.

Keeping the pressure on: Campaign literature

Regardless of his response in the Leader, it was important that we keep reminding voters that Ron Phillips wasn't listening, had taken them for granted and really was the "absent Member for Miranda" — in our literature and, if I got the chance, in the media.

By mid-February, we'd gone beyond our single-page A4 pamphlets to produce our two major pamphlets, on General Issues and on Overdevelopment. Letterboxed by campaign volunteers across the electorate, both pamphlets also sought to reinforce the importance of electing '*A Local who Listens*' — for voters would then have an *advocate* to act on their behalf.

Our 'General Issues' pamphlet noted my work as a practising barrister, then implored voters to: "Let Barry Collier be **your advocate** in State Parliament from 27 March" [7–12].

A local who listens . . .

The people of Miranda want an MP who puts them first. They don't want someone so involved with leadership struggles and party politics that he has no time for them. The people of Miranda need a *local who listens* to their concerns, then works hard to get the best results for their families, their loved ones and themselves. Barry Collier *is* that local.

Barry has lived in the Shire for 27 years. Married with 2 children, he has worked in the Shire as a teacher at Port Hacking High and as a public solicitor at Sutherland Local Court. Barry is now a practising barrister. He is well qualified to represent you.

Let Barry Collier be *your advocate* in State Parliament from 27 March.

Barry Collier
Labor for
Miranda

BARRY COLLIER'S TOP PRIORITIES FOR MIRANDA

- *Stopping rampant overdevelopment*
- *Upgrading our Sutherland Hospital*
- *Cleaner, safer beaches, rivers and bays*
- *Ensuring our fair share of funding for education, youth services and seniors*
- *Opposing the sale and privatisation of our electricity industry*
- *Continuing the police crackdown on crime*
- *Completing the Woronora Bridge and Bangor bypass*

7 – 12: Extract from our General Issues pamphlet

We also included an 'advocacy statement' in the signed letter forming part of our Overdevelopment pamphlet:

"Why has our elected Council approved more flats than any other Council in Sydney?

"Why is it that 81% of new developments approved by Council do not even comply with its own codes?

"The people want answers. The Liberals — including Ron Phillips — have been strangely quiet. Why?

"We need a local Member of Parliament prepared to ask the hard questions- and determined to get the answers.

"As your MP, I will advocate an inquiry to get to the truth."[118]

We followed our strategy of continually painting Mr Phillips as the absent member for Miranda who really wasn't listening to his

---

[118] See 7 – 4: The defining overdevelopment pamphlet (inside).

community in other pamphlets we produced, both on State-wide and on local issues.

In our *Don't Privatise Our Power* pamphlet, we noted that the privatisation of the New South Wales electricity industry by the Liberals meant higher electricity bills, blackouts and power cuts, job losses and foreign ownership of our electricity industry. But we didn't leave it there. We then went on to point out that:

> "Ron Phillips is the architect of the electricity sale. He and his Liberal mates want to sell off our power industry to pay for their costly election promises...."[119]

A very, very local issue

There was also one very local, suburb-specific, issue which provided a very firm platform upon which to draw attention to my opponent's apparent lack of action.

In late 1997, the local bus company, South-Trans, cut its services from the suburb of Gymea Bay to Gymea Village, depriving many local seniors and the disabled of easy access to their traditional local shopping centre. Residents, and the Gymea shopkeepers themselves, had been doing it tough for two years, and it seemed that Mr Phillips had not addressed the problem at all.

Here was a very real problem, identified by the politically astute Paul Smith, upon which we could campaign and, at the same time, take a well-deserved swipe at my opponent.

---

[119] See 5−4: Extract from my anti-privatisation pamphlet.

Paul wrote an excellent pamphlet headed "Barry Collier, Labor for Miranda says... Let's Restore Our Gymea Bay Buses!" After briefly setting out the history of the problem, the pamphlet screamed out:

"OUR SENIOR CITIZENS ARE REALLY SUFFERING ... AS ARE THOSE WHO RELY ON PUBLIC TRANSPORT ... AND OUR GYMEA SHOPKEEPERS ARE SUFFERING.

"They say that Ron Phillips doesn't care about this problem.

"What can *you* do? Support Barry on March 27!

"As your future Member of Parliament, Barry Collier is working hard to get the Gymea Bay Buses restored.

"Phone Barry NOW and tell him your problems with the Gymea Bay Bus Service."

This very specific, very local issue resonated throughout the entire suburb of Gymea, from households to local business owners. And, while I had absolutely no idea how I was going to fulfil my promise to restore the buses after I was elected, this very specific campaign issue must have put pressure on my Liberal opponent!

More media

While media opportunities were relatively rare during the election campaign, I took what opportunities that did present themselves to continue portraying Mr Phillips as the absent Member for Miranda who had taken his constituents for granted.

Five weeks out from election day, Alison Megarrity and I were interviewed by a journalist with the Sutherland-Menai Express, a newspaper then covering the western end of the Shire.

The subsequent article began by characterising us as 'Two first-time ALP candidates fighting to win the State seats of Menai and Miranda in the coming State election', and gave us the opportunity to comment on the key issues in our respective campaigns.[120]

I took no time in connecting overdevelopment with Mr Phillips ' apparent failure to take an interest in his electorate:

> "The Liberal councillors have favoured developers over the residents and our State MPs have looked the other way," Mr Collier said.

> Mr Collier reserved his worst criticism for his opponent who he believes has ignored his electorate in favour of factional politics. "Ron Phillips has been the absent member for Miranda," he said.

> "He's preferred factional politics in Macquarie Street and Woolloomooloo and now he's attending to the Olympics. Stephen Mutch and Peter Collins can tell you what Ron Phillips has been up to."[121]

> "What he should have been doing is working constructively within the shire to find better ways to manage shire development."

---

[120] *Sutherland-Menai Express*, Fight for vital seats, 23 February, 1999 (extracts).
[121] Woolloomooloo is the Sydney suburb in which the Liberal Party headquarters are located.

I don't know whether the highly experienced Mr Phillips was feeling the heat three weeks out from election day, but an article appearing in the Leader in early March just might have given him cause for concern, both as the sitting Miranda MP and as the Deputy Leader of the Liberal Party itself.[122]

Entitled *ALP looking for another 'Wranslide'*, journalist Murray Trembath gave the impression that, for the first time in 15 years, the seat of Miranda was about to change hands:

> It has been a long time between drinks for the ALP at the eastern end of the Sutherland Shire.
>
> However, some of the party faithfuls with long memories are quietly confident that a 15-year drought is about to break.
>
> The seat of Miranda, held since 1984 by Deputy Opposition Leader Ron Phillips, would fall to the ALP with a swing of 5.3% — a distinct possibility if several polls are an indication ...
>
> Barry Collier, the ALP candidate for Miranda at the forthcoming election, believes history can repeat itself.
>
> "Miranda is a marginal seat and very winnable," Mr Collier said.[123]

There it was in black and white! The Labor candidate saying publicly, for the very first time — and three months into the

---

[122] *St George & Sutherland Shire Leader*, 9 March 1999.

[123] Murray Trembath is said to have coined the phrase *Wranslide* after Labor Premier Neville Wran's historic 1976 victory with a 13-seat swing and the largest primary vote for any major Party in a century.

campaign—that Miranda could be won by the ALP! That was something of a bold move, especially given that I had no knowledge of any polling beyond what I read in the local newspaper.

But having made that statement off the cuff, it really worried me that I may have endangered 'the underdog status' we'd been so careful to preserve throughout the campaign. I later rationalised my statement with the notion that, regardless of whether it put any more pressure on my opponent, it might have given swinging voters some hope that things really could change in Miranda, and vote for me. After all, people generally like to be on the winning side!

While that remained to be seen, it was important to keep reminding voters that I really *was* different from my opponent; that I was around and that I would listen to them. What better way to do that with my ads in the Leader during the pre-poll in the final two weeks of the campaign?

My ads to one side, the paper also published its own series of feature articles on candidates in each of the local State seats. I was interviewed by journalist Merryn Porter, and really couldn't believe my good fortune when I read the Leader article which followed only four days out from election day [7 – 13].

I could not have wanted a more positive article! The heading alone was just gold! The content clearly laid out what Labor was really all about: tackling overdevelopment, opposing electricity privatisation, rebuilding Sutherland Hospital and fighting crime.

The article also allowed me to paint a picture of my opponent as the absent Member, more concerned with leadership struggles and back room party brawls than his constituents. I can only describe the article as every first-time candidate's media dream!

ELECTION '99 *key seats*

Pressing the flesh and prepared to lend an ear

By MERRYN PORTER

BARRY Collier's campaign material describes him as a local who listens.

He says the people of Miranda do not want a local member who is too busy with leadership struggles and party politics to leave time for their constituents.

He said a number of voters had told him during the campaign that they were disillusioned with incumbent MP Ron Phillips.

"They see him as a person who is more concerned with back room party brawls," he said.

"They see him as a bit of an absent member.

"(And) a lot of people ... have not forgotten what he did to Stephen Mutch and Peter Collins, and that is something that is around when you talk to people."

Not that Mr Collier has centred his campaign on knocking his main political opponent.

Instead, the 49-year-old father of two has been out doorknocking and handing out campaign material

■ BARRY COLLIER

at local railway stations in a bid to find out what people are concerned about.

He said the Coalition's plan to sell off Energy Australia has been the

main talking point of the campaign.

"A lot of people are concerned about the privatisation of the power industry," he said.

Over development of

the Shire is also a cause for concern.

"Over development is the major issue in this electorate .., for young and old," he said.

"I have been advocating an inquiry into (Sutherland Shire) Council and the reason why it has not been following its housing strategy."

On a positive note, Mr Collier points to Labor's record on health (they have pledged $79 million to the redevelopment of Sutherland Hospital) and crime (the introduction of tough new laws).

He also denies claims made by the Opposition in recent weeks that crime rates are up in the Shire.

Mr Collier said he had met with the commanders of Miranda and Sutherland police patrols, who had reported a "significant success" in fighting crime.

"The new knife laws and new powers to break up gangs are really working ... the police are telling me that," he said.

A barrister who specialises in criminal law, Mr Collier says convicted felons are also spending more time in jail.

7 – 13: St George & Sutherland Shire Leader, 23 March 1999

One of our senior volunteers who'd grown used to Labor defeats in Miranda and had often complained that the Leader was biased in favour of the Liberals, was very surprised indeed:

"I can't believe it!" he said. "For the first time in living memory, the Leader looks like it's endorsing a Labor candidate! What's going on?" he asked me with a smile.

The article's timing could not have been better, both because of its appearance in the last week of the campaign and because that edition also carried 'my commitments' advertisement.

Were we being unfair to Mr Phillips?

You might think that we were being unfair in labelling Mr Phillips the 'absent member for Miranda.' After all, he was the Deputy Leader of the Liberal Party and, as such, his duties required him to promote his Party's policies and support his newly installed leader, Kerry Chikarovski, as well as other Liberal candidates in an effort to win back Government.

While all that is understandable, there is also the view that his first duty as an MP was to those who elected him — namely, his constituents in the seat of Miranda. That meant being there to meet with them, listen to their issues and to act upon their concerns. Let's look at the public attention Mr Phillips gave his constituents throughout the campaign.

Ron's local campaign record

In the 3½ months before the election, I only came across my opponent on the campaign trail twice - the first in early February at the public meeting about Oyster Creek, and the second, soon afterwards, at a street stall outside Kareela shops where we agreed to come to some arrangement about railway station visits.

Despite that arrangement, I had no reports of anyone seeing Mr Phillips personally at any railway station in the electorate after his early morning encounter with the ETU at Gymea. The continued absence of my opponent was not lost on train travellers, as one commuter at Kirrawee Station in the last week of the campaign had made very clear.[124]

Of course, there were other campaign activities in which you would have expected Mr Phillips to participate personally. Yet, throughout three months of my own doorknocking, not one resident told me they'd also been visited by Mr Phillips himself. Neither did any of my campaign workers out letterboxing report seeing him doorknocking anywhere.

Mr Phillips did not attend the ballot draw at the Returning Office in early March and, unlike me, didn't personally hand out How to Votes at any time during the two weeks of the pre-poll.

My Liberal opponent was virtually nowhere to be seen on the hustings throughout the entire campaign. That could only add weight to our claim that he was 'the absent Member for Miranda.' Indeed, given media reports of negative polling, Mr Phillips' apparent lack of involvement was astonishing.

So where was Ron?

There really is only one rational answer to this question. Ron Phillips was out and about elsewhere, fulfilling his role as Deputy Leader of the State Liberals in trying to win back government for his Party. That was surely a task made much more difficult following the dumping of Peter Collins and Collins' replacement by the untried and untested Kerry Chikarovski just three months out from a general election.

---

[124] See Section 5.7: *Persistence Pays.*

This was not mere speculation. During the last week before election day, Ron Phillips was reported to have been out and about in the country seat of Northern Tablelands (in the New England Region), campaigning against Independent candidate Richard Torbay, then challenging sitting National Party Member, Ray Chappell.[125]

You can judge for yourself whether we were being unfair in claiming that Mr Phillips was not listening and was the absent MP for Miranda. You might also form the view that he had taken the seat for granted, partly because he did not take me seriously.

7.6. Last week, last day

Five days out from the election, our campaign ramped up again — something I had thought impossible the previous week.

No stone was to be left unturned, no task to be left to the last minute, no pamphlets to be left lying in the Campaign Office and of course, nothing to be taken for granted. That translated into long days for our still very enthusiastic volunteers — not to mention days of 16 hours and more for my Campaign Director, Bob Rogers, and myself. The adrenaline was clearly pumping!

Whilst the last week would see me continue all my usual campaign activities, I devoted more and more of my time to the pre-poll. With the number of early voters steadily increasing as the days rolled on, that not only made good sense, but required some adjustments to my usual routine.

It meant, for example, short bouts of *spot doorknocking* (doorknocking only for an hour or so in a chosen street here and

---

[125] Torbay went on to win the seat and later become *Speaker* from 2007 to 2011.

there) during the quieter times at the pre-poll. But, of course, there was much to do outside the advertised pre-poll times, during that frantic week.

Scully appears again ...

With five railway stations in the Miranda electorate, and five days left before election day, the mathematics were abundantly clear: we needed to hand out at one station each morning, beginning at 5.00AM on Monday at Como, the smallest station in the electorate.

As we were packing up after Como, I got a call out of the blue from Carl Scully's Office, asking if I'd like the Transport Minister to visit Miranda Railway Station with me the next day during the morning peak. Of course, I jumped at the chance and arranged to meet him at the Station entrance with volunteers at 7.00AM.

Now as a general rule, candidates aren't allowed to canvass for votes on railway platforms; they only ever did so at station entrances. This was to be different. I was delighted when Scully arrived and invited me to do a 'station walk' with him. Who was going to stop the Minister from going onto one of his station platforms to meet morning commuters?

Commuters were taken by surprise and genuinely pleased as Scully introduced himself, introduced me as our candidate and invited them to tell him personally about any problems they were having with the timetable, the station or the rail system itself.

Long serving Station Master, Peter Stearman, and his staff were absolutely delighted to have the Minister ask them how he could improve facilities for them and their customers at Miranda.

This was first-class campaigning in action. Needless to say, Carl Scully was a big hit with commuters. I have no doubt that I picked up a lot more than a handful of votes during my station walk with the Transport Minister at Miranda that morning.

God knows, Mr Collier!

Late on Tuesday afternoon, I got an unexpected call from John Goschin. He told me that Father Constantine from the local Greek Orthodox Church was visiting his home and invited me to join him and his wife, Maria-Grazia, to meet his Parish Priest. I had no hesitation in accepting.

I'd never previously met Father Constantine, but was very impressed with this humble, down to earth, and obviously very caring, man of God. We spoke of his work in his Shire-based Parish and of his hopes and prayers for the building of a Greek Orthodox Church on the Kingsway at Gymea.[126]

With the State poll just days away, discussion naturally turned to the election. We talked in very general terms about the issues facing the Shire and the challenges ahead for NSW, regardless of which side won. Father Constantine played with 'a straight bat', and did not criticise either Party or mention any candidate. But I will never forget the following exchange:

> "Father, which Party do you think is going to win the State election: Liberal or Labor?" I asked.

---

[126] Father Constantine had been conducting the Orthodox Services (Liturgy) each Sunday for his parishioners in the nearby Gymea High School hall for several years.

"I know Mr Carr is very popular," the Priest replied diplomatically.

"What about Miranda? Who do you think will win here? Mr Phillips or me?"

"God knows, Mr Collier," Father Constantine said, quietly and so very sincerely.

How do you respond to an answer like that from a very wise man of the cloth? I didn't answer because the priest was right: *He* would be the only one who knew the winner at that point.

I only knew that I had done everything I could to cross the finishing line first. I had always believed we would win. I just hoped God was on my side and didn't have other plans for me!

I enjoyed the evening with Father Constantine and my friend's family. But it occurred to me that I hadn't spoken to any of the Church leaders in the Shire during the entire campaign.

That was a flaw; something I'd overlooked, probably because I hadn't been a Churchgoer since my own Catholic Priest at Revesby was just so outraged at the fact I wanted to marry Jeanette— a Protestant—many years before! I just hoped that my oversight in not contacting any of the Churches in the electorate would not cost me votes come Saturday.

What's this? Direct mail from Bob?

Shortly after arriving at my own home from meeting Father Constantine, Jeanette handed me a letter saying "here's some mail that came today you might be interested in."

The letter, headed 'From the desk of Bob Carr, Premier of New South Wales', dated 22nd of March was addressed to 'The Collier Family'. It not only set out some of his Government's major achievements; the letter actually encouraged recipients to vote for me!

Here was the Premier, in a costly direct mail letter, telling Miranda voters that "Saturday's election will be very close," and:

"Miranda needs a strong voice in Government, and Labor's candidate Barry Collier won't be afraid to speak out on your behalf."

"...I urge you to support Barry Collier on March 27. He'll be your voice in the Labor government...

"P.S: *The Liberal's electricity policy is risky and confused. Don't risk it. Vote 1 Barry Collier.*"

Wow! This was the stuff that any first-time candidate's dreams were made of, and the timing was, of course, impeccable. While I'd had absolutely no input into the letter, absolutely no idea that it was being written or who wrote it, I was, of course, grateful to the Premier for his support.

Naïvely as it seems in hindsight, I did not read anything into the fact that Bob Carr had written to every household in the Miranda electorate supporting me.[127] I just thought how good it was to see our Premier supporting all his candidates regardless of whether he thought they would win or lose.

---

[127] These were the days before the Internet and emails had really taken hold.

But wait ... there's even more!

The direct mail letter from Minister Knowles supporting my stance on overdevelopment arrived the very next day.[128]

Direct mail from the Premier and one of his senior Ministers? I couldn't have asked for more. And yet, on Friday, 26th of March — the day before the election — a second letter from Bob Carr arrived at all homes in the electorate, again urging residents to vote for me!

This letter began with "Tomorrow your vote will decide the future of the Shire" and went on to tell residents:

> "Labor's candidate for Miranda Barry Collier cares about the future of this area, that's why he's developed a plan to look after your needs and to keep Mirada a great place to live."

> "Working together we've developed a local plan which includes... Building a better Sutherland Hospital...and... Fighting the increase in high-rise developments by the Liberal-controlled Sutherland Council."

> "In contrast, the Liberal's candidate Ron Phillips has spent all his time developing a policy to sell off our electricity industry which will lead to blackouts and higher power bills."

> "That's why I urge you to Vote 1 for Barry Collier tomorrow. He will be your voice for a better future for Miranda."

---

[128] See Section 7.2: *Direct Mail.*

Powerful stuff from a popular Premier for families to discuss at the dinner table the night before the election! It could only help get us across the line.

Gathering the troops ...

Organising and staffing polling booths on election day is an enormous undertaking and my Campaign Director, Bob Rogers, had done an outstanding job in doing so. Each of our 21 polling booths in Miranda would be fully staffed by local Labor Branch members, volunteers, family members and friends.

But the task of actually setting up the Labor material at each booth (typically in the very early hours of the morning and well before voting began at 8.00AM), managing the workers throughout the 10 hours of polling, and overseeing the scrutineering after the poll closes at 6.00PM falls to the Booth Captain.

Bob had arranged a meeting with all our Booth Captains at our Campaign Office on Thursday night, some 36 hours before the big day itself. The most obvious reason for the meeting was to provide our Booth Captains (all of whom had worked on the campaign) with all the material they needed for their respective polling booths (the How to Votes, coreflutes and so on).

The second reason was for Bob and me to thank them for all their work to date and give them some last-minute instructions. Sitting together on the stairs leading to the rear of the Campaign Office, our Booth Captains were in high spirits, determined, and looking forward to walking that last mile together "down the Miranda Road into Macquarie Street."

I told our Booth Captains, "I know it's going to be close. But we've all worked very hard together for three months, and with that little extra push on Saturday, I sincerely believe we can do it; we *can* win Miranda back for Labor!"

Their cheers were enough to tell me that they believed it too! The atmosphere was just so positive; the camaraderie overwhelming.

There were, of course, observations made and questions posed by the Booth Captains. Chief among the observations were the very encouraging *vibes* being reported by our workers at the pre-poll and the favourable feedback from my doorknocking.

Ray Plibersek reported that he had spotted Ron Phillips and spoken to him briefly in a local shop the previous day. Ray observed that "Phillips looked like the rabbit that had just seen the headlights coming!" Observations like that could only help further inspire and motivate our Booth Captains and workers on polling day.

Naturally perhaps, the first question from a Booth Captain following Ray's revelation was about polling:

"Do we know if any Labor polling has been done in Miranda?" he asked.

"Not that I know of," I replied sincerely, looking at Bob Rogers who nodded in agreement. "So, it seems we're still the underdogs," I said.

"OK, that's good," the Booth Captain responded. And there the matter ended.

My response was genuine. I had no knowledge of any polling being done beyond that reported in the Leader in early February.[129] If polling was being done by Labor, nobody had told me; certainly not my Campaign Director. And Head Office would have told Bob, surely! I thought.

Bob finished up by giving our Booth Captains some final instructions and some last-minute requests. My only request was for them to ensure that their booth workers said "Barry Collier for Miranda" or just "Barry Collier" as they handed out my HTV.

I explained my reasoning to the Booth Captains as I had to our workers at the pre-poll earlier.[130] It made good sense to me. The last thing we wanted voters to hear before they went into the booth was my name.

I could see that some of the older Members who for many years had simply been saying: "ALP" each time they handed out a Labor HTV weren't comfortable with my instruction, but they agreed to follow it in the interests of "Party unity."

Speaking of Party unity, I was surprised to see the reappearance of Paul Ellercamp at the Booth Captain's meeting. Despite his initial support and promised involvement, Paul had been missing in action for three months — apart from his recent cut to our SEC funding. In the end, it was Bob, rather than Paul, who alone had carried almost all Campaign Director's workload!

---

[129] See 7 – 11: St George & Sutherland Shire Leader, 11 February 1999.
[130] See Section 6.6: The importance of being 'Barry'.

Last day: Jannali and pre-poll

I woke well before dawn on Friday, the 26th of March. The last day of campaigning had arrived. I was determined to make the most of it, as I had every other day since I was endorsed as the candidate.

I had always been driven by the belief that, with hard work, we would win Miranda. Yet there was always that niggling thought in the back of my mind how dreadful it would be to lose by one or two votes, all for want of that little extra effort. That thought spurred me on, and so I was up and off for a 5.00AM start at Jannali, the last of our railway stations.

Somewhat unusually, we handed out 'packages' of five pamphlets to each commuter. Jeanette and her stepfather, Ernie Grinstead, had spent four hours the previous night folding every leftover A4 pamphlet we could find at home and making up these packages. There was clearly no point in having any pamphlets left over!

Commuters were generally polite and had no hesitation in taking the packages. We'd certainly provided them with plenty of reading material for their long train trip ahead!

We wrapped up our last station visit around 8.30AM, less than 24 hours from election day. We'd received a very positive response from commuters at every railway station throughout the week — and Jannali was no exception. It seemed to me that change was in the air, and if the response at Jannali translated into votes the next day, we'd be on our way to Macquarie Street.

But of course, it was too early to count our chickens, and so, after a quick bite to eat at home, I was off to the Miranda pre-poll. With the number of early voters picking up towards the end of the final week, it made good sense that I should spend the remainder of the last day handing out there personally.

Apart from Max Remy, I was the only other candidate who turned up to the pre-poll booth that day. Early voters seemed genuinely pleased to see a candidate from one of the major Parties there handing out and more than one remarked that I'd actually doorknocked them. As with Jannali station earlier, the response towards me at the pre-poll was very positive! But again, I reminded myself, that it's not over until it's over!

Bolters and long-shots

I took short breaks form the pre-poll throughout the day to call in to our Campaign Office nearby.

On that last day, and under Bob's experienced direction, the old run-down shop was just a hive of activity. The Office front door was even propped open for all the enthusiastic volunteers coming and going, running errands, arranging to drive the elderly and disabled voters to pre-poll and picking up all those left-over pamphlets to deposit in letterboxes of their choice.

After pre-poll closed, I returned to the Campaign Office for a cuppa and catch up with Bob. Everything was ready to go. Branch members, volunteers and supporters had worked very hard, and Bob and I had worked ourselves into the ground. There was really nothing more we could have done during the campaign on our shoestring budget. Tomorrow, the voters of Miranda would decide whether we'd done enough to secure their support for a Labor MP after 15 years in the political wilderness.

Naturally, the discussion turned to what we'd be doing after the polls closed at 6.00PM the following day. I'd left all those arrangements to Bob. Sitting by ourselves in the Campaign Office, we had one of those conversations which demonstrated my inexperience:

"What's happening tomorrow night?" I asked Bob.

"The scrutineers will phone in the results to me, starting about 6.30 for the smaller booths. Donna Spears and her friend Charles have set up their computer and they'll be feeding the results into it as they come in.[131] We'll have a good idea how we're going by 7 or 7.15," Bob said.

"OK," I replied. "Once I've finished at Port Hacking High, I'll go home, have a quick shower and get back here with Jeanette and Michael as soon as we can."[132]

"Good," he said. "After we know the result, we're all going to *the Tradies* for a get-together and a celebration.

Surprised, I said "I thought we were doing that here! I really want to thank all our workers and celebrate right here, where all the work was done! What's changed?"

"The media has taken a great interest in the result here, because of Phillips' electricity privatisation. There'll be TV cameras at *the Tradies* as part of the election coverage."

"News to me! Why can't they come here?" I asked.

---

131 Donna Spears was a brilliant criminal lawyer with whom I'd worked at the Office of the Director of Pubic Prosecutions. Sadly, she passed away in 2013.

132 Port Hacking High School was the last booth I'd planned to visit on election day.

"It's too late! It's already arranged! I reckon that after months of working here, all our Members and supporters deserve a better place to celebrate!"

I couldn't argue with that! But I couldn't help but ask, "so why all the media interest now? Except for the Leader, they haven't really shown any interest in what's been going on down here for last three months!"

"One of the Channel 9 people I spoke to said that Miranda is a bolter!" came the unexpected reply.

"What's a bolter?" I asked, never having heard the term.

"It means an unexpected winner. They're expecting you to win!" said Bob with a smile.

"How come? There hasn't been any Labor polling that we know of, has there? What's Head Office saying about all this?"

"No internal polling. Nothing in the Herald or the Tele about Miranda that I know of! I rang Della Bosca today and asked him what he thought of our chances — and he just said 'we were a long shot'!"

"Well, there you go! We're still the underdog! Typical bloody media!" I said.

"Go straight home; get a good night's sleep. You'll need it. Tomorrow's going to be very hot! I might see you at one of the booths. If not, I'll see you tomorrow night…and good luck!

"To both of us, Bob. Thanks for everything," I said, leaving him to lock up our old Campaign Office.

7.7. Last doorknocking story (#16)

I didn't go straight home. Oh, no! With an hour of daylight-saving time left, I decided to do some doorknocking in a quiet Sylvania Heights street. Driven by the thought that 'every single vote counts', I just couldn't resist!

Not everyone I doorknocked was as supportive of me as the residents of Honeysuckle Street. While some were very positive, and most were very polite, there was one notable exception in the gathering twilight.

Having knocked on a door, and waited for some time, I heard a gruff male voice call out "yeah!" from above. Standing back, I looked up to see a man who appeared to be in his 60s, with both hands on the balcony railing.

"What the hell do you want?" he asked, angrily.

"I'm Barry Collier, I..."

"I know who you are!" he said, cutting me off. "What are you doing around here, you arsehole?"

"I'm seeking your support tomorrow" I responded, knowing I obviously didn't have it.

"I'm not voting for a piece of shit like you" he said.

"That's OK. It's a democracy" I responded. "But there's no need for the language!"

"Bullshit, there isn't!", he yelled. "You're wasting your time!"

"Well, I obviously am here" I said, determined to remain calm.

"Nobody with half a brain would vote for you. You are a fucken' idiot if you think you are going to win. This is a Liberal seat: L-I-B-E-R-A-L ...Liberal! Get it?" he said.

"Yeah", I said, "I know I'm the underdog, but we'll see how I go tomorrow."

"You won't get elected, you loser!" came the stern reply.

"Well, if I do get elected, I'll work for you, whether you voted for me or not!" I said, knowing full well the extreme rusted-on Libs hated that line.

"What are you going to do for *me*?" he yelled.

"What do you *want* me to do for you?" I asked, knowing from experience now, that people who asked that question usually had no specific idea of what they wanted.

"I just want you to fuck off!" he yelled, seemingly even more infuriated with my question.

"OK" I said, leaving and walking to the next house, as the man slammed his balcony door and went inside.

Undaunted, I continued doorknocking in the same street until darkness fell and I began making my way back to my car — a route which took me past that angry man's house once again. I simply couldn't resist popping the last handful of my pamphlets into his letterbox as I went by.

The response from the man on the balcony was by far the worst I'd encountered in 3½ solid months of doorknocking. But it was also timely reminder that, regardless of the positive litmus test in Honeysuckle Street and my strong belief we would win, we still had to fight for every single vote until the close of the polls at 6.00PM the next day.

Perhaps the man on the balcony did me a favour, if only by adding just that little bit more to my determination to be first across the line!

PART C: ELECTION 1999

8. THE BIG DAY FINALLY ARRIVES

8.1. Kicking off on home turf: Kareela

Saturday, 27th of March 1999, 5.00AM. It was hard to believe the big day had finally arrived. And it was going to be yet another stinker — and yet another learning experience!

I'd slept remarkably well, drifting off sometime around 10.00PM the previous night, visualising, as I had every night for months, all those votes going into that giant ballot box with my name on it. Belief aside, I lay there for a moment with a remarkable sense of calm knowing that, with the help of my fabulous campaign team, I had done everything I possibly could over the last 3½ months to win Miranda.

But this was no time to be distracted by the morning radio or to be trawling through the newspapers looking for optimistic predictions about the future of the Carr Labor Government. It was time to get going. It was up, into the shower and a quick breakfast.

Despite the prospect of being on my feet at polling booths for 10 hours straight on what would be another very hot day, I didn't give a moment's thought to what I'd be wearing. I dressed in my black suit, white shirt and tie — the outfit matching exactly my photo on my coreflutes; the same outfit I'd worn handing out at every early morning railway station.

I'd always followed the principle that if I wanted to be an MP, I had to look the part. Besides, if my dress matched my photo on my coreflutes, voters would have no problem spotting me at each of the polling booths I'd planned to visit.

The plan

The Miranda electorate comprised 21 polling booths, the majority of which were located in public school halls, with several in church halls and one in a retirement village. And, with the benefit of local experience and the helpful estimates provided by the Returning Officer, we had a very good idea of the number of voters likely to attend each of the booths on election day. The numbers varied from under 200 to around 3,500.

For the candidate, it is both physically impossible and uneconomical (if not insane) to attempt to visit every booth during the 10 hours the polls are open. From an Economics viewpoint, the aim of visiting the polling booths is to maximize your vote per unit of time. At the very least, that means being seen by as many voters as possible for each hour you put in at each booth. That was, and remains, the conventional wisdom.

This common-sense reasoning could only mean one thing — turning up at each of the larger polling booths in the Miranda electorate and spending an hour or two greeting voters, handing them my How to Vote (HTV), and personally asking them for their support, before moving on to the next booth. The order in which I chose to attend these booths was up to me. My list had me starting off at my home booth at Kareela Public School before the polls at 8.00AM and finishing at the Port Hacking High School booth when the polls closed at 6.00PM.

My family would inevitably play its role on the big day with Jeanette and our daughter Sarah rostered on at Kareela later in the morning and our son Michael, getting up his hours behind the wheel by driving me from booth to booth in our campaign car (displaying his L-plates) — and handing out with me to give our Labor booth workers a break.

Michael had done it all during the campaign— everything from letterboxing with Jeanette and helping Big John set up his 'flying pickets' to working on the pre-poll, and, given his gift for IT, setting up our donated computers in the Campaign Office. So when he came up with the idea of driving me around on the big day, how could I say "no"?

Kareela booth

Having arranged for Michael to pick me up later, I walked the short distance from my home to the Kareela booth.

I remember standing for a moment, opposite the School at the signalised pedestrian crossing, momentarily taken aback, as I waited to cross Freya Street.[133] For any first-time political aspirant, I can tell you that seeing a row of your own coreflutes tied to a school fence and nailed to garden stakes outside your very first polling booth on your first election day is something very special indeed. Wow!

But reality soon hits home. After months of hard slog, the big day had finally arrived! Decision time! My future was now in the

---

[133] This was the same pedestrian crossing outside my kid's School that Ron Phillips told me couldn't be done years before.

hands of thousands of voters. The ultimate four-year job interview was just about to begin!

I arrived at the Kareela booth around 7.30AM, just as the first of the early voters were lining up outside the School hall to have their say at the ballot box. John McCracken and other Branch members had been at the booth since 5.30AM and had done a great job in setting up all the Labor material — including several *Bob Carr: Achieving More for NSW* coreflutes sent out by Head Office at the last minute.

While there were many more of my general 'Barry Collier for Miranda' coreflutes on display, there was also our 'Help Barry Collier Stop Overdevelopment' and the 'Don't Privatise Our Power' coreflutes in prominent positions. And, to emphasise the fact that I actually lived in the same suburb as most of the voters attending that booth, I'd also had two blue and white coreflutes made up with 'Vote 1 Barry Collier: A <u>Kareela</u> Local who Listens!' Who knows? Some voters might actually like the idea of having their State MP living in the same suburb or maybe even in the same street!

Branch members were dressed in the blue and white *Help Barry Collier Stop Overdevelopment* T-shirts. We only had two of these for each of the 21 booths. Despite the heat of the day, these same two T-shirts had to be worn by other booth workers rostered on later.

Present too, was a feature of every local Labor stall in living memory: the ubiquitous card table, with pamphlets, my HTVs, and information for absentee voters. But amongst these was something I hadn't previously seen: a green pamphlet reading:

"Thinking of Voting 1 *Democrats* but want to stop Mrs Chikarovski's power sell-off?

"Give your Preference 2 to Barry Collier."

Conscious of the importance of every vote, I thought that was very clever, given there was only one Democrat coreflute on display and no one was there handing out for that Party.[134]

The Liberals had also been busy setting up Ron Phillips' coreflutes and their Party bunting since early morning. The Greens, too, had been busy, despite arriving much later at the booth than both major Parties (as usual).

As I was having a quick chat to John, I saw an older man roll up, breathing heavily and struggling with a box of One Nation How to Votes. On arrival, he plonked himself down heavily into the fold-up chair he'd also been carrying up the steep Freya Street hill to the school driveway entrance. While he was obviously not a well man, you had to admire his commitment!

Grabbing a pile of my own HTVs, I went to the school gate ready to start and, on the way, introduced myself to the booth workers from the other Parties. That's not only courteous; it's also good PR, if not plain common sense. Like our own booth workers, other booth workers would be out there all day in the hot sun too — and it's important that all booth workers be as pleasant and polite to each other as possible. After all, and despite our political differences, we weren't at war: we live in a democracy and that

---

[134] These Labor pamphlets had been a very late delivery from Head Office and were being distributed on the day to our candidates throughout the State.

means respecting the rights of others holding views different to our own.

When handing out at a polling booth, there's nothing worse than being harangued by zealots from another Party wanting to make a nuisance of themselves by starting an argument over some issue or complain over some trivial matter as if the entire election outcome and the survival of mankind depended upon it! Regardless of their Party affiliations, most booth workers don't want any unnecessary hassle and are happy to simply 'get on' with the other side. It's not uncommon to find them chatting with each other about everything *but* politics in those inevitable gaps between voters arriving at the booth.

From what I saw, and from all reports later, Kareela booth workers on all sides "got on well together" throughout the day. The Labor and Liberal booth workers were even helpful and sympathetic to the One Nation man: picking up the pile of HTVs he was continually dropping and handing them back to him, saving the old fellow the trouble of getting out of his fold-up chair to retrieve them.

Handing out ... personally

Soon after I arrived, the Official in charge of the Kareela booth appeared and began putting up signs directing voters to the school hall.

Having introduced herself to nearby booth workers and me, she laid down the law regarding the minimum distance we all had to maintain from the school hall when handing out our HTVs. That meant going no closer to the polling booth than the driveway gate, some 30 metres from the hall away along the driveway. The distance between the two was, if you like, an official 'campaign no-go zone'.

I stood in the middle of the driveway on the very edge of the Presiding Officer's imaginary line introducing myself to voters, shaking their hands, giving them my HTV (if they hadn't already been given one by our workers) and saying "I'm asking you for your support today."

I was really encouraged by the fact that many voters were greeting me with "Hello Barry," and reminding me that we'd already met at Jannali station or the shops or at their front door.

Some voters took the opportunity to mention my major election commitments with comments including "you've got to stop this overdevelopment, Barry" and "for God's sake, don't let the bastards sell off our power stations!" Others were more specific, telling me what they wanted me to do for them locally: "if you get in, please do something about the Five Ways."[135]

Whilst most voters gave no indication as to how they were voting, a significant number said they were voting for me. Some indicated that with a knowing wink, some with an "OK"; others with an encouraging "you'll be right, mate!"

As was to be expected, there were voters who declined to take my HTV — mostly with a polite "no thanks" or with a shake of the head. A few abruptly said "no way," or told me they "hated Labor," or "always voted Liberal," or "couldn't vote for Carr" or were "supporting Pauline" or "only ever voted Greens."

---

[135] At the time, the *Miranda Five Ways* was a very large roundabout which was later proven to be the State's *No 1 blackspot* for minor accidents.

Knowing that winning or losing the election might ultimately come down to preferences, I asked those who told me they were "voting for the Greens" (and those who had obviously only taken the Greens HTV from booth workers) to consider giving their second preference to me. This made eminent sense given the fact my name was second on the ballot paper, immediately below that of the Greens candidate.[136]

But of course, election day wouldn't be election day without some complaint by some Party hack. From time to time, and in an effort to meet as many voters coming through the wide gate as possible, I'd inadvertently took one or two steps backwards, crossing the Presiding Officer's imaginary 30 metre boundary line into the 'campaign no-go zone.' And who, from the other Parties, complained the loudest about my minor transgression? You guessed it! The One Nation man in the fold-up chair whose pamphlets we were constantly retrieving from the ground!

Some surprises

As encouraging as my visit to my home booth was, it was not without several surprises.

Firstly, and very early on, I was astonished to hear one older voter tell me he'd "never seen a politician shaking hands on election day before!" I don't know how long he'd been living in Kareela, but perhaps his comment was just another reflection of the fact that Miranda had for too long been regarded as a safe Liberal seat and had been taken for granted by my opponent.

---

[136] The problem with the Greens votes is that it they tend to *exhaust*. That is, they *only* vote for the Greens and do not allocate any 2nd preference.

In any event and whatever the reason, standing there, shaking hands with voters appeared to be a big plus for me. At least the old One Nation fellow and the Young Liberals handing out for Mr Phillips seemed to think so. Clearly, political aspirants should never underestimate the power of a genuinely friendly handshake with voters at the polling booth on election day!

A second surprise was the manner in which several voters approached the ballot box. While the vast majority of voters walked directly towards me on their way to the school hall, I was somewhat puzzled to see a couple of Asian heritage actually stop on the kerb, three metres outside the school gate, and take a long look at me. They then looked down at my HTV they'd been given by our booth workers, then at my coreflute, and then at me again, looked down at my HTV once more, nodded to each other, looked at me with a smile and the male of the pair said, "ah!"

The penny dropped. They had been comparing me with my photograph on my coreflute and on my HTV, and had assured themselves it really was *me*: the same person on the Labor material as the one standing there in the flesh. I shook their hands and asked for their vote. They both appeared very pleased but did not say anything. The man simply nodded and as he pointed to my photograph in the Chinese newspaper he also held in his hand![137] I responded with a nod and off they went to the School hall, talking happily to each other in their own language.

While I had no doubt that they'd go in and vote for me, there were some lessons in all this. On the one hand, the appearance, at the Kareela booth, of the ad we'd put in the Chinese newspaper could only be taken as yet another endorsement of Bob Roger's

---

[137] See Section 7.4: *I like Chinese*.

experience and attention to detail. On the other hand, and more importantly, the appearance of the Asian couple who obviously could not speak English was a clear signal that the ethnic and cultural composition of the Shire was changing.

The third surprise came in the form of an unnecessarily offensive response from a Kareela resident whom I thought I knew reasonably well.

If you are handing out in your own suburb on election day — whether for yourself or for some other candidate — you naturally expect to meet friends, neighbours and other residents you know at the polling booth. You greet them using their first name, and as with every other voter, you ask them to vote for you — because if you don't, you may not get it! The reason is quite simple: they may well believe that, because they know you personally (perhaps for a long time) and you haven't bothered to ask them for it, you are simply taking their vote for granted!

So, when the mother of one of my daughter's primary school friends approached me, I greeted her by name, handed her my HTV and asked for her support. She snatched it from my hand, screwed up my pamphlet in front of my face, threw it at my feet and, without a word, stormed off towards the polling booth!

I was dumbfounded! This was something I'd never encountered at the thousands of homes I'd doorknocked, or at any of the railway stations or street stalls I'd attended. I'd known this lady throughout virtually all of my daughters' primary school years. I'd spoken to her at the local shops and she always seemed friendly to me and my family.

What made this episode even more bewildering was the fact that, several days earlier, I'd actually called in at her Kareela home during some late afternoon doorknocking, where we'd had what I thought was a very friendly chat.

But this was no time to stand there reflecting on the lady's behaviour, which was just so completely out of character. I just had to continue handing out as if nothing had happened!

Suffice to say, I never saw the lady again, anywhere. Even to this day, I do not know the underlying reason for her behaviour at the polling booth. Perhaps I'll never know what had happened — or what had been said by some third party — between our seemingly friendly discussion at her front door several days earlier and her arrival at the polling booth. But I do know that, for whatever reason, she and her family moved out of Kareela several months later.

Some special locals

At every polling booth there'll always be one or two important locals or well-known public figures turning up to vote. And I had two turn up at the Kareela booth on the big day.

Around 8.30AM, I noticed the local Magistrate arrive to vote. I had appeared before him at the Sutherland Court House for years as the Legal Aid Duty Solicitor representing clients facing criminal charges.

As he approached the booth, he took a HTV from every booth worker, regardless of the Party they represented. I greeted him using his first name and asked for his support, even though I really did not expect any response or commitment from him (one way or the other).

Having gone in and voted, the Magistrate returned back through the School gate carrying all the literature he'd taken in. He gave me back my HTV, telling me "it's better for the environment." I wasn't offended. Indeed, as a lawyer who had appeared before him in Court on a daily basis, it was important that there had been no suggestion of bias so far as his decisions were concerned.

To make the point perhaps, he then walked over to booth workers from each of the other Parties and gave them back their HTVs as well. Clearly, and as in his Court, the Magistrate wanted to give all and sundry the impression that he was always impartial. He certainly didn't want any gossip around about him being too friendly with any member of a political party. Call it 'judicial independence' if you like.

And, while he gave no indication as to how he voted, I wouldn't have bet my house on him voting for me! The lesson here is that you cannot expect people to tell you how they are going to vote or if they are going to vote for you, even if you know them very well!

Local Magistrate aside, Kareela was also home to a top international tennis player of the 1930s and 1940s who'd actually competed in four Grand Slam doubles finals (winning the US Open) and had represented Australia in the Davis Cup. He regularly drove past my home and, if he saw me in my front yard, often stopped for a quick chat. Talking to him during the election campaign however, he was rather cynical about my candidature and I got the distinct impression he thought I was wasting my time in running for Parliament.

As I stood handing out on election day, I saw our still very fit, former tennis star walk across the pedestrian crossing to the school, to be presented with my HTV by my booth workers. Walking a little further down the hill towards the school gate where I was handing out, our aging star turned a few heads when he called out loudly "where's Barry?" — in a tone and with an emphasis clearly suggesting that I should be there in person, but I wasn't!

I yelled back just as loudly, "I'm over here, Bill!" Clearly, he hadn't seen me! Looking a little taken aback (if not a little embarrassed) at being caught out, and not wanting to look foolish, he called back, "good to see you, Barry!"

A casual observer would have thought that while this man tried to make mileage out of his belief that I hadn't even bothered to turn up at the booth, his attempt to do so had backfired badly.

Yet, I believe that Bill's calling out had two positives for me. On the one hand, it drew voters' attention to the fact that I really *was* there at the polling booth. Indeed, one of the voters about to take my HTV embarrassed the Liberal booth workers when he yelled out, "Barry's here, but where's Ron?"

On the other hand, the former tennis star saying it was good to see me, sounded like something of an endorsement — when in reality it was more about saving face than anything else.

Of course, I'll never know just how Bill voted. But again, it would have been reckless of me to put my house on the line in the expectation that he voted for me. Even so, and for years afterwards, he'd still often stop and chat if he saw me as he drove past my home.

There was never any mention of election day by either of us — nor should there have been. He and I both knew that, like tennis at the top level, politics is tough and competitive. But you must accept the umpire's decision and once the game is over, you have to put the result behind you and move on!

One special vote

As a first-time candidate, it's very easy to get caught up in the election-day frenzy with its mix of excitement, tension, anxiety and anticipation. Indeed, you can be so focused on getting as many votes as possible that you forget about the one vote you will most assuredly get: your own!

As silly as it seems, it's not unknown for candidates to cop a fine from the NSW Electoral Commission for failing to vote on their big day! I well recall the last piece of advice my very experienced Campaign Director, Bob Rogers, gave me about election day: "...Oh...and Barry, don't forget to vote yourself!"

I didn't forget, but I chose my moment carefully: waiting for a distinct lull in the number of voters tuning up, and then handing all but one of my HTVs to a Labor worker before crossing the Presiding Officer's imaginary line and walking the 30 metres along the driveway to the polling booth in the school hall.[138]

The driveway at Kareela was lined with those enduring School P&C fundraising activities which characterise every election day: the sausage sizzle, the cake-stall, the giant raffle, the book stall and even the face painting. On my way to the booth, I stopped and spoke briefly to the parents and grandparents operating the stalls, many of whom I knew personally, and I promised to grab a sausage sandwich on my way back out.

As tempting as it was to ask for their vote or support, I couldn't. It was really against the rules. I was in the official 'campaign no-go zone'. That meant, no handing out; no shaking

---

[138] I needed one HTV because it also contained the Labor ticket for the NSW Upper House. As usual, an election for the *NSW Legislative Council* was also being held the same day as a general election for the *NSW Legislative Assembly*.

hands; no canvassing for votes; no Labor or Liberal T-shirts, hats or badges, or anything to suggest you are trying to persuade people to vote for you or for your Party. The same is true for the polling booth itself. It's sacred territory!

Having entered the hall with my one Labor HTV and having my name marked off the Miranda Electorate Roll, I duly voted for myself. There was something surreal about seeing your own name on the official ballot paper, putting the number 1 beside it, and then stuffing the completed ballot paper in the ballot box!

'Yes!' I told myself, 'this really *was* happening'. And, for one fleeting moment, I reflected that my vote was just as important as everyone else's: mine counted too! Indeed, mine was one of the many votes I'd visualised going into that big ballot box with my name on it, before dozing off every night for months.

'Claytons campaigning'

After voting and on my way back to the school gate, I stopped and, as promised, ordered a sausage sandwich and a drink at the P&C stall in the 'campaign no go zone'.

While I didn't ask any of the school volunteers to vote for me, and didn't think that buying a sausage sandwich would help me in that regard, the parents and grandparents seemed to appreciate the fact that I was spending time with them on my big day. And it certainly didn't do my candidacy any harm for me to be seen supporting my local school by voters on their way into the booth!

I stood with my sausage sandwich facing the school entrance so that any voter doing the 30-metre walk on the narrow driveway to the polling booth couldn't help but see me. As they passed by, many said: "Hello Barry" or, "Good to see you", or wished me good luck. I figured that it might also help my prospects at the booth if the last (and only) candidate they saw before going in to vote was me! It was a 'Claytons Campaign' — the kind of campaign you have when you're not campaigning!

I thought about buying another sausage sandwich, but decided against it. After all, there were many more school polling booths to visit on the day, and I'd be tempted to buy a sausage sandwich and drink at most of them!

And so, I was soon back at the school gate, standing on that invisible demarcation line, shaking hands and handing out my HTVs until, during a lull in voter traffic and in keeping with my timetable, it was time to move on to another booth.

The early vibe

To me at least, *the vibe* during my first polling booth visit of the day was overwhelmingly positive for us. My son Michael agreed.

But it's so easy for candidates to get carried away, especially early on election day. You need to remember that the booth workers helping you will also be picking up *the vibe* — and it's worth getting their take on how things are going.

Before heading off to our next booth, I had a quick chat to John, who had worked on the Kareela booth for Labor candidates over many elections. According to John, "It's much better than it usually is for us here!" Good news!

It was also as abundantly clear to John, as it was to Michael and me, that *overdevelopment* was the key issue for voters in Kareela. In choosing this as our major platform, we'd been right all along!

8.2. Moving on ... Gymea Bay and Sylvania Heights

Having thanked our workers, Michael and I headed off in our campaign car to the Gymea Bay Public School booth. With 3,500 voters, this was the largest booth in the Miranda electorate.

While our campaign car had always attracted attention throughout the campaign, it was something else again on election day, when the immediate focus was voting itself! With Michael in the driver's seat and the Barry Collier coreflutes on the car's roof, the response was nothing short of phenomenal—with waves and shouts of approval, people giving us the thumbs up, pointing and laughing, and yelling encouragement everywhere along the route. I was also waving out of the front passenger window to the people we passed, and getting positive responses including "Yay, Bazza!"

Our old Mitsubishi Magna was doing us proud! It certainly didn't pass unnoticed by shoppers in the busy Gymea retail strip or by voters heading towards Gymea Bay Public School as we drove up and down outside the booth, looking for a parking spot!

When we finally got out of the old Magna, one voter saw Michael's L-Plates on the back of the car and called out laughingly to his mate on the other side of the road, "Look! A learner politician with a learner driver!" Michael and I both laughed too. Our mobile advertising was proving to be a real bonus on the big day too!

Gymea Bay

Standing beside the car, putting on my suit coat, I was astonished at the plethora of different A-frames, coreflutes on stakes, Party posters and bunting both on the green verge and along the school fence. If I thought for one moment that the Kareela booth was saturated with election material, this was a step up again!

Looking ahead along the council footpath, it seemed there were people everywhere. It was almost as if every voter in the Gymea area had turned up at the same time to exercise their democratic right in the growing Saturday morning heat—many accompanied by their kids and their dogs. But for the slight bulge in the crowd at what I knew to be a narrow gate, it would have been virtually impossible for any first-time visitor to the school to spot the entrance to the polling booth!

Walking with Michael the 100 metres or so towards the gate, I introduced myself to voters who were making their way to the booth, shaking their hands, saying hello to their kids, occasionally patting their dogs, and, of course, asking for their support. If the voting going on inside the booth matched the positive feeling I was getting outside on my way there, I couldn't help but feel that we were on our way to winning, notwithstanding candidate's disease.

Being there

Our Labor booth workers standing just inside the school gate in their 'Help Barry Collier Stop Overdevelopment' T-shirts quietly confirmed that the feeling at the booth had been positive since the polls opened at 8.00AM. Most voters coming through the gate, they said, were taking my HTVs, with some actually asking for the "Barry Collier one!"

I then stood a little further inside the school gate on the short path leading to the school playground for 10 or 15 minutes, greeting voters, shaking their hands and handing out to those who didn't already have my HTV. I have to say that it was pleasing to hear our Labor booth workers following our instructions, saying "Barry Collier for Miranda" as they handed out my HTVs — and doubly pleasing to hear some voters respond with "Good! That's the one I want!"

Voters walking up the path seemed pleased to see me, with one lady looking up from the HTV she'd been handed to see me and say "Oh, it's you!" in a tone suggesting she never really expected to see one of the candidates at her polling booth.

Now, regardless of how quick, enthusiastic or agile our booth workers were, the surges of voters coming through the school gate meant they'd inevitably miss handing out my HTV to some voters. Spotting these voters, I'd make sure that I did so as I asked for their support.

But of course, there are also voters who simply refused to take my HTV from one of our booth workers, and here is a curious thing. When many of those same voters came along the short path to me and I shook their hand, they were more than happy to take my HTV from me! While you may well think these voters were just being polite, this apparently contradictory voter behaviour at the polling booth serves to highlight the importance of the candidate being there on election day!

The heat is on

With more than 800 pupils, Gymea Bay Public was the largest primary school in the Shire, and it had grounds to match. From the end of the short pathway, voters had to walk some 50 metres, without any vestige of shade, across an enormous bitumen playground towards the polling booth before encountering the 'campaign no-go zone'. And it was there, in the full sun, about 10 metres from the school hall, that the workers from each Party had set up their A-frames and were handing out their HTVs.

I'd always taken the view that I wanted my face to be the last face the voter saw before entering the polling booth. So there, on the edge of the no-go zone, I stood beside my corflute, in my black suit and tie, shaking hands and handing out my HTVs as the morning heat really built up. Suffice to say I wasn't wearing a hat or sunscreen, and in the blistering heat, I knew full well my face was going to get very, very burnt. But like Scarlett O'Hara, at the end of *Gone with the Wind*, I'd think about that tomorrow.

Even so, voters on their way to the school hall seemed genuinely pleased to see me as I introduced myself and shook their hand — with many remarking they'd already met me during the campaign. All that personal contact with voters in the electorate over the past 3½ months looked like it was paying off when it really counted!

There's always one

But of course, there's often just one zealot handing out for the other side who simply can't resist the opportunity to have a go and make their presence felt in an apparent effort to make a name for themselves.

This particular young man in a Liberal T-shirt decided to complain about my blue coreflute in the same tedious way as others in his Party had done earlier in the campaign: "Why isn't yours red like other Labor candidates? Blue is the Liberal colour!"

Determined not to be distracted and ignoring the young man completely as voters approached, I eventually gave him my stock standard answers: blue always being my favourite and there being no copyright on the colour. Not happy with that, the young man then sought to engage me in some kind of policy debate, reminiscent of a disgruntled early morning rail commuter. Taking something of a punt, I asked the young zealot, "You're not from the Shire, are you?" When he responded "no," I asked, "so how much are they paying you to hand out here?"

There was no response. I'd obviously hit a raw nerve. Seemingly embarrassed, he soon handed his HTVs to another, much more pleasant, Liberal worker nearby and walked off towards the front gate. I saw that same young man at another booth later in the day— but he didn't come anywhere near me.

Good vibes at the Bay

Minor annoyances to one side, *the vibe* at the Gymea Bay Public School booth was very encouraging, given the size and importance of the booth in the overall scheme of things.

As attractive as it was to stay longer and just lap up the positive *vibe*, time waits for no man and very few women. We needed to move on to our next polling booth. But before doing so, I enjoyed the mandatory sausage sandwich and a drink, as well as a quick chat, with the P&C volunteers. They were quick to tell me that pupils attending Gymea Bay Public needed a Wombat Crossing outside the school on the very busy Gymea Bay Road.[139] Careful not to make promises I may not be able to keep, I responded by saying I would do everything I possibly could to get one for the school if I was elected.

On my way out of the school grounds and walking back to our campaign car with Michael, I took every opportunity to shake hands and speak with voters making their way to the booth. You don't stop campaigning on election day until the voting closes at 6.00PM!

---

[139] 'Wombat crossings' are especially designed, raised pedestrian crossings outside schools which are funded by the NSW State Government.

Sylvania Heights

Our campaign car continued to attract attention from shoppers and other motorists as we made our way through the slow Saturday morning traffic to Sylvania Heights Public School— the second largest booth with just over 3,000 voters.

Shoppers waiting at pedestrian crossings were waving with amused looks on their faces. Stopping in traffic near playing fields, we saw parents seemingly talking about this odd-looking car to their puzzled-looking kids in sports uniforms; drivers were double-beeping their horns in approval, while their passengers were leaning out of the car windows smiling, laughing and giving us and our *Beverly Hillbillies*-style car the thumbs up!

As we arrived at the school and sat waiting for a parking spot, I noticed a young mum with a baby on her hip, standing open-mouthed at the sight of the old Mitsubishi Magna with the coreflutes on the roof secured by ropes! It was as if she was having a 'Close Encounter of the Third Kind'. Maybe she was simply appalled at what she saw as an astonishing lack of sophistication by a candidate for Parliament. I'll never know.

But whatever her thoughts, and regardless of the encouragement we were getting in driving between booths, I got the distinct impression that the people of the Miranda electorate had never seen a car like this one on election day— or if they had, it must have been many moons ago!

The booth

Now with five separate entrances to the school grounds, the large Sylvania Heights booth just had to be the most difficult to manage effectively, so far as handing out our HTVs and organising our workers were concerned. But our Booth Captain, Rhodes, and the Sylvania-Taren Point Branch members, assisted by our volunteers, had it all under control.

On arrival at the main gate, I offered to give Bert a break, but he wouldn't hear of it! The energy and commitment of this senior Branch member, whom I'd first met during my preselection attempt for Cook was simply extraordinary!

Bert had a job to do and was determined to do it, regardless. Certainly, there was no way he was going to be distracted by the Young Liberal in the blue Party T-shirt who tried to draw him into some kind of political argument. I didn't hear what Bert said to him in his lowered tone. But whatever it was, the young man obviously realised that he'd bitten off more than he could chew, giving up and walking away with a sheepish look on his face.

While Michael helped handing out at one of the other school entrances, I stood in the middle of the main, tree-lined driveway leading down to the end of a long line of voters waiting to get into the small school hall. Grateful for the shade, I followed my now established routine: greeting voters, shaking their hands, giving my HTV to those that didn't yet have one, and asking for their support, without crossing that imaginary line drawn by the booth's Presiding Officer. But there was a problem.

A significant number of voters were joining the queue outside the hall from the four other entrances to the school! For the candidate, it was impossible to make that all important personal contact with voters on their way into this booth. Frustrating as it was, I resisted the temptation of entering the 'no-go zone' with my HTVs. That became increasingly difficult when the end of the growing polling booth queue snaked its way closer and closer to me, from time to time!

Still, the response to me personally at the Sylvania Heights booth was very encouraging. Even allowing for the dreaded candidate's disease, it seemed that change really *was* in the air!

The quiet man

That thought quickly passed as I saw the same angry man who'd yelled and sworn at me from his balcony the previous evening coming down the driveway towards me. He was accompanied by a younger woman who appeared to be in her thirties holding the hand of a child clutching her dolly.

I don't know who was more surprised: him or me! What are the odds of coming face to face with that same bloke in less than 24 hours at a booth with 3,000 voters and five different entrances? 'This'll be good,' I thought to myself. The last thing I wanted was a big confrontation at the polling booth!

But if I expected a heated argument or a display of animosity I was wrong. I put my hand out and offered him my HTV without a hint of recognition or mention of our meeting at his home the previous evening. But while I was still expecting some negative comment from him, there was none.

Chastened, perhaps, by the presence of his daughter and granddaughter, the man shook his head, declined to shake my hand, then looked down at the Liberal HTV he was holding and said gruffly, "no thanks." His daughter, with a slight look of defiance, did the exact opposite. She not only shook my hand and took my HTV, she asked her daughter to "hold the paper for dolly!" Now that must have really grated on grandad!

The Heights vibe

Anyone who has worked in a shop knows something of the natural ebb and flow of customers. The same is true of voters arriving at certain polling booths on election day, and seasoned Booth Captains like Bert Rhodes well knew the quiet and the busy times at his Sylvania Heights booth.

Having spent a very busy two hours handing out on the main driveway, the time was fast approaching for me to move on to the next booth. I'd already spoken to Bert about my timetable and my wish to spend some time with our Booth workers at each of the four other school entrances before leaving.

After what can only be described as a major rush of voters, Bert walked down the driveway to me saying "it's really going to drop off for the next couple of hours, so it's a good time now." So off I went, walking along well-trodden paths between the school buildings and across the vast school playground to the other entrances — not only to hand out my HTVs but to personally thank the Branch members and volunteers for their work.

On the way, of course, I met and shook hands with voters and their families walking towards the school hall, many holding my HTV. I also stopped at the fundraiser for my now mandatory sausage sandwich and can of soft drink.

The P&C members running the BBQ were quick to tell me about needs of their school: in this case a COLA (or Covered Outdoor Learning Area). They were impressed when I told them I'd already met with the Principal, Mr Dennis Burke, during my campaign and that I'd do what I could to help them, if I was elected. That not only demonstrated my genuine interest in their school, but added to my credibility. Other parents coming to the booth would soon learn of my conversation with these P&C volunteers. Hopefully, that all-important word-of-mouth would play its part in adding to my votes at the Sylvania Heights booth.

Branch members and volunteers at each of the other entrances were quick to tell me the feeling was "pretty good for us." My son, Michael, confirmed that. And, as I stood handing out at each gate for a short time, I got the same *vibe*.

I walked back to the main entrance with Michael and couldn't believe just how quiet it had become there. Bert Rhodes obviously knew the booth like the back of his hand.

"How do you think we're going here, Bert?" I asked as we left for the campaign car.

"This is the best I've seen for us in years," Bert said with a knowing grin.

Coming from Bert, who always told it like it was, that was fabulous news! Like the big Kareela and Gymea Bay polling booths, Sylvania Heights was one we had to win — or at least to go very close to winning — if we were to get across the line!

8.3. Taking the pulse elsewhere

Booth workers aside, there was another person out there taking the pulse on the big day with whom I kept in constant contact: my Campaign Director, Bob Rogers.

He had the task of going to each of the booths, checking if anything was needed and addressing any problems. Bob also had the job of delivering the sandwiches and soft drinks that had been donated to us for our booth workers.

Conflict at the ballot box

As I left the Sylvania Heights booth, Bob phoned to tell me that "things were generally going very well at all the other booths except Oyster Bay" where Ray Plibersek had allegedly been assaulted in the early morning.

It seems that Ray had really upset the Liberals by drawing attention to the fact that their HTVs did not have the appropriate authorisation printed on them as required by law— and had further set the cat among the pigeons by drawing that fact to the attention of booth's Presiding Officer.

From what I could make out, the Libs were not permitted to hand out their HTVs for Mr Phillips for about an hour, until the problem was rectified. I had no sympathy for the Libs in any of this. The problem appeared to be down to their failure to observe the rules—and when it comes to the State Electoral Commission's Presiding Officers and the rules, there are no shortcuts!

When I told Bob that I'd find out more when I visited the Oyster Bay booth later in the afternoon, he told me not to bother. "It's over; the problem's been resolved. Don't waste your time getting into petty squabbles at the booth; just concentrate on getting votes for yourself!" Good advice for all candidates!

Jannali East

It was time to move on to other booths on my list, starting with Jannali East Public School, at the very western end of the Miranda electorate.

At the time, Jannali East could best be described as traditional working class with low to middle income earners as well as a significant number of public housing tenants and seniors living in 1950s fibros.

I was told by one Branch member that Labor had always "done well" at the Jannali East booth and we should win it this time as well. But another Branch member, suggested that, for the same reason, I should "give Jannali East a miss." He argued that I'd be better off spending my time trying to pick up swinging voters at other booths which tended to favour the Liberals!

That was advice I just wouldn't accept. I was not about to avoid the more than 1,800 voters expected to attend the Jannali East booth just because they tended to favour the Labor Party! Our supporters in the Jannali area were just as entitled to meet their Labor candidate on election day as everyone else— and I wasn't about to ignore them or take them for granted!

In fact, I believed it made very good sense for me to turn up at the Jannali East booth for an hour or so. No one likes to feel ignored, especially those who support you. Even if the candidate appears at the booth for only a short time, that all important word-of-mouth will kick in. Other locals will soon learn that you had taken the time to come to their polling booth, and you thought they were important enough for you to do so. And who knows? I might even attract some swinging Liberal voters to our side and even deter some disgruntled Labor voters from swinging the other way. In the end, we could go on to do better than "well" at the Jannali East booth.

As it turned out, the response I received personally at the booth was tremendous. While it wasn't exactly in the rock star category, I left Jannali East Public School after an hour or so with the distinct feeling that I would win this booth relatively easily!

Other booths

I visited other booths throughout the day- including those at St Catherine Labouré Church Hall in Gymea, Yowie Bay Public School and Kirrawee High School.

Our workers at each of these confirmed *the vibe* that I'd been picking up myself during my time there: that the mood towards Labor had been very positive all day. Good news! But there was one booth that deserves a special mention in its own right.

8.4.   Oyster Bay: Why people vote for you!

It was around 2.30PM when I arrived at the Oyster Bay Public School booth. By that time, I'd been on my feet for more than six hours straight in my suit and tie without a hat or sunscreen on what, to me at least, was an extraordinarily hot day.

But there was no relief at Oyster Bay. Standing in the middle of the asphalt school playground in my suit which was by now wringing wet, I gave my HTV to a woman in her 30s on her way to the booth with a young boy aged seven or eight in tow. Of course, I did my usual spiel and asked for her support.

I later saw the woman came from the booth talking with the boy, who appeared to be very interested in what was going on.

As they walked several metres past me towards the school exit gate, I heard the little boy ask:

"Mummy, who did you vote for?"

"The man back there in the black suit," she said.

"Why?" asked her son, looking quickly over his shoulder at me.

She said, "anyone who stands out here in a black suit on a day like today deserves my vote!"

People vote for you - or don't vote for you for all sorts of reasons. But that one really took the cake!

A lesson about voting

Stunned by her response—but grateful for her support—it occurred to me that there really is no point in trying to figure out why any particular individual votes the way they do.

You can talk all you like about your promises or your stance on a particular issue. You could even have the most charismatic Party Leader imaginable. But at the end of the day, and unless they tell you, you can't really *know* what drives a particular individual to favour you over your opponent on election day.

It could be anything: from the way you spoke to their children when you first met them at the shops to the fact you patted their family dog as they made their way past you to the polling booth; it might be the fact that you attend the same Church or follow the same football team ; it could be that you took the time to admire the roses in their garden when you doorknocked them. But it could also come down to the fact that they just 'like something about you' without being able to identify what that 'something' is!

The simple lesson for me was this: never dismiss or underestimate the importance of the personal factors voters take into account in deciding where they'll put their number 1 on the ballot paper. When it comes right down to it, many voters will make their decision on the day and at the very last moment, based only on their personal assessment of you, the candidate.

So what did that young mum at Oyster Bay make of me? Having never previously met her, I'd like to think that, by standing out there in my wringing wet black suit, I'd given her the impression that I was genuinely committed to working hard for the community if I was elected – and I certainly wasn't going to get a little matter like the heat get in my way!

8.5. Miranda suburban booths

Lesson learnt, it was time to move on from Oyster Bay to the last big booth of the day at Port Hacking High School in the heart of Miranda itself.

On our way, I decided to depart from the now very damp list of booths I'd had my coat pocket all day and make a short unscheduled stop at the other, smaller booth in the suburb.

Miranda Central

Tucked in behind the gigantic Westfield complex at the small Community Centre, the Miranda Central booth was only expected to attract around 1,200 voters during the day.

Big John McLean lived nearby and had run this booth himself for years: setting it up around 5.00AM on State, Federal and Local Government election days and working until the polls closed at 6.00PM, typically without taking a break.

John was personally very proud of his booth, and justifiably so. It was one of the very few that Labor had consistently won – at least since he'd been in charge as its designated Booth Captain. In local Labor circles, Miranda Central was 'Big John's booth'.

Several days out from the poll, John had invited me to drop into his booth on election day to 'see his set-up' if I got the chance. This was the same Branch member who had come up with the ingenious hand-painted sign on the Campaign Office roof, and had devoted every available moment he had to help ensure a Labor victory in Miranda. While I couldn't give John a commitment, I really just couldn't say "no"!

Michael and I called into the Miranda Central booth. Big John's "set-up" can best be described as extraordinary! I don't think there was even one vantage point he hadn't exploited in positioning my coreflutes. Indeed, a casual observer might well have thought Barry Collier was the only candidate for Miranda!

In handing out for half an hour with John, Michael and I thought *the vibe* was very positive! He told us, "everyone's really worried about overdevelopment: a lot of people weren't taking the Liberal HTV at all!" Good, I thought, the issue is really biting when it matters most: on election day!

John confirmed that since his booth opened at 8AM, the feeling had been "very good for you, Mr Barry." He expected that to continue until the polls closed, when, of course, he would also be my scrutineer and phone in the results to the Campaign Office.

Whatever the overall outcome, Big John was determined to keep his winning record for Labor at Miranda Central intact!

Port Hacking High

With more than 2,400 votes expected to be cast, the main Miranda polling booth at Port Hacking High School was certainly worth two hours of my time on election day.

Local Labor wisdom had it that, so far as voter numbers were concerned, the best times for candidates to attend this booth were early in the morning and towards the very end of the day after the Saturday afternoon shop by locals at the Westfield complex across the road.

Voters could only access the door to the school hall in one of two ways: via a short flight of concrete stairs from the busy Kingsway or via a long asphalt driveway from Wandella Road, taking them past the school hockey field and the teachers' carpark. Arriving in our campaign car, Michael and I were impressed with the row of my coreflutes on garden stakes on the grass verge along the driveway. Mine were interspersed with those of my opponent— and clearly, he had more coreflutes on display than me.

"So be it," I thought to myself as we got out of our campaign car in the teachers' carpark. But no sooner had that thought crossed my mind, when Branch member Chris Hunt rolled up with more coreflutes of mine on garden stakes in the back of his ute, got out and proceeded to hammer them into the ground, more than matching those of Mr Phillips!

I'd later discover that Bob White had been busy throughout the day in his Gymea garage, putting my 'left-over coreflutes' on garden stakes. The left-overs included those we'd used for advertising in the Campaign Office as well as some we'd held back as a kind of insurance— in case a lot of them were knocked off by the Libs! Bob Rogers had given Chris Hunt the task of delivering these extra coreflutes to booths where there appeared to be an "imbalance" between ours and those of the Libs.

Determined voters

Like most of the voters arriving by car, some with young children, Michael and I walked the 50 metres or so from the teacher's carpark to the polling booth.

But there are also a host of other cars being driven the length of the driveway, delivering elderly parents, friends and relatives as well as those with disabilities right to the polling booth door. The drivers as well as booth workers, helped these passengers out of the vehicles — some into wheelchairs and some onto walking frames — and assisted them into the school hall.

I couldn't help but admire these voters who, despite their age and obvious disabilities, had ignored the availability of a postal vote, and were just so determined to exercise their democratic right at the ballot box in person on election day itself!

The importance of working locally

Like other polling booths, the Presiding Officer at Port Hacking High had established the official 'campaign no-go zone' outside the school hall. As I had done at other booths earlier, I stood just outside it doing my (by now) very practised spiel, sometimes at the foot of the stairs and sometimes the end of the driveway.

The voters were generally very positive with many noting they'd already met me during the campaign and some actually telling me upfront that they were actually voting for me! But amongst those arriving at Port Hacking High were two groups which deserve special mention: former students and former clients.

In the late 1970s and early 1980s I'd taught Economics, Commerce and Geography at Port Hacking High School itself. Not surprisingly and given the tendency for kids who grow up in the Shire to stay in the Shire, I met former students who took the opportunity to remind me that I'd actually taught them. Some I recognised by sight and some I remembered by name; some even still called me "Sir." Several introduced me to their children who accompanied them, saying "this is Mr Collier. He taught me here when I was your age." Some even said they were going to vote for "their old teacher."

But there was a second group of late afternoon voters who were far more reluctant to talk about their previous encounters with me. These were my former clients charged with criminal offences whom I'd represented in my role as their Legal Aid Duty Solicitor at Sutherland Local Court.

They knew that I knew all about their past and looked a little sheepish as well as somewhat apprehensive that I might say something about their encounters with the local police or the outcome of their Court cases. Of course, I didn't mention either!

Indeed, I didn't give the slightest hint I knew them, socially or professionally. I treated them as I did any other voter whom I'd never previously met, and they seemed to appreciate that. And, while I'd hoped I get to their vote (regardless of the outcome of their cases), there was absolutely no way I could be sure one way or the other. All I knew was that I'd done my best for each of them in Court and that every vote counted.

If anything, these two groups of voters brought home to me the importance not only of being a local but of having a good solid history of working locally as well. In our parochial Shire, particularly, that counted for a lot!

Six o'clock rock

Polling booths in New South Wales all close on the dot of 6.00PM. As that magical time approached, we saw some voters taking the steep stairs down from the Kingsway two at a time and voters actually running from their cars in the teachers' carpark, hoping to make it into the school hall before the doors closed. It was as though the last train that would get commuters into town on time for work was just about to pull into Miranda station.

There was simply no time for me to shake voters' hands; no time to give them my standard spiel; and no time to ask for their vote. There was only just enough time to hold out my HTV and say "Barry Collier" and hope they grabbed it as they continued on through the still open door into the polling booth.

But there was another rush. The rule is that scrutineers — those appointed by each candidate to oversee the counting of the votes — had to be inside the polling booth before the doors closed on the stroke of 6.00PM.

As the booth's Presiding Officer appeared at the door of the hall several minutes from the closing time, our Booth Captain Tony Iffland called out "scrutineers!" With that, three of our booth workers left their posts and quickly disappeared into the school hall, clutching my signed scrutineer appointment form, moments before the Presiding Officer shut and locked the doors.

As with commuters running for the train at Miranda Station, some voters just didn't make it before the booth doors shut. One disappointed man told me "I just forgot it was voting day today!" Another voter actually banged on the hall door begging to be let in saying "I can't afford the fine!" Opening the door, the Presiding Officer told him, rather sympathetically, "I'm sorry but I can't break the rules!" and shut the door again.

That was it! Our 3½ month election campaign for Miranda was officially over. There was nothing more I could do now but wait for our scrutineers at each booth to phone in the vote counts to our Campaign Office, where my friends Donna and Charles were waiting to feed the results into their computer program.

But where was Ron?

While Michael walked off to the Campaign Office, I was off home, driving our trusty campaign car. On the way, it occurred to me that the entire time voting was taking place, I never once spotted my opponent, Ron Phillips, at any of the booths!

You would've thought that over the 10 hours of election day, we'd cross each other's path at least once, and more likely than not, at one of the bigger booths. But no!

I must admit being a little puzzled as to why I didn't see him. After all, he did not have the list of the polling booths I had decided to attend or the times I'd chosen to do so. Besides, Bob Rogers had never once mentioned spotting Mr Phillips anywhere else during my short phone conversations with him.

Surely, he would have attended some booths on election day! I can only think that Ron was somehow tracking my movements throughout the day, and went to booths he knew he would have to himself! That would be a smart move by my much more experienced opponent— and was the only thing that made sense.

After all, and as I had discovered throughout election day, being the only candidate for a major Party on the spot and effectively having the polling booth to yourself can be a real advantage. Another lesson, perhaps, for the future!

8.6. At home with Mr Knight

I arrived home to see the TV news on in the lounge room, filled with election day reports including comments from reporters and voters at a host of suburban and country booths across the State.

The full election night coverage on Channel 9, with a panel of experienced political commentators and high-profile MPs from both sides, was advertised to commence at 6.30PM. There was just enough time for a shower and a quick change of clothes before Jeanette and I had to leave so as to be at our Campaign Office as the results came in.

As I was getting ready, the TV coverage began and, of course, we just had to watch some of it before going out the front door.

The election night coverage began with introductory comments about key electorates and the number of seats the Liberals had to win if they were to wrest government from Labor. Next came preliminary observations by each of the panel members, including Michael Knight, Labor's Minister for the Olympics.

Knight predicted the return of the Carr Labor Government with an increased majority and went on to stun other panel members by saying:

"...and Labor is going to win Miranda!"

With a look of astonishment, the panel moderator questioned Knight's prediction saying "it's only four minutes into the telecast and you are predicting that Ron Phillips, the Deputy Leader of the Liberal Party, will lose his seat?"

"Yes," replied Knight confidently.

"Wow! I hope he's right," I said to Jeanette, having always believed we would win but astounded by Knight's confirmation so soon after the polls had closed and without seeing any results.

"He's right," said Jeanette, firmly.

"How would Knight know? I've never spoken to the guy, and there's been no polling by Head Office," I said. "Do you really think he's got it right, this early?"

"He *has* got it right! You'll see!" said my very supportive wife.

We soon left home in our trusty campaign car, heading off to our Campaign Office, anxious to see the results as they came in.

9.   ELECTION NIGHT

9.1.   Early evening

Buoyed by Michael Knight's confident prediction of a Labor win in Miranda four minutes into the television broadcast, the adrenaline kicked in, overtaking the sheer exhaustion I'd felt at the close of the polls.

Anticipating a life-changing night ahead, there were a host of thoughts running through each of our minds as Jeanette and I drove to our Campaign Office. Jeanette specifically recalls one of our short conversations on the way:

> "I think Knight's right. We will win, but I don't think it'll be a walk-over," I said.
>
> "When do you think we'll know for sure?" Jeanette responded.
>
> "I don't know. I think it's going to be very long night, but I believe we'll scrape over the line," I said.
>
> "Hopefully, we'll do better than that!" Jeanette replied. "But do you think the Party should've preselected you earlier and given you more time to campaign? Maybe you could have done some more doorknocking?"
>
> "No," I said, "I couldn't have done any more. Another day of doorknocking and I think I'd be dead!" I replied.

We parked behind the Campaign Office and had to bang on the back door for someone inside to open it. We didn't have a key; in fact, there was no key. There hadn't even been a lock on the back door throughout the entire campaign. Our security at the rear of the Office consisted of a metal bar jammed across the door on the inside. We simply didn't have the money to pay for a locksmith and anyway, the bar seemed to work just fine!

Campaign Office buzz

Inside, the Campaign Office was the tidiest I'd seen it since it had been opened by Treasurer Michael Egan.

The folding tables were empty. While there were some A-frames and coreflutes brought back from some booths, there was no campaign literature left on the shelves: our volunteers had distributed all of them as we had asked—in letterboxes, somewhere; anywhere! It didn't matter. There was no point having any of our pamphlets lying around in the Campaign Office gathering dust on election day, of all days.

To say that there was buzz of excitement in the Campaign Office is an understatement of the first order. Supporters who'd come directly back to the Office from nearby polling booths had already seen Michael Knight's prediction on the old TV set Bob had borrowed from someone for the night. Provided no one touched the temperamental indoor aerial or stood too close to it with a mobile phone, we continued to receive reasonable, though at times, intermittent, reception.

Bob Rogers was busy taking phone calls from our scrutineers, quickly writing the results on scraps of paper and handing them to Donna and Charles, who'd punch these into our borrowed computer—ably assisted by my son Michael, already proving himself to be something of a budding computer whiz at age 17.

Smaller booths

As expected, the first preference (or primary) votes recorded at the smaller booths were the earliest to be phoned in.[140] First preference figures for each candidate at the bigger booths would naturally come in later.

Results for Frank Vickery Village in Sylvania were among the first in. Located inside the grounds of this large retirement village, the booth accounted for about 850 voters, half of whom were residents of the facility itself. With many aged residents in poor health and in nursing home accommodation, management strictly prohibited both doorknocking and letter-boxing inside the Village precinct. Not surprisingly, postal voting always played a major role in determining the final result for the booth.

No Labor candidate had ever won Vickery Village and so, over time, it had gained a reputation as a natural Liberal booth. Not having had the benefit of doorknocking or letter-boxing or the money to mount a postal voting campaign, we didn't expect to shatter that long-standing Liberal record in 1999!

Even so, the figures phoned in by our scrutineers for the Vickery Village booth were far better than we had expected. I was told that being only 150 votes behind Ron Phillips on first preferences was one of Labor's best results at the booth ever!

---

[140] The first preference (or primary) votes are those with the number 1 written beside the candidate's name *before* the voter's individual preferences (numbers 2, 3, 4, etc.) are taken into account. The second and subsequent preferences are then distributed to the two candidates recording the highest number of first preference votes. The voting results are then said to be on a 'two-party-preferred' (or 2PP) basis. The candidate with the highest number of votes 2PP (*after* all preferences have been distributed) wins the seat and is declared elected as the MP.

Indeed, one of our senior Branch members saw our primary vote at Vickery Village as an early sign that "the swing was on!"

I hoped she was right. To me, it was a clear sign that the direct mail letters about overdevelopment and Sutherland Council sent by Bob Carr and Craig Knowles to Village residents personally might have done their work!

The Liberal lead on primary votes at Vickery Village was soon erased with a Labor win of around 150 at the Como booth, and another at Caravan Head. Small booths for sure; but positive signs nevertheless.

Next cab off the rank was Big John's booth, Miranda Central. Labor had polled more than 49% of first preferences, putting us ahead of the Libs by some 160 votes! John had clearly won his booth, and had kept his personal record of Labor successes intact!

As we were congratulating Big John, Bob Rogers shoved a scrap of paper in my hand, simply saying "Jannali East." Wow! We had polled 52% of the first preference votes and were 400 ahead of Ron Phillips! The distribution of preferences later was also likely to favour Labor, putting us further in front again.

One of our very seasoned Branch members watching Donna put the figures for Jannali East into our computer pointed out that the result was "better than usual" at this 'traditional' Labor booth. Perhaps it was my doorknocking and the street stalls we did in Jannali; perhaps it was turning up at the booth on election day; perhaps a combination of both. But whatever the reason, the lesson for any candidate is very clear: never ignore your base!

As the figures for other booths were coming in, Donna Spears turned from the computer to me and said, "it's really starting to look good for you. Let's hope you get a phone call from Mr Phillips!"

A doubt and a declaration

As Donna said that I realised I'd left my mobile phone in my car. Walking out the back door to retrieve it, I was surprised to find Big John sitting on a plastic chair by himself in the dark, head down, obviously exhausted but seemingly upset.

"What's wrong, John?" I asked, very concerned at the thought of him collapsing.

"I'm really worried we're going to lose, Mr Barry," he responded. "Maybe I didn't do enough; maybe if I'd worked harder..."

"No!" I said abruptly, cutting him off. "If we lose to the Libs, it won't be because of you! You've done more than I could have asked of anyone! You could not have done any more!"

"But..."

"No buts! Think about it. You've done it all: stations, street stalls, flying pickets, letterboxing, pre-poll, everything; the only thing you didn't do was doorknocking—and I wanted to do all that by myself anyway! And look, you won your booth!" I said,

"But..."

"Listen! And what about the sign on the roof? That was all *your* idea! I know that got us a heap of votes! The people loved it! John, I couldn't not have had a more hardworking and loyal worker than you! I'm very proud of you; and I'm sure Labor, your Union and Bob Carr are also very proud of you!"

"You really think we'll win? John asked, seeming to brighten up.

"Well, I said, "the figures are looking good; Michael Knight's already predicted a win for us on the tele. But I'll let you into a little secret just between you and me: I've always believed we'd win from the very start! And we will win thanks to the work of members like you!"

"Tonight?

"Yes, tonight!" I said in a very confident tone. "OK?"

"Yep!" John said, my response having appeared to lift his spirits a little more again.

"Now, come inside with me and get yourself a coffee!"

"OK, Mr Barry," John said, his faith seemingly restored.

This was one of those unforgettable election-night conversations, for two reasons. Firstly, here was Big John, who'd worked so hard right throughout the campaign and who was always so positive about our chances from the beginning, entertaining a doubt for the very first time and at the very last hurdle.

In many ways that was understandable, given that the Liberals had held Miranda for 15 years. But I was also moved by John's humility in reasoning that we might lose the election because he hadn't done enough work. Anyone could come up with a hundred reasons why the Libs might win on the night, but Big John working his heart out could never ever be one of them!

Secondly, my conversation with Big John was also the very first time I'd told anyone outside my immediate family that I really believed I would win from the very beginning. There were very few, if any, in the Party who believed that when I nominated for Miranda, and it was so important to continue being seen as the underdog—especially when everything about our shoestring campaign clearly supported that very valuable status. And, of course, any early declaration by me that I believed I would defeat the Deputy Leader of the Liberal Party would attract the claim I was suffering from candidate's disease!

Swings and in-house predictions

Back inside the Campaign Office, the atmosphere was far more upbeat than when I'd left it 10 minutes before. Optimism was everywhere!

Some of the bigger booths had begun to come in and the results were looking good. All three booths in Kirrawee had us ahead on first preferences; we were 100 in front at Oyster Bay and some 400 in front at St Catherine's. Our scrutineers at Port Hacking High also had us in the lead by 200 votes.

At the same time, we were behind on first preferences at other big booths — Gymea Bay Public School, Sylvania Heights, Yowie Bay and, disappointingly, my home booth of Kareela—but not by the huge margins that had been recorded at each of these in previous State elections.

But the disparity between Mr Phillips' first preference votes and mine on these booths was not insurmountable. No doubt the result was going to be close. It would probably all come down to preferences and here, we had further cause for optimism.

It was more than just my name being Number 2 on the ballot paper after the Greens and picking up their preferences as well as the donkey vote. The One Nation candidate, Max Remy, was polling remarkably well, running third behind Ron Phillips and me, with just under over 7% of the total first preference votes. All indications were that Remy seemed to be taking votes from the Liberals and if his supporters followed the One Nation ticket, the majority of his 2,800 first preference votes would flow on to us.

Things were not only looking good; there was the talk of a Labor victory starting to find its way into the many enthusiastic and increasingly noisy conversations taking place around the computer and in the Campaign Office itself. The TV screen was beginning to show Labor leading in Miranda, lending support to Michael Knight's prediction of victory within half an hour of the polls closing.

There was no doubt that the "swing was on!" But the $64,000 question, of course was, would the swing be big enough? After all, we needed a swing of 5.3% just to get across the line!

A final Litmus test

About 7.30PM, as we were tossing this question around, Paul Smith walked into the Campaign Office, hat in hand. Paul had been working all day and scrutineering at a big booth in Caringbah for Scott Docherty, our candidate for Cronulla.

Paul strode directly over to me and we had one of those memorable conversations:

"How's it all going?" he asked.

"Bob reckons we're looking good. The swing's definitely on according to the figures," I reported.

"How'd you go at Gymea North?" Paul asked me.

"We won the booth by about 50 votes on first preferences," I said. "Why?"

"Well, if you've won Gymea North, you've won the election!" was Paul's astonishing, but confident, reply.

While I must admit being astounded at first, I'd learnt to rely on Paul's experience and judgment. Here was our 1995 candidate for Miranda, who'd put our overdevelopment strategy together and who knew all the previous statistics like the back of his hand, telling me I'd already won the seat on the basis of the primary votes in one particular booth!

Paul had already provided me with one litmus test which I'd passed: getting a positive *vibe* when I was doorknocking in Honeysuckle Street, Jannali.[141] Winning the Gymea North booth on first preferences, it seems, was the second of his personal litmus tests which I needed to pass for success!

Paul's prediction at 7.30PM was more than encouraging; it was fantastic! Michael Knight and now Paul Smith! Victory was in the air!

9.2. Jubilation!

By 8.00PM, our scrutineers had phoned in the first preference figures for all of the Miranda booths. We were looking very good —

---

[141] See Section 6.7: Doorknocking Story #14.

to the point where a favourable distribution of preferences would see us first across the line with a swing of more than 5.3%.

While our expectations were understandably high, it was too early to celebrate. As one of our volunteers was quick to point out, "it's not over until a certain lady sings, Barry!"

Around 8:30PM, amongst all the noise and mounting expectations in the campaign office, Bob Rogers' mobile rang. As he took the call, he walked away from the crowd around the computer and the TV set towards a quieter corner of the Campaign Office.

After a short conversation, Bob came towards me, phone to his ear, waving his free hand up and down in a motion that could only be interpreted as telling everyone else to quieten down.

"Ron Phillips would like to talk to you!" Bob said, handing his phone to me.

"Hello, Ron," I said, with a hint of nervous anticipation.

"Barry," he said, "I'm ringing to concede defeat and to congratulate you on winning the seat of Miranda."

"Thank you," I said, "I really appreciate your call."

"It's been a great privilege for me to serve the people of Miranda for 15 years and I wish you well as you seek to serve them in the Parliament," came Ron's reply.

"I'll certainly do my best. Thank you again," I said, impressed by both his apparent sincerity and his graciousness in defeat.

Throughout my rather short conversation with my opponent, Bob Rogers was standing looking at me wide-eyed, with a somewhat knowing look, but waiting for me to tell him what Ron Phillips had said.

"We won! We won!" I yelled out, the moment I clicked off Bob's phone.

A giant cheer went up! Jubilation! Victory!

I immediately hugged Bob saying, "We did it! We did it!"

"Yes! We did it!" he repeated.

I kissed and hugged Jeanette, "thank you!"

"I knew you could do it!" she said.

"Yeah," but I couldn't have done it without you!" I replied, kissing her again.

"Congratulations Dad," Michael said, as I hugged and thanked him for all his hard work as well.

"Proud of you, Dad," my daughter Sarah said as I hugged her.

These were the first of many thank yous, congratulations, kisses and hugs throughout the remainder of the night. Smiles and laughter were everywhere as I went around our "ramshackle" Campaign Office thanking all our Branch members and supporters present who had contributed so much to our Labor victory in Miranda, including Bert Rhodes, Jim and Pat Foy, Big John McLean, Paul Smith, Tony Iffland, Maurie Bevan, Thelma Deacon, Donna Spears and Trevor Romer.

After 15 years of Labor in the political wilderness, the taste of victory in Miranda was very sweet indeed. But the night was still young, and the celebrations were just beginning. They'd continue later at *the Tradies*, up the Kingsway in Gymea. In the meantime, all attention turned back to our TV set.

9.3. Mr Knight's second announcement

News travels very fast in the world of Party politics. Less than 10 minutes after receiving the call from my opponent, an enormous cheer went up in our Campaign Office as Michael Knight fulfilled the prophesy he'd made only four minutes into the Channel 9 Election telecast – by telling the viewing audience: "Ron Phillips has rung Barry Collier to concede that he's lost Miranda!"

To the disbelief of other members of 9's Expert Panel— Laurie Oakes, Ray Martin, senior Liberal John Hannaford and moderator Helen Dalley—Michael Knight confirmed that Phillips had conceded defeat at 8.30PM.

A very Liberal explanation

I've included the following transcript of the Panel discussion immediately following Knight's announcement, because it provides an insight into reasons for the loss of Miranda to Labor from the Liberal Party's perspective.

Given John Hannaford's role, along with Ron Phillips, in the removal of Leader Peter Collins and the installation of Kerry Chikarovski the previous December, you may find his comments and exchanges with other panel members particularly interesting!

Knight: It's Ron Phillips' own view. He's rung the Labor candidate to concede.

Dalley: So he hasn't done it publicly? But he's done it to your candidate?

Knight: Done it privately, yeah.

Dalley: That's pretty amazing! So that is rather extraordinary news! What do you put that down to?

Knight: Barry Collier campaigned really hard. For about six months he's been out there knocking on doors. Quality candidate; moving very quietly. And Ron Phillips picked this up a few weeks ago.

              And I was at a function with Ron where he said that he had to leave early because his seat was in trouble! So I think he'd worked it out.

Dalley: Do you think it was one of those instances where it was down to individual campaigning or was this a real message for the Liberal Party? Deputy Leader; he'd ousted Collins; helped put in Chikarovski. Do you think it was a message like that to him?"

Knight: Labor has done very well in the southern suburbs; we've done very well in places like Heathcote, Georges River, Kogarah: and I think part of that's happened in Miranda as well.

Dalley: Do you think they're becoming Labor Party territory now?

Knight: Oh, things move back and forth. It's Labor territory tonight. We're pleased about that but we've got to fight the next election at the next election.

Dalley: I can hear John Hannaford disagreeing!

Hannaford: Well Helen, whilst Ron Phillips has conceded to his colleague, my understanding is that on information we're getting, the figures are coming back, so it might have been a premature concession by Ron.

But what was a major issue down in that electorate — and I have said before there's been a lot of local issues — overdevelopment has been a major issue in Miranda. You've had a Liberal-controlled Sutherland Council. There's been a large amount of controversy aimed at the Liberals because of the overdevelopment down there..."

Dalley: So are you saying that he's absolved from any of this? That it's not his fault that he may have lost this seat?

Hannaford: He's lost this seat not because of any of the State-wide issues. The issue down there and there's a lot of...

Dalley: Are you seriously saying there was no anti-what he might have done to Peter Collins?

Hannaford: Down in Miranda there was a very, very strong campaign on local issues. And Ron actually had to go back during the course of the campaign... back there to deal with that because of what was clearly...the issue of Sutherland Council and their very strong pro-development attitude. A lot of issues on high-rise development and density development...

Oakes: But John, do you deny that Liberal Party's polling down in Miranda kept picking up the word backstabber in the context of Ron Phillips?

Hannaford: Absolutely, I deny that!

Oakes: You deny that?

Hannaford: Absolutely, Laurie! That was not an issue down there, whatsoever!

Oakes: Well, my Liberal sources tell me that it was. And if that was an issue, don't you have to deny it because you were his partner? He tapped one shoulder of Peter Collins, and you tapped the other one?

Hannaford: Laurie, I don't know where you're getting that information from, but it certainly was not an issue down in Miranda at all!

Oakes: Leadership wasn't an issue? Liberal leadership not an issue?

Hannaford: No, it wasn't Laurie. You've had, across-the-board as I understand it, a State-wide swing of about 3%. Down in that particular electorate though, that was particularly affected by local issues and particularly in the Miranda end of the electorate.

Dalley: But surely the point is this: Ron Phillips should have realised that there were local issues that he had to go and fight hard on long before just a couple of weeks ago?

Hannaford: I think that's part of the problem that you get with people in Shadow Minister's positions and in the Leadership position. You are out there fighting a State-wide campaign and when a swing is on, as we've seen it happen, then sometimes you've overlooked your own backyard, and Ron has clearly done that!

Martin: This is the same part of Sydney that David Hill had so much trouble with in the Federal election; it's the same part of Sydney that Sutherland went for the Liberal Party before. This is an area where the Liberal Party have been doing very well until now.

Hannaford:	Exactly. But Ray, what you've highlighted there is it's the way in which you run your local campaign....
Dalley:	So, Ron Phillips didn't run his own local campaign very well: you'd have to say that!
Hannaford:	Well, clearly if he hasn't won the seat, he hasn't run his campaign as well as he would have liked. And clearly, he hadn't picked up early enough that local development issues and the issue of Liberal control of Sutherland Council hadn't been registered there early enough.
	Now I understand that there was, in fact, some late polling done in that seat which indicated that these were particular issues and he went back there to deal with them.
Dalley:	Well, hopefully we'll sort that out as to whether in fact he has conceded and whether, as you say, the figures are coming back to you.
Knight:	He's conceded! The interesting thing is that John Hannaford says he can't count. I think he proved in the leadership challenge he can count!
Martin:	He's an old warhorse, John, as well. I mean he's not going to ring up anybody and give it away!"
Hannaford:	He is an old warhorse...
Dalley:	That would be a major concession for him to make.
Hannaford:	And I'm surprised he made it at this hour of the night. Let's see what happens as the night goes on...

Campaign Office comments

While nothing could wipe the smile of victory from their faces, Branch members and supporters gathered around the TV were far from impressed with Hannaford's attempt to exonerate Phillips personally for the loss of Miranda.

Some stood there quietly with looks of incredulity on their faces, while others were much more vocal with grunts, groans and comments such as "you've got to be joking" at the milder end of the range.

John Hannaford's claim that leadership issues played no part in Ron Phillips' defeat received a "does he think we're stupid?" from a Branch member. His questioning of the fact that Ron Phillips' had conceded early attracted very loud "bullshit!" from one of our supporters who was present when I took the phone call at 8.30PM from my opponent!

But of course, winners are grinners, and as the focus of the television coverage shifted from Miranda to the numbers showing Labor achieving an overall majority in the 93-seat NSW Parliament, one Branch member turned to me and said "by God, the Libs are poor losers, aren't they?"

My early take

It was only to be expected that in the coming hours and days, the television and print media would dissect, and analyse in detail, the factors underlying the swing to Labor and the return of the Carr Government. There would, of course, include further discussion of the reasons for the "extraordinary" loss by Ron Phillips' of his own seat.

You may well ask what was going through my mind as I stood watching Hannaford's explanation of Ron Phillips' defeat in Miranda.

For a start, Knight's statement that Phillips' had only "worked it out" that "his seat was in trouble" "a few weeks ago" simply beggars belief. Some six weeks out from election day, the front page of the widely-read Leader reported that an opinion poll indicating that Phillips "would lose his seat of Miranda as part of a Labor landslide win."[142] Ron must surely have known, or at least had some inkling, that his hitherto 'safe seat' was in jeopardy!

John Hannaford's assertion that State-wide issues played no role in the loss of Miranda to Labor was just plain nonsense. Electricity privatisation was clearly a major issue for households across New South Wales, and one which impacted on the architect of that Liberal policy: Miranda MP, Ron Phillips himself.[143]

It was equally ridiculous for Hannaford to argue that the Liberal leadership wasn't an issue in Miranda "at all!" Ron Phillips' role in the removal of Party Leader Peter Collins and an installation of Kerry Chikarovski was something raised consistently with me during my doorknocking.[144]

As Laurie Oakes said, the word "backstabber" was used more than once to describe Deputy Leader Ron Phillips' role in Peter Collins' ousting—not to mention his earlier role in the overthrow of Stephen Mutch, the Federal Liberal MP for Cook, and the subsequent installation of Bruce Baird.[145] Interestingly enough,

---

[142] See 7−11: St George & Sutherland Shire Leader, 11 February 1999.
[143] See: 5.8. Electricity privatisation: A case study.
[144] See 4−2: St George & Sutherland Shire Leader, 15 December 1998 and 7−13: St George & Sutherland Shire Leader, 23 March 1999.
[145] See also Section 2.7 A visitor to the booth.

most of the residents I came across who used this and other terms to denounce Phillips' role in the removal of Collins and Mutch were traditional Liberal voters themselves. Australians generally hate disloyalty!

The overdevelopment issue

But John Hannaford's most astonishing statement of all concerned the key issue of the entire campaign: overdevelopment! Having correctly identified this as "a major issue in Miranda" he went on to say "there's been a large amount of controversy aimed at the Liberals...the Liberal-controlled Sutherland Council.... and their very strong pro-development attitude..."

Hannaford goes on to argue that Ron Phillips had "not picked up" the issue of overdevelopment "early enough" and only did so after some "late polling in the seat!"

On the 15th of December 1998 — more than three months out from election day, the Leader published its first article about my candidacy for Miranda. The very first line in that article entitled *Labor takes aim* clearly spelt out my platform and my stance on the issue of overdevelopment in the Shire:

> 'The Labor Party will target "rampant overdevelopment" in the Sutherland shire in its bid to win the seat of Miranda at the March election.'[146]

But our campaign on overdevelopment did not stop there. Every pamphlet we handed out at railway stations and at every street stall listed tackling the Shire's 'chronic overdevelopment' as my top priority; we letterboxed the entire electorate with our

---

[146] See 4 – 1: St George & Sutherland Shire Leader, 15 December 1998.

pamphlet devoted entirely to overdevelopment and which called for a State Government Inquiry into the Sutherland Council's Housing Strategy. I wrote to the Editor of the Leader attacking the Council's pro-development stance on overdevelopment and referred to it in newspaper articles. We had displayed coreflutes encouraging voters to 'Help Barry Collier Stop Overdevelopment' for more than two months of the campaign. To my great surprise, there was no response by my opponent Ron Phillips to any of this!

How could Ron Phillips *not* have known overdevelopment was the major issue of the election campaign, when the battle lines had been publicly drawn on day one and our literature had listed it as our top priority ever since? Even if he'd never read any of these, he must have surely seen coreflutes nailed to the telegraph poles!

The 'late polling' bit was just plain nonsense! I suspect that Ron only really got interested in the issue following the much-publicised visit of Minister Craig Knowles to Miranda and his announcement of a Government Inquiry into the Council's Housing Strategy on the 18th of March.[147]

Until then, Ron Phillips did not take the issue of overdevelopment seriously. Indeed, and consistent with our portrayal of him as the "absent member for Miranda," Hannaford made it clear that the sitting MP hadn't spent enough time in the electorate and "had to go back there to deal with" the issue. Clearly, by that time, it was far too late. The horse had bolted.

But it was also abundantly clear that this very high profile, 15-year veteran of State politics did not take me or my candidacy seriously, despite some of his local Branch members telling him to

---

[147] See 7 – 8: The Leader, front page, 18 March 1999.

do so![148] Perhaps that reflected the kind of personal arrogance that can develop—consciously or otherwise—from being a long-time incumbent in what is widely regarded as a 'safe seat'.

In the end, Hannaford effectively put the loss of Miranda down to the way Phillips had run his "local campaign," politely summing it up by saying Ron had clearly "overlooked (his) backyard".

At that point, and despite Hannaford's analysis, I really had no sympathy for Mr Phillips over his election loss. If he had taken the issue of overdevelopment and my candidacy seriously from the beginning and come out all guns blazing, pulling his Liberal colleagues on Sutherland Council into line, election night 1999 might have had a very different ending for him (and me). But I'll leave all the 'if only' stories for Ron and the political historians.

Telecast over, Bob began marshalling the troops, saying it's time to get to *the Tradies*: "the media and the Labor supporters were waiting!"

9.4. At *the Tradies*

I was walking on air as I walked through the doors of *the Tradies* with Jeanette. There were smiles, handshakes, congratulations and pats on the back everywhere we went.

One doubting Thomas who bailed me up was quick to let out a loud "yes!" after I personally confirmed that we had done it! Finally, it seemed, all Branch members and our supporters in the Shire really had something to celebrate: A Labor victory!

---

148 See Section 5.7: A Como experience.

And we weren't just celebrating victory in Miranda. First time Labor candidate, Alison Megarrity was well out in front, with TV commentators all agreeing that she would be the MP for the newly-created seat of Menai. Veteran Labor MP Ian McManus had easily defeated Lorna Stone, capturing the newly re-instated seat of Heathcote. And while he had not won the Liberal stronghold of Cronulla, Labor's Scott Docherty had achieved a very creditable swing of more than 5% against long-time sitting MP Malcolm Kerr.

Three of the four State electorates which, taken together, covered the whole of the Sutherland Local Government Area, were now safely in Labor hands. It was as though a political tsunami had appeared from nowhere, leaving the Cronulla electorate isolated— an island in what had, for too long, been the sleepy Shire's sea of Liberal blue.

Introducing the Labor Member for Miranda ...

On election night at *the Tradies*, however, it was all about returning Miranda to Labor, and, having made our way through the enthusiastic crowd to catch up with him, Bob Rogers had more news. Channel 9 Panel wanted to interview me — soon!

But in the meantime, Bob said, I had to get on the stage and be formally introduced as the new Labor Member for Miranda to everyone gathered in the Club's auditorium!

In anticipation, he'd already assembled a large group of local Branch members, booth workers and key supporters on the Club stage holding my coreflutes. Their job, Bob had told them, was to wave the coreflutes and cheer enthusiastically as I came onto the stage to be introduced. As I looked at them, Bob told me he had no trouble finding volunteers for the 'welcoming party'.

Yet, even now, with the time for the interview fast approaching, there was, for me, at least, one last fly in the ointment. The question was: who would actually introduce me to the Party faithful as the new Labor MP for Miranda? After all, no one had had the job for 15 years!

Two choices and two firsts

According to Paul Ellercamp, the task of introducing the winning Labor candidate to supporters on election night traditionally fell to the President of State Electorate Council: in Miranda's case, Paul himself! That presented a real problem for me, personally.

Paul had started out promising his full support as one of two 'Campaign Directors' after my preselection for Miranda in December 1998, and produced one media release as well as my Introductory Card. But by mid-January 1999, he'd disappeared completely from our campaign scene, without any explanation.

Paul resurfaced a week out from election day, put on his hat as President of Miranda SEC and, along with SEC Secretary, Troy Bramston, refused to provide our campaign with any more funds — when victory was in sight and we were really struggling to pay for those vital last few newspaper ads.[149]

Bob Rogers also wanted to introduce me to the audience. It was Bob who suggested that I consider running for Miranda after my defeat in the Cook preselection ballot, and he had been beside me all the way — from the very moment I was preselected until election night. Bob had worked just as hard as me on the organisational side of the campaign. Indeed, I was (and remain) in

---

[149] See Section 7.4. Newspaper ads, flies and loyalty

no doubt I could not have won the election without his continued commitment, support, and first-class people skills.

So here was my problem: Paul Ellercamp wanting to introduce me and Bob Rogers also saying he'd like to introduce me as the new Labor MP for Miranda to the waiting crowd in the auditorium. But as Connor McLeod said in the movie, *Highlander*, "there can only be one!"[150] It was my call. Even so, this wasn't the most difficult decision I'd ever had to make.

Regardless of the so-called Labor tradition, I believe it would have been morally wrong for me to choose Paul over Bob, and I simply told Paul that Bob would do the introduction.

While he appeared disappointed, Paul didn't argue with me. I'm sure he understood my reasons without me stating them. But there was yet another reason for choosing Bob over Paul. It was quite clear that, unlike Bob Rogers, Paul Ellercamp never really believed I could win!

I was also mindful that our success in winning back Miranda had brought with it two firsts! It was, of course, my first win. And, despite having worked hard in managing Labor campaigns at all three levels for many years in the Shire, it was also Bob Rogers' first big win. We'd proven to be a great team and Bob deserved to share both the credit for our win and the limelight with me!

And so, with Labor supporters towards the rear of the stage, Bob stood front and centre saying:

---

[150] The 1986 movie starred Christopher Lambert.

"Ladies and Gentlemen, it is my great pleasure to introduce Barry Collier, the new Labor Member for Miranda!"

The feeling was hard to describe as I was greeted with cheers and applause as I walked onto stage and shook Bob's hand — with supporters behind us joining in, enthusiastically waving my coreflutes.

The interview

No sooner had I thanked everyone involved in the campaign for their support — including Jeanette, my family and *the Tradies* itself — when Bob got the message that I'd soon be interviewed by Laurie Oaks and Ray Martin. I have to admit being a little nervous ahead of my first appearance on national TV with two giants of the political media, starting in five minutes.

Bob and I stayed on the stage with our supporters in the background holding my coreflutes, waiting for what seemed an eternity for the interview to begin. The transcript said it all.

Martin: I can see Barry Collier in Miranda waiting for us right now. Barry, can you hear me?

Collier: Yes, I can.

Martin: Congratulations on tonight. Are congratulations in order?

Collier: Yes! (At which point our supporters behind me waving my coreflutes drowned out Ray Martin with their very loud cheering and shouting.)

Martin: Could you clear something up for us please... there's some confusion. Did you get a call from Ron Phillips tonight?

Collier: I can't hear a word you are saying!

Martin: Well, you've got to calm down those enthusiastic supporters of yours! (At which point, I signaled our supporters behind me to lower the volume.)

Martin: Did you get a call from Ron Phillips tonight?

Collier: Yes. I got a phone call from Ron about half past eight and he conceded defeat ...graciously I might add.

Martin: Well, John Hannaford here says that he can't count.

Collier: Well, Ron certainly can! (Laughter from the Panel.)

Martin: Now again, I guess to be a politician you have to be optimistic, but two weeks ago did you think you had any chance of taking this away from the Deputy Leader of the Liberal Party?

Collier: Yes, we did. We ran a very strong grassroots campaign on overdevelopment down here, which was a local issue!

Martin: Fair dinkum?

Collier: We did! Privatisation was another issue which the people down here were very anti... So we focused on local issues rather than State-wide issues. Sutherland Hospital was another one.

Oakes: Barry, Ron Phillips, of course, was the Shadow Minister in charge of the privatisation policy. Do you think that was the main reason he's lost his seat?

Collier: That was one of them. Overdevelopment was another. There were quite a number of people around here who were quite dissatisfied with his involvement in the affairs of Peter Collins and Stephen Mutch. That was something coming through in my doorknocking. It was a grassroots campaign of doorknocking, railway stations...and those sorts of things...people were telling me that all the time.

Oakes: You've written five economics textbooks, I understand. Are you a threat to Michael Egan for the Treasury job?

Collier: Probably, probably (laughing).

Oakes: Or the Attorney General? You're a criminal barrister as well...

Collier: Yes, I'm a barrister; I practice criminal law. Of course, my interests are in both economics and law, so I'd be happy to take either of those. However, I must say the incumbents are very experienced and very competent...

Oakes: All right... Michael, are you busting there to say something?

Knight: No, no. I was just going to congratulate Barry. A fabulous campaign. He did really, really well and Ron Phillips only woke up to it near the death. But congratulations Barry! A great win!

Collier: Thank you, Michael. I think that Ron was out of the campaign — out of the arena — a fair bit with his other duties, being Deputy Leader and with the Olympics and so on.

Martin: You're being polite! You called him the "absent member."

Collier: Where did you get that from? (Laughing.)

Martin: All right, we're almost out of time. Barry, congratulations! Thanks for talking to us.

Collier: Thanks very much. My Campaign Manager's here... I shook hands with Bob Rogers on camera and patted him on the back, saying "good on you Bob," as the view widened to show our supporters behind me cheering and waving my coreflutes.

Martin: Congratulations from the mob. All right, Barry Collier there at Miranda.

Apart from the thrill of being interviewed by two of the most respected political commentators around, it was really gratifying to be able to thank my Campaign Director, Bob Rogers, publicly on national TV!

For the second time, and on election night, I said I believed we could win: something I'd never said publicly throughout the entire campaign, even though I'd always believed it in my heart of hearts. It didn't matter now.

Interview over, the Leader photographer turned up and, of course, we obliged with a celebratory shot with my family and supporters gathered around me. The photographer said that their senior journalist, Murray Trembath, would call me for comments sometime the next day for the paper's Tuesday edition. I couldn't wait.

9.5. Other news reports

In the meantime, the celebrations continued at *the Tradies*, with Labor members and supporters still talking excitingly about our winning campaign and their involvement in it— but with one eye on the nearby TV being switched from channel to channel by a beaming supporter.

As soon as the seat of Miranda was mentioned, a loud ssshh! reverberated around the crowd and all attention focused on the screen. Here's a smattering of what the commentators were saying.

The ABC's Panel anchored by the well-respected Kerry O'Brien with election analyst Antony Green said it all.

O'Brien: Now to the seat of Miranda where there's a
             sorry tale to be told about Ron Phillips the

Deputy Liberal Leader and sitting member who had held a margin of 5.3%.

Green: Barry Collier is leading for the Labor Party on primary votes. We have all the booths in from within Miranda itself. The only other one is about 60 votes from Sydney Town Hall, and comparing all those booths with last time, there is a 6% swing and it would be very hard for Ron Phillips to turn that around. I had a report that he was doing very badly with the postals and the absents...that was the perception at the booths and in the pre-polls earlier this week.

Later, and during a call through all the seats, a cheer went up with:

Green: Alison Megarrity, a Liverpool Councillor, will be the new Member for Menai.

O'Brien: On to Miranda, one of the major upsets of the night. The Deputy Leader of the Liberal Party, Ron Phillips, has been defeated.

Green: He can't turn that result around. That's with all the booths in. He's 2½% behind on primaries, and we're estimating with preferences that there's in fact a 6% swing and Labor will gain that seat.

O'Brien: The new Member for Miranda will be Barry Collier. He's a criminal law barrister and he's written five Economics textbooks.

And over to Channel 7 with Presenter Stan Grant and political commentator, Glenn Milne:

Grant: Glenn, let's go through some of the losses now for the Coalition. Coming up on the screen here now we can see seats lost to the Liberals: Menai, Ryde, Georges River, Miranda, Strathfield, Tweed, Northern Tablelands.

The Labor strategists here are now predicting that the Liberals will lose possibly up to 13 maybe even 17 seats. Let's go through some of the key areas here and in fact some Shadow Ministers who've lost their seats, most notably, of course, Ron Phillips (whose photograph appears on the screen).

Milne: That's right, the Deputy Leader there: he's gone in Miranda! And that was an early shock, Stan, during the night.

Our scrutineers here were not expecting him to lose that seat. Obviously, there's been a big shift against him.

Grant: You'd have to think though, that he's paid the price for getting rid of Peter Collins and installing Kerry Chikarovski.

Milne: I think that's right. There was panic in that seat in the last week when they realised that he was losing ground and obviously voters have been unimpressed by the shift to Chicka!

And what of Ron Phillips himself?

Late in the evening, Channel 7 newsreader, Ross Symonds began a report on the result in Miranda with the lead-in:

> "Opposition Leader, Ron Phillips, after holding the seat for 15 years, was beaten by Labor's Barry Collier. The swing: 7.6%. Mr Phillips blames his job of selling the electricity privatisation plan for his loss..."

The report went on to show Ron Phillips, with his wife Anne Maree, addressing his Liberal Party members and supporters in his own Campaign Office.

Regardless of what he may have said to the media earlier, this short speech for TV was measured and dignified. Ron did not criticise his own Party nor, for that matter, the Labor campaign, as others would have done. Rather, he spoke of the honour and the privilege of serving the people of Miranda for 15 years, representing them and the Liberal Party in Government and having been the State Minister for Health. He went on to say:

> "But at the end of the day, there is nothing certain about a lifelong career in politics... and it's now time to pass the mantle onto others."

Finally, and with a hug, he thanked his wife saying how much he was looking forward to spending more time with his family:

> "Let me say, I may have lost the seat of Miranda, but I get my wife and my kids and my five grandchildren back and am looking forward to it..."

From what I saw, Ron Phillips had been as gracious in defeat publicly as he was during our private telephone conversation earlier at 8.30PM.

A new beginning?

Around 11.00PM, and with the crowd dwindling, it was time for Jeanette and I to say our farewells and drive home our campaign car — still sporting the Barry Collier coreflutes and ropes à la The *Beverly Hillbillies*.

As we drove along the Club's exit driveway, the heavens opened. It had been a long, hard 3½ months of doorknocking day after day in the heat, and, apart from one overnight shower which only served to raise the humidity, this was the first really heavy shower I could remember in the whole campaign.

But coming as it did on the very night we'd won, this heavy shower of rain was significant. To me, at least, it heralded the dawn of change and a new beginning for the people of Miranda — and for me.

10. WHAT DO WE DO NOW?

10.1. Early morning, early thoughts

As Sunday morning, 28th of March 1999 came to consciousness, both the reality and enormity of our victory set in. We'd actually done it! We'd won! I was now the State MP for Miranda!

Ron Phillips had actually conceded defeat last night as early at 8.30PM! The Carr Labor Government had been returned with an increased majority!

You may well ask: what goes through the mind of a previously unknown, first time candidate who defies the odds and defeats a very high-profile, 15-year MP to win a seat in Parliament? How did this newly-elected MP feel the morning after such a victory, with all the congratulations, the praise and the backslapping of that unforgettable, life-changing night on waking?

Laying there in that early morning light, thinking about the extraordinary events of the night before, I was still over the moon of course! For a start, it was hard to believe that I'd been interviewed on national TV by such respected journalists as Laurie Oaks and Ray Martin.

But as excited and as delighted as I was with our victory, I felt an extraordinary sense of humility, along with the deepest sense of responsibility. Humility came in the realisation that thousands of local residents had actually chosen to put their trust in me to represent them and their families in the NSW Parliament. A great privilege accorded to so few, that trust carried with it a huge, as yet unspoken, responsibility to fulfil my commitments and to serve my constituents to the best of my ability—whether they voted for me or not. For one so inexperienced in public life, the magnitude of the task ahead did not escape me.

I was, of course, just so grateful and so thankful for the honour which had been bestowed upon me. Yet, and as strange as it may seem, there was no great sense of personal pride in what was being regarded by so many as an outstanding political achievement. The pride I felt was pride in my family who loved me and believed in me every step of the way, and pride in all our local Labor Branch members, volunteers and supporters who had worked so hard to secure our victory.

A measure of respect

And as odd as it may seem to the Party hard-liners, I could not but help feel a touch of sympathy for my defeated opponent.

In one fell swoop, Ron Phillips had lost both Miranda and the Deputy Leadership of the NSW Liberal Party. That must have been an exceptionally hard kick in the guts, after 15 consecutive years in public life, including three years as the State Minister for Health.

Yet Mr Phillips had the personal courage and the professionalism to telephone me to concede defeat and congratulate me as early as 8.30PM on election night, at a time which must have been very soon after he saw the writing on the wall! While I may have just entered the political arena, I'd seen enough as a player on the sporting field to know that was not something everyone on the losing side would do.

I had no doubt that the NSW Liberal Party would lay the blame for its most decisive defeat since the 1978 *Wranslide* at the feet of Ron Phillips. I also knew the media would have a field day in attributing the Liberal loss to his key role in removing Peter Collins as Leader and his failed electricity privatisation policy. Both would be bitter pills for Phillips to swallow.

I then recalled last night's late broadcast of Ron Phillips addressing the Party faithful in Miranda with his wife, Anne Maree, by his side. I hoped that if the day ever came when I lost my seat in Parliament, I'd accept defeat with the same grace and dignity. While some Labor hard-liners would see it as a kind of political weakness, in the end, and after 3½ months of campaigning against him, I came to have a measure of personal respect for my defeated Liberal opponent.

Early morning reflections aside, it was time to get up and make Jeanette breakfast in bed — something I had not done for a long time. And after listening to the radio coverage, I was off to buy the Sunday papers from my local newsagent: my very first constituent to congratulate me on Day One!

10.2. What the Sunday papers were saying

While I'd have to wait until the following Tuesday for The Leader to hit the Shire streets, the Sydney newspapers were full of reports and analysis of the 1999 NSW State election.

I've chosen extracts from the major Sunday metropolitan newspapers, quoting so much of the analysis and comments as are relevant to Miranda [10 − 1 to 10 − 6].

CARR-NAGE:
Chikarovski crushed by big swing to Labor

PREMIER Bob Carr was swept back into power last night with an increased majority and a 4.9 per cent swing across the State. Mr Carr appeared last night to be heading for a 13-seat majority, having won 53.7pc of the vote.

The Coalition appeared to have lost more than 12 seats, handing Labor its biggest landslide win since Neville Wran's victory in 1978.

Deputy leader Ron Phillips lost Miranda and Michael Photios failed to win the new seat of Ryde. They were the key plotters in the coup which toppled Peter Collins in December. Mr Collins said last night: "The result is worse than anyone predicted."

10 – 1: The Sun Herald, 28 March 1999

Chicka rolled
Even North Shore dumps Liberals

The Liberals were last night said to be devastated. They lost several key MPs including deputy leader Ron Phillips, who was surprisingly defeated in his southern Sydney seat of Miranda... and MP Michael Photios.

Both were key plotters of the coup which toppled Liberal leader Peter Collins in December and saw themselves as future leaders of the Liberal Party.

Major recriminations are expected within the Coalition over the coming weeks, but Mrs Chikarovski is expected to stay on as leader for the time being.

Liberal party state director Remo Nogarotto, who will undoubtedly be in the firing line, strongly defended the decision to topple Mr Collins.

10 – 2: The Sun-Herald, 28 March 1999

Amazing victory
Labor bolts in with big swing

PREMIER Bob Carr stormed back into office last night as the Coalition was humbled across NSW.

The outcome was a stunning confirmation of the campaign skills of Mr Carr and his right-hand man, Labor secretary general (now MLC) John Della Bosca. "He is simply the best campaign director there is," Mr Carr said.

Coalition figures moved quickly last night to signal the death of the Opposition's controversial plan to sell off the State's $25billion electricity industry. Defeated MPs blamed the privatisation plan for their demise.

The Coalition's worse casualty was the loss of deputy Liberal leader Ron Phillips, who was soundly beaten by Labor's Barry Collier in Miranda.

One Nation's strong showing was the surprise of the night…

10 – 3: Sunday Telegraph, 28 March 1999

Careers in tatters

Liberals' deputy leader heads list of big-name losers

LABOR'S election victory left a trail of broken political careers in its wake last night.

The biggest scalp was that of Ron Phillips, the Liberal deputy leader and Coalition heavyweight of the past decade who lost the safe seat of Miranda.

The victor, Labor candidate Barry Collier, was jubilant. "We ran a very strong grassroots campaign and people were very anti-privatisation," he said.

"We fought the campaign on local issues. Privatisation one of the reasons why Mr Phillips lost his seat."

10 – 4: Sunday Telegraph, 28 March 1999

Phillips & Photios — the big losers

RON Phillips and prominent Liberal frontbencher Michael Photios bowed out of State politics last night, the Liberal Party Deputy Leader's demise providing the biggest shock.

Mr Phillips was one of the first to lose his seat — Miranda — to a surprisingly strong Labor Party showing in Sydney's South.

Mr Phillips, Coalition Health spokesman and representative on the Sydney 2000 Olympics Organising Committee, lost with 40.68 per cent of the primary vote to high profile Sutherland Shire criminal Lawyer Barry Collier (43.21pc).

10 – 5: The Sun Herald, 28 March 1999

Election'99: The Verdict

The contentious electorates:

MIRANDA

Held by: Ron Phillips, Liberal.

Main contender: Barry Collier, ALP

Margin: 5.3 per cent.

The drill: An unexpected fight for the Liberals, with Labor closing the big margin late in the campaign.

Verdict: Phillips concedes by 8:30PM to the affable Collier.

10 – 6: Sunday Telegraph, 28 March 1999

As expected, the Sunday newspapers let loose on my former opponent Ron Phillips. No doubt the Party heavyweights and those Liberal MPs who'd lost their seats would also put in the boot behind the scenes.

Clearly, and as the papers would have it, the Deputy Leader had paid the price for both his disloyalty and for attempting to sell a major Liberal policy which was not only ill-conceived, but plainly unacceptable to the electorate as a whole.

But for those of us out there on the ground, there were a host of other factors that contributed to Ron Phillips' defeat— not least of which was the problem of overdevelopment.

Still, there were some interesting comments in the extracts worth mentioning. Firstly, and quite clearly, the metro media didn't expect Ron Phillips to lose his seat. That enabled us to maintain the important 'underdog status' up until election day.

Secondly, while I practiced criminal law and I worked in the Shire for Legal Aid, I was not the 'high profile Sutherland Shire criminal lawyer' the Sun Herald made me out to be. In reality, I was not a high-priced silk in the public eye; I worked full-time for Legal Aid clients at Sutherland Local Court. The elevated status was flattering, but untrue.

Thirdly, while Bob Carr proclaimed Della Bosca as "the best campaign director there is," I am yet to receive any reply from him to my requests in early 1999 for assistance to help me "capture the seat of Miranda."[151] While Della Bosca didn't think I could win in January 1999, a simple reply wouldn't have hurt. Party officials, including General Secretaries, should at least be in touch with all their candidates, regardless of their prospects of success.

10.3. Sunday morning and a question

Late morning, after having read the Sunday papers—admittedly with a measure of satisfaction— I received a call from Herald journalist, Tim Jamieson, asking for an interview (complete with photographer) at the Campaign Office. Of course, the newly-

---

[151] See Section 4.6. Letters to Della.

elected Labor MP for Miranda was more than happy to oblige and arranged a time mid-afternoon.

No sooner had I put the phone down, when senior journalist Murray Trembath rang to interview me for the next edition of the Leader. Grateful for the opportunity, I did the interview over the phone without hesitation, knowing full well that, having seen Mr Trembath in action with his shorthand notebook during the Knowles visit, he wouldn't miss a word.[152] I recall putting the phone down, thinking maybe that was a little brave, and hoping for a good story the following Tuesday.

Jeanette, who had been sitting at the dining table with me while I answered Mr Trembath's questions, said that from the sound of things, she thought the interview went well. But it raised an important question for both of us — one to which neither of us knew the answer.

Jeanette said, "Why don't you ring Bob Rogers? He'd know!" An eminently sensible suggestion, I thought, given Bob's vast experience. And so, my first call as the MP-elect for Miranda was to my trusted Campaign Director with our burning question.

Before going on, I need to note that, as I would discover much later, my question to Bob was far from unique. Let me explain.

The Candidate

Several years after my election, I was given a DVD by one of my supporters: a 1972 movie entitled The Candidate, starring Robert Redford. The supporter, who'd contributed hours of work to our

---

[152] See 7 – 7: With Minister Knowles & Journalist Murray Trembath.

428

1999 victory, said he could see some parallels between Redford's campaign in the movie and our campaign in Miranda.

The Candidate chronicles the election campaign of local legal aid lawyer, Bill McKay—a first time, unknown aspirant for a seat in the United States Senate.

McKay, who is initially not interested in politics, agrees to run for the Democratic Party after the powerbrokers persuade him that he can use his candidature to get his own agenda for legal and social reform out there in the public domain. He would, in effect, have *carte blanche* to say whatever he wants. McKay's is given only one instruction which is written by the Campaign Director on the inside of a matchbook cover: "you lose!"

The reality is that no high-profile Democrat was willing to risk yet another humiliating defeat at the hands of the very popular, long-serving Republican Senator, Crocker Jarmon, who is widely regarded as "unbeatable". In effect, Bill McKay is asked to 'fly the flag' for the Democratic Party. With the polls showing an overwhelming victory for the Republicans, McKay's race for the US Senate is effectively over before his campaign has begun.

Yet, spruiking all that is wrong with the political system and campaigning on his own platform that "there must be a better way," McKay's message resonates with voters. Against the odds —and contrary to the powerbroker's instructions and early polls— McKay goes on to comfortably win the Californian Senate seat.

But moments after being told he's won, and as the victory celebrations are about to begin, McKay grabs his Campaign Director by the arm, leads him through the crowd of supporters into a nearby hotel room and shuts the door.

In the final scene, with the media and supporters clamouring outside in the hallway, we see our newly-elected Democratic Senator looking his Campaign Director in the eye and asking him a vital question. And there the movie ends — with the question hanging in the air, unanswered!

It was the very same question I asked my Campaign Director, Bob Rogers, in that phone call to his home just before lunch on Sunday, the 28th of March 1999:

"What do we do now, Bob?" I asked, sincerely.

"I don't know!" came his astonishing reply. "I've never got past a Saturday night before!"

The reality was that, despite being the Director of many previous State and Federal Labor campaigns, Bob had never had a winning candidate! Despite all his hard work, every Saturday night at the end of each election had ended in disappointment for our Shire candidates and for him personally as their Campaign Director.

This was a *first* for him, as well as for me! We were both in the dark, and just as in the movie, no answer was immediately forthcoming. After a few seconds, Bob did answer:

"After 15 years without a Labor Member, I'm just looking forward to putting my feet up on Phillips' old desk!" he said.

"You can be the first!" I replied, giving Bob my first post-election promise.

We eventually decided that we couldn't do anything much until Ron Phillips and his staff vacated his Miranda Electorate Office in Urunga Parade, Miranda. For that, we had to wait until the poll was declared.[153] And sometime or other after that, I'd have to be sworn in as the new MP for Miranda and get my own Office staff. Clearly, there was a very steep learning curve ahead — for both of us.

10.4. More media

It was only to be expected that the next two days would see a plethora of newspaper articles, analysing and dissecting the election— everything from the statistics and commentary on the Party Leaders to articles on the changes in individual seats and the new MPs.

The Carr Labor Government had been comfortably returned, winning 55 of the 93 seats in the New South Wales Legislative Assembly. The Liberal-National Coalition had won only 33 seats, with the remaining five seats being won by Independent candidates. Independents aside, Labor had increased its majority in the NSW Legislative Assembly from 1 seat in 1995 to 22 seats in 1999.

In what many described as a Liberal disaster, the Coalition's primary vote had collapsed in many of its seats. Throughout the State, Labor had won seats regarded by commentators as "notionally Coalition seats."

Three of the four seats serving the Sutherland Shire— Heathcote, Menai and Miranda were now in Labor hands. Like Ian

---

[153] The declaration of the poll takes place after all the votes have been counted. The Returning Officer officially declares a candidate to be the winner of the election (the poll), and publishes the result in a local newspaper. The poll is typically "declared" a week or two after election day itself.

McManus and Alison Megarrity, I was delighted to be going to Parliament as a member of the Carr Government.[154]

I'd be in a far better position to do more for my community than I would on the other side of the House in Opposition.

Recriminations continue

For several days after major elections— and more so when there's been large swings or even landslides— there'll always be recriminations and finger pointing (if not weeping and gnashing of teeth) on the losing side of the ledger. This 'finds its way' into the media, often with the help of disaffected and disgruntled Party members.

Not surprisingly, the Monday newspapers picked up from where the Sunday papers left off, focusing the reasons for the Liberals' record loss. While I'm not going to go through these ad nauseam, I can't help but recount one little gem I came across written by Ken Hooper, Chief of Staff to former Premier Nick Greiner for 10 years [10−7].

We were absolutely astonished to learn that the Liberals had spent "more than $300,000" attempting to retain Miranda— especially when compared to the $20,000 we'd struggled to raise and spend to actually win it.

Put simply, Ron Phillips had lost his seat despite outspending me by 15 to 1! On the one hand, and while funding is always important, this vast disparity in election spending between

---

154 Labor's Scott Docherty did not win Cronulla. He later went on to serve two terms on Sutherland Shire Council, from September 1999 to September 2008.

our respective campaigns clearly demonstrates the value of a genuine grass-roots campaign based on local issues.

The missing pieces

Why did the Liberal party perform so dismally on Saturday?

KEN HOOPER

...Deputy Leader, Ron Phillips... was so engrossed in campaigning for his own faction within the party, he took his eye off his own seat of Miranda and didn't notice it was slipping from his grasp.

A series of fights within the Miranda branches had also seen bitter factions develop and by the time party officials woke up to what was going on, it was too late.

The Liberals reportedly threw more than $300,000 at Miranda (its original budget was $120,000) in the dying days of the campaign, creating yet another problem.

A shortage of funds – and an equally desperate need – saw the Liberals transferring funds from electorate to electorate as the campaign progressed. Marginal seats got the big top up and lesser seats were relegated to looking after themselves.

10 – 7: The Daily Telegraph, Monday 29 March 1999

On the other hand, the fact that we actually won despite being outspent 15 to 1 by the Liberals was not only a tribute to the magnificent efforts of our local Branch members and volunteers; it was an added reason why our victory over such a high-profile Liberal as Ron Phillips came to be regarded by many in the Labor Party as so very special.

A Herald special

Any doubts the public may have had about just how special our victory really was put to rest by Tim Jamieson's article in the Sydney Morning Herald the same day [10−8].

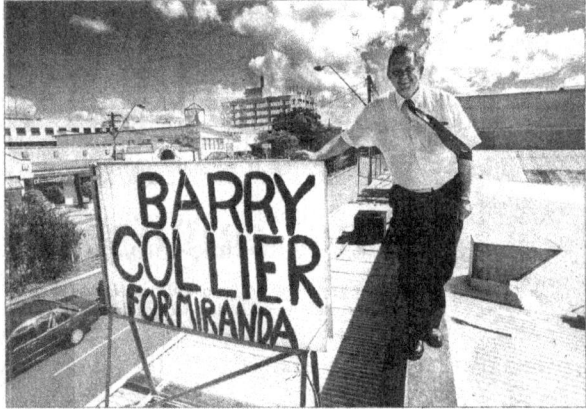

Phillips tripped by a shoestring

10 − 8: *A Herald Special, Monday 29 March 1999*

The heading, the story and the photograph of me on the roof of our Campaign Office with Big John's hand-painted sign really said it all. When it came to the seat of Miranda, the Herald article must have seemed like something of a "follow-up" story to the 'Missing Pieces' story in its rival Sydney paper, the Daily Telegraph.

I can only think that the angry Liberal members who read both articles must have been outraged by the fact that Ron Phillips, having spent $300,000 worth of Party funds on his campaign, was beaten by a very basic, unsophisticated Labor campaign costing only $20,000! Looked at in this light, I have no doubt that some Liberal heavyweights and staunch Liberal Party members would have regarded the loss of Miranda as humiliating.

The Leader

The headline of Tuesday's St George and Sutherland Shire Leader screamed out the impact of the election results in Sydney's South: Of the region's eight seats in Parliament, only one remained in Liberal hands: Cronulla [10 – 9].

Our election night photo on the front page – with Big John's arms raised in victory – must have been the last straw for the local Liberal diehards.

10 – 9: The Leader, Tuesday 30 March 1999 (Front page)

Election 1999 — *and the winners were . . . . .*

The true believers

The winners:
- Cronulla – Malcolm Kerr (Lib)
- Georges River – Kevin Greene (ALP)
- Kogarah – Cherie Burton (ALP)
- Heathcote – Ian McManus (ALP)
- Lakemba – Morris Iemma (ALP)
- Menai – Alison Megarrity (ALP)
- Miranda – Barry Collier (ALP)
- Rockdale – George Thompson (ALP)

By MURRAY TREMBATH

HOMEMADE signs above his campaign rooms and fixed to his car roof-racks helped Labor's Barry Collier to a shock win in the seat of Miranda.

"We had a very limited budget and had to make do the best we could," said Mr Collier, a 49-year-old barrister and former schoolteacher, who lives at Kareela.

"Charlie, my next-door neighbour, painted a big sign which I fixed to the roof racks of my 1987 Mitsubishi Magna.

"I drove around with it on for the best part of two months and people couldn't help but notice.

"It was like something out of the Beverly Hillbillies. Kids would yell out, 'On ya, Bazza'."

Campaign worker John McLean, a transport worker at Sydney Airport, painted the amateurish sign atop Mr Collier's campaign rooms on Kingsway, opposite Westfield Shoppingtown Miranda.

"At least it stood out," said Mr McLean, who gave up two weeks of his holidays to work on the campaign. Mr Collier said he had run a grassroots campaign, concentrating on visiting railway stations, door knocking and street stalls.

"My campaign team and I always believed we could do it," he said.

"There were some encouraging signs about but the only advice we got [from ALP head office] was on Friday afternoon when they told us we were a long shot."

■ BARRY Collier and his 17-year-old son Michael pose yesterday with the car and sign that helped Labor win Miranda from the Liberals.

Mr Collier said Mr Phillips had rung him at 8.30 pm on Saturday to concede defeat and congratulate him.

"He was very gracious and I appreciate that," he said.

Mr Collier said overdevelopment was the major local issue, and he would like to see the inquiry announced by Urban Affairs and Planning Minister Craig Knowles expedited.

"A lot of people were opposed to electricity privatisation and there was also a fair bit of disappointment about Mr Phillips' activities in relation to Stephen Mutch and Peter Collins."

Mr Collier said he would strive as the new MP to be accessible and effective.

"As my campaign slogan said, I want to be 'a local who listens and works hard for them'."

Labor needed a 4.5 per cent swing and got nearly 8 per cent.

Phillips won't play blame game

By MURRAY TREMBATH

RON Phillips attributes his downfall to community concern about overdevelopment in the Shire.

However, in an interview with The Leader, he refused to comment on whether he felt he had been made a scapegoat.

"I am not going to give a commentary on the election results, or to lay blame," he said.

"One of the truisms in politics is not whether you win or lose but where people lay the blame.

"That's not the sort of game I play."

Asked whether he had an inkling of his defeat, he said, "In the election run-up, I said to people that if ever the Labor Party was going to get me, this would be the election.

"I think they ran a substantial campaign against me on overdevelopment and I thought that was successful.

"People can work out themselves whether what they said was true or untrue.

"The main point I want to make is that it has been an honour and a privilege to serve the people of Miranda and NSW for 15 years.

"I gave a substantial part of my life to politics and I fought for what I believe in.

"I fought for the people of Miranda, and I am proud of my achievements, including being the Minister for Health for four years."

10 – 10: The Leader, Tuesday 30 March 1999, page 2

The Leader's second page on Tuesday 30th of March continued the story of our winning shoestring campaign, complete with a photo of Michael and I with our campaign car [10 – 10].

From our perspective, the Leader could not have chosen a better heading. After Shire Labor's 15 years in the political wilderness, winning back the seat of Miranda really was, to quote Prime Minister Paul Keating, "a victory for the *True Believers*, the people who in difficult times have kept the faith!"[155]

In the same article, notably, Ron Phillips attributed his "downfall to community concerns about overdevelopment." There's a lesson in that for every candidate: if you ignore the local issues, you do so at your peril!

10.5. More to do

The week after the election was no time to be sitting around enjoying the fruits of victory over countless cups of coffee.

The following Monday morning would see Jeanette and I and a host of still smiling Branch members descend on 581 The Kingsway, Miranda to clean up our humble Campaign Office before handing it back to the real estate agent.

Cleaning up aside, we had to return all the borrowed furniture and equipment to its owners and unscrew hundreds of my coreflutes from A-frames and garden stakes. We'd store the coreflutes in the expectation that I'd use them again at the next State election in 2003 (should I be preselected for Miranda again). The A-frames and stakes would be recycled for use by future Labor candidates.

I can only imagine what it must have been like for Bob and all those other committed Labor branch members cleaning up Campaign Offices, election after election, defeat after defeat. This

---

[155] Paul Keating, *Election Victory Speech*, 6 August 1993.

time however, with victory and a real sense of achievement still in the air, I don't believe branch members saw the dismantling of our 1999 Miranda Campaign Office as a chore!

The final campaign decision

There is no doubt that we left the old run-down clothing shop in a better state than we found it. But, having closed up for the last time, Bob and I had to make one last decision: when to have a victory dinner for all those who'd worked on our campaign.

We'd already decided in February *where* we'd hold our post-election dinner, win or lose: the *Miranda Palace* — that little Chinese restaurant on the Kingsway whose owners had refused to remove my coreflutes from their front window despite being pressured to do so by two Liberal heavies.

We settled for a $20 a head banquet (BYO) on the 8th of April, 1999. Bob Rogers sent out invitations to Branch members with the heading:

> The Party We've Waited Fifteen Years for…
> *(This is not a fundraiser: just a night to remember.)*

Even so, that question still hung there at the back of our minds: what do we do now? No doubt we'd find out sooner or later. But that, of course, is the subject of another book in itself.

EPILOGUE

On the 27th of March 1999, the Labor Party won 55 of the 93 seats in the NSW Legislative Assembly, returning the Carr Government for a second term with an absolute majority of 17 seats.

In one of its worst results ever, the Coalition Parties secured only 33 seats, having lost 12 seats to Labor and five seats to Independent candidates. In addition to the finger pointing, blame shifting and recriminations which typically accompany losses of this magnitude, the Liberal Party went on to conduct a 6-week inquiry into the reasons for its defeat.

Our efforts in Miranda saw a 7.6% swing to Labor, slightly better than the State-wide average swing of 7.2% to the Party overall. We now held the seat with a slim margin of 2.3%. Clearly, there was much to be done over the new 4-year term in Parliament if we were to keep Miranda in Labor hands.

As this book comes to an end, I want to share a few interesting snippets that came to light in the wake of our Labor victory in Miranda.

The Liberals' polling

'By March, the reports are almost uniformly gloomy... Figures were now pointing to a looming disaster. In Miranda, the seat Phillips had held since 1984 and where 55% of voters had never heard of the Labor candidate, Labor came from behind in November to hold a four-point lead on the two-party preferred vote. Fortunately, there was someone to blame.'

(From *The Liberals, a History of the NSW Division*, Ian Hancock, Federation Press, 2007.)

The Former Opposition Leader, Peter Collins

In October 2000, Peter Collins, the Opposition Leader deposed by Ron Phillips and John Hannaford launched his own book, *The Bear Pit*, in the Legislative Assembly chamber itself. I received an invitation and like many others who attended, lined up after the launch to have my copy signed personally by the author. To this day, I treasure the words he unexpectedly wrote on the title page:

> *For Barry-*
> *To the man who took Miranda from one of my assailants*
> *With every good wish*
> *Peter Collins*
> *26 October 2000*

The Premier, Bob Carr

But the last word on our 1999 campaign which returned Miranda to Labor after 15 years in the political wilderness should go to Bob Carr himself.

Having watched my TV interview shortly after we had won Miranda on election night, the Premier reportedly turned to his media advisor, Walt Secord, and asked "where did we get *him* from?"

APPENDIX

THOSE WHO MADE IT POSSIBLE

Success, they say, has many parents. But, as politicians with very busy and demanding lives, we often tend to overlook those at the grass-roots who made our successes possible though their work and commitment at the very beginning of our careers.

I've listed some of the names of those who contributed to our success in Miranda in 1999. To them, their local Labor Branch Members and our supporters, my thanks and my gratitude.

Bert Rhodes	John McLean	Bob White
Paul Smith	Jim Foy	Pat Foy
Martin Iffland	Iffland family	Trevor Romer
Anne Long	Dan Long	Maurie Bevan
Joy Hall	Edwina Hall	Betty Lewis
Carole Ashworth	Luke Ashworth	Alan Bell
Dawn Emerson	Phil Blight	Mary Hunt
Graham Hill	Ken Smith	Ray Plibersek
John McCracken	Chris Hunt	Tony Iffland
Hazel Wilson	Tim O'Connor	Peri Young
Lawrie Daly	Paul Ellercamp	Charlie Low
Michael Forshaw	Bob Armstrong	Jim Ayling
Warren Elder	Graham Piper	Olivia Ayling
Thelma Deacon	Donna Spears	Ken Long
Ernie Grinstead	John Goschin	Doug Edwards

INDEX

D

R

S

T

www.ingramcontent.com/pod-product-compliance
Lightning Source LLC
Chambersburg PA
CBHW072058040426
42334CB00041B/1332